POLICING FUTURES

WITHDRAWN

D1471950

Policing Futures

The Police, Law Enforcement and the Twenty-First Century

Edited by

Peter Francis
Lecturer in Criminology and Sociology
University of Northumbria at Newcastle

Pamela Davies
Senior Lecturer in Criminology and Sociology
University of Northumbria at Newcastle

and

Victor Jupp
Principal Lecturer in Criminology and Sociology
University of Northumbria at Newcastle

First published in Great Britain 1997 by
MACMILLAN PRESS LTD
Houndmills, Basingstoke, Hampshire RG21 6XS and London
Companies and representatives throughout the world

A catalogue record for this book is available from the British Library.

ISBN 0–333–68965–8 hardcover
ISBN 0–333–68966–6 paperback

First published in the United States of America 1997 by
ST. MARTIN'S PRESS, INC.,
Scholarly and Reference Division,
175 Fifth Avenue, New York, N.Y. 10010

ISBN 0–312–17597–3

Library of Congress Cataloging-in-Publication Data
Policing futures : the police, law enforcement, and the twenty-first
century / edited by Peter Francis, Pamela Davies, and Victor Jupp.
p.   cm.
Includes bibliographical references and index.
ISBN 0–312–17597–3 (cloth)
1. Police—Great Britain.   2. Law enforcement—Great Britain.
I. Francis, Peter, 1968–   . II. Davies, Pamela, 1962–
III. Jupp, Victor.
HV8195.P65 1997
363.2'0941—dc21   97–13024
                                                                    CIP

This book is printed on paper suitable for recycling and made from fully managed and
sustained forest sources.

10   9   8   7   6   5   4   3   2
06   05   04   03   02   01   00   99

Printed and bound in Great Britain by
Antony Rowe Ltd, Chippenham, Wiltshire

Contents

Acknowledgements

Many of the papers on which this collection is based were originally presented at the University of Northumbria's Annual Criminal Justice Conference held in Durham during the spring of 1996. Our thanks go to all those who presented papers at the conference, as well as to our colleagues and students at the University of Northumbria, without whose combined efforts the conference would not have been the success it was. In particular we are grateful to the administrative support of Nancy Noon and Heidi Robinson in the run-up to and during the conference weekend.

The various papers presented at the conference have been revised (in some cases extensively) for this volume, while others have been specifically commissioned, and we would like to thank all the contributors for their support in the production of this book. Finally, our thanks go to Annabelle Buckley at Macmillan for the support she has provided during the period it has taken to collate, edit and publish this volume.

Newcastle

PETER FRANCIS
PAMELA DAVIES
VICTOR JUPP

Notes on the Contributors

Jennifer Brown is Senior Lecturer in Psychology at the University of Surrey, where she also obtained her doctorate. Previously she worked as a researcher for Hampshire Constabulary and as a Lecturer in the Institute for Police and Criminological Studies at the University of Portsmouth. She has been actively researching the experiences of women in the police service and is also interested in occupational stress amongst police officers. She recently authored *Stress and Policing* (with Elizabeth Campbell) (1993).

Elaine Campbell is Lecturer in Social Policy at the University of Newcastle. She has teaching interests in the areas of criminal justice, crime and deviance and qualitative methodology. She is currently finishing her PhD on the implementation of a prosecution and diversion policy in a police force area. Her other research interests are in the areas of crime prevention and the private sector of policing.

Pamela Davies is Senior Lecturer in Criminology and Sociology at the University of Northumbria at Newcastle. She specializes in the teaching of crime as work, along with victimology and explaining crime and deviance. Previously she worked for Northumbria Police. Her research interests include women, crime, gender stereotyping and the informal economy. She has recently edited *Understanding Victimization* (with Victor Jupp and Peter Francis) (1996).

Peter Francis is Lecturer in Criminology and Sociology at the University of Northumbria at Newcastle. He is currently coordinating a research project into young people, drugs and social exclusion in North East England, and evaluating a programme of child-caring services for parents in prison. His publications include *Prisons 2000: An International Perspective on the Current State and Future of Imprisonment* (with Roger Matthews) (1996) and *Understanding Victimization* (with Pamela Davies and Victor Jupp) (1996). He is also on the editorial board of *Criminal Justice Matters* (Institute for the Study and Treatment of Delinquency).

Paddy Hillyard is Director of the Centre for Socio-Legal Studies in the School for Policy Studies at the University of Bristol. He is a former chair of Liberty and is a member of the editorial board of *Social and Legal Studies: An International Journal*. He is a regular contributor to *Statewatch* and has written widely in the fields of the sociology of law and civil liberties. His last book was *Suspect Community: People's Experience of the Prevention of Terrorism Acts* (1993).

Les Johnston is Reader in Criminology and Head of the Criminology Section at the University of Teesside. He has research and teaching interests in public, commercial and civil policing, the politics of law and order, criminal justice policy and social theory and the state. He is author of *The Rebirth of Private Policing* (1992) and of numerous articles on policing and criminal justice. At present he is working on two books, *Governing Diversity: Explorations in Policing* (with Clifford Shearing and Philip Stenning) (forthcoming) and *British Policing in Transition* (forthcoming).

Victor Jupp is Principal Lecturer in Sociology and Criminology and Head of the Division of Sociology at the University of Northumbria at Newcastle. He specializes in the teaching of research methods and criminology. In addition he undertakes work for and acts as an assessor to the Open University. His publications include *Methods of Criminological Research* (1989), *Understanding Victimization* (with Pamela Davies and Peter Francis) (1996) and *Data Collection and Analysis* (with Roger Sapsford) (1996).

Barry Loveday is Principal Lecturer and Research Coordinator at the Institute for Police and Criminological Studies at the University of Portsmouth. He has published widely on policing, including the recent book *Core Issues in Policing* (with Frank Leishman and Steve Savage) (1996).

Eugene McLaughlin is Senior Lecturer in Criminology and Social Policy at the Open University. His publications include *Out of Order? Policing of Black People* (with Elias Cashmore) (1991), *Managing Social Policy* (with John Clarke and Alan Cochrane) (1994) and *Community, Policing and Accountability* (1994).

Karim Murji is Senior Lecturer in Social Policy and Sociology at the Roehampton Institute. His publications include *Traffickers: Drug Markets* *and Law Enforcement* (with Nicholas Dorn and Nigel South) (1992) and *Drug Prevention* (with Nicholas Dorn) (1992) as well as a number of articles about policing.

Nigel South is Reader in Sociology and Director of the Health and Social Services Institute at the University of Essex. His current research includes work on crimes and the environment and several other projects in comparative criminology such as prison systems and cross border crimes. His recent books include *Eurodrugs: Drug Use, Markets and Trafficking in Europe* (with Vincenzo Ruggerio) (1995), and the *Social Construction of Social Policy* (with Colin Samson) (1996).

David Wall is Deputy Director of the Centre for Criminal Justice Studies at the University of Leeds. He coordinates the Masters programme in criminal justice and lectures in criminal justice and policing. He has conducted research and has published articles on the themes of access to criminal justice, policing information technology and the sociology of the legal profession. He is co-author of *The Impact of PACE: Policing in a Northern Force* (with Keith Bottomley, Clive Coleman, David Dixon and Martin Gill) (1991) and is a co-editor of and contributor to *Access to Criminal Justice: Legal Aid, Lawyers and the Defence of Liberty* (with Richard Young) (1996).

1 New Millennium 'Blues'? Policing Past and *Policing Futures*

Peter Francis, Pamela Davies and Victor Jupp

INTRODUCTION

It is approximately four decades ago, during the 1950s, that the British police first came under the gaze of the sociological and criminological telescope, since which time policing and law enforcement have become central to much intellectual, popular and political discourse and debate. Conventional wisdom on the trajectory of this relatively short period, as Downes and Morgan (1994) succinctly put it, is generally apocalyptic; things have deteriorated irreversibly since the golden days of the 1950s and the future of the police and policing looks bleak. Indeed, for some commentators it is a period in which the community 'plod', epitomized by Ted Willis's PC George Dixon, first in the 1950 film *The Blue Lamp* and later in the BBC television programme *Dixon of Dock Green*, has been replaced by the 'reactive pig' or 'reluctant bobby', with a visored 'Robocop' or 'Darth Vader' armed and waiting around the millennium corner.

However, the reality is more complex and less sensational than the trajectory and images highlighted above suggest. As Downes and Morgan go on to point out, police and policing 'are now in a healthier state than before, but look worse because far more is known about their shortcomings' (1994: 221). This is the outcome of three factors: first, a mixture of academic research; second, changes in the politics of policing, crime and order; and third, broader socioeconomic and cultural developments affecting late modern society. Taken together, these factors provide a degree of guidance as to the changing past and current nature of British policing, and provide some understanding as to why it continues to face momentous change in the light of the coming millennium. It is these changes and the consequences of them for policing futures as seen by the various contributors to this volume which is the focus of this introductory chapter.

1

THE RECENT PAST OF POLICING

It was an epistomological break during the 1960s which first opened the intellectual floodgates to the study of policing. During this period, a number of sociologists and criminologists (see the work of Becker, 1963; Lemert, 1967; Cohen, 1971; Young, 1971), working on both sides of the Atlantic, became critical of the dominant positivist view that the starting point for any criminological inquiry into the causes of crime should be either the individual offender or the social environment in which they resided. Instead, they began to explore crime and deviance in terms of the 'social reaction that *other* people – including state officials – have towards offenders' (Lilly, Cullen and Ball, 1995: 114). Offenders were to be viewed not as in some way different, but as human actors whose activities were to be appreciated; indeed all they had in common was that they had been 'labelled' (Reiner, 1994). As Becker (1963) argued, deviance was not the quality of the act a person committed, 'but rather a consequence of the application by others of rules and sanctions to an offender' (Becker, 1963: 9). This 'intellectual' focus on the application of rules specifically, and the process of control more generally, shifted much intellectual inquiry towards social control, its nature and form. This departure meant that criminologists and sociologists began to problematize the role and function of criminal justice, including the police and law enforcement agencies, focusing specifically on the ways these agencies create and amplify deviant behaviour (Reiner, 1992b).

This intellectual shift did not develop in a vacuum. The emerging intellectual preoccupation with the actions of the state and its agencies coincided with broader developments in the realm of policing, and in particular to what has been referred to as its 'politicization' during the second half of the twentieth century (Reiner, 1992a; Morgan and Newburn, 1997.) Prior to this period, modern policing was viewed by many with pride and as a powerful symbol of Britain's 'greatness'. It was a period in which the post-Second World War cross-party consensus appeared to construct and reinforce the view that, of the major institutions of the state, the police were the least problematic, certainly when compared with countries such as the United States of America (Reiner, 1994). In contrast, during the second half of the twentieth century a number of changes internal to the police forces of England and Wales have highlighted various organizational and operational shortcomings (Rose, 1996). As Reiner (1992a: 74) argues, 'from a position of almost invisibility as a political issue, policing has become a babble of scandalous revelation, controversy and competing agendas for reform'. Revelations about corruption, malpractice and miscarriages of justice from the late 1950s have destroyed for many the notion of a lawful, disciplined and professional police force. Controversies surrounding technological advancements in everyday operational matters, the use of increasingly sophisticated hardware in the control of industrial disputes and urban unrest, racial and sexual discrimination and harassment, and centralization and accountability have raised questions as to the police role within and support for the community; while the increasing involvement of the police within the political process since the 1970s has tarred the organization's non-partisan image.

More recent party political involvement in policing during the 1980s and 1990s, combined with growing police demands for increased levels of personnel, resources and funding have continued to highlight shortcomings surrounding contemporary policing styles and structures (Loveday, 1996; Morgan and Newburn, 1997), as have concomitant developments resultant from the 'privatization' and 'globalization' of criminal justice. With regard to privatization, for example, a variety of hybrid, commercial, private, individual and non-public forms of policing have re-emerged throughout western democracies including the United Kingdom (Johnston, 1992; Shearing and Stenning, 1987; South, 1988); while at a global level policing has been effected by the development of European-wide law and order policies (Hebenton and Thomas, 1995; Sheptycki, 1995; 1997).

Alongside these developments, the exponential growth of crime in the United Kingdom since the 1950s has highlighted further shortcomings about the British police, especially regarding their ineffectiveness at controlling crime. In their authoritative account of crime and policing published during the 1980s, for example, Kinsey, Lea and Young (1986) put it thus: 'the police face a crisis of considerable proportions – and it is crime which is the motor of this crisis' (1986: 12). Moreover, they identified two key stages in the development of this crisis: 'The first, in the period 1955 to 1975, was a crisis of effectiveness: an inability ever to catch up with the rising crime rate. The second – what we might term the "hyper-crisis" – extended from 1975 onwards, when police effectiveness ... passed below the level at which the police could reasonably be said to be "capable of tackling the problem at all"' (Kinsey, Lea and Young, 1986: 12).

Up until the 1950s approximately half a million indictable offences were recorded across England and Wales (McClintock and Avison, 1968). However, since then, and despite periods of both affluence and depression, recorded crime rates have soared throughout most western democracies (and more recently in the new emerging eastern democracies), and England and Wales are no different. There has been 'a doubling of the figures within ten years (from roughly half a million crimes in 1955 to a million in 1964), another doubling over the next ten years, and yet another by 1990' (Maguire, 1994: 257). By 1995 the recorded crime rate stood at just over five million (Home Office, 1996), while the British Crime Survey for the same year estimated nineteen million crimes were committed against individuals and their property (Mirrlees-Black, Mayhew and Percy, 1996).

Moreover, in acknowledging a plethora of literature problematizing the measurement of police effectiveness (Bottomley and Pease, 1986) and the use of the clear-up rate as an index of police efficiency (Kinsey, Lea and Young, 1986), there has been a coextensive decline in the proportion of crimes which have been cleared up, from approximately 47 per cent during the 1950s (McClintock and Avison, 1968) to a current figure of around 38 per cent. This decline in the level of police effectiveness over the recent past is compounded by evidence which shows decreasing levels of police detection, increasing levels of unreported crime (Kinsey, Lea and Young, 1986; Mirrlees-Black, Mayhew and Percy, 1996), and increasing levels of government spending on policing (Uglow, 1988: 58).

Finally, underlying these factors, deeper and more fundamental structural, cultural and economic transformations have increasingly problematized the nature and form of policing in late modern society. Described at length in discussions on 'postmodernism' (Lyotard, 1984; Giddens, 1990; Reiner, 1992c; Eagleton, 1996) and involving disparate themes, the most common of which include fragmentation, pluralism and diversification, such transformations point towards an increasingly turbulent social order, bifurcated between those socially excluded and the majority 'two-thirds' included (Hutton, 1996); the former identifiable through their relative deprivation, 'underclass' and political and economic marginalization (Lea and Young, 1984), the latter characterized by attempts to distance themselves from the former in their public and increasingly private and virtual worlds of work, leisure and play (Davis, 1992a, 1992b).

It is in the response to these 'end-of-century transformations' that the various shortcomings of the police organization can be witnessed most clearly. For example, the use of aggressive policing tactics and styles against those with little or no possibility of reincorporation into the mainstream has increasingly generated unprecedented levels of antagonism towards the police in many communities across the United Kingdom (Campbell, 1993). Moreover, the inability of the police to provide an adequate level of patrol in areas of relative affluence has resulted in a plurality of policing systems emerging, delivered by public and private agencies and shaped around notions of community safety, surveillance and security (McManus, 1995). And to compound matters further, the emergence of new forms of criminal activity as a result of technological developments, such as the computer and the Internet, has further problematized the structure and role of policing at the end of the twentieth century.

THE COLLECTION

The preceding discussion of changes affecting British policing is important since this volume is predicated on the assumption that understanding the past is an important task in reconciling the present and anticipating future prospects. In the rest of this chapter, such thinking is related to current trends and future prospects as seen by the various contributors to *Policing Futures*. However, before that, there follows a brief discussion of the concepts 'police' and 'policing' as utilized in this collection, along with a brief review of the title, theme and structure of the volume.

As Les Johnston (1992: 4–6) has documented, the concepts 'police' and 'policing' have been carelessly conflated throughout much of the literature on the subject, with historians, sociologists and criminologists invariably assuming the two mean the same thing. However as Reiner (1994: 716) distinguishes:

> 'Police' refers to a particular kind of social institution, while 'policing' implies a set of processes with specific social functions. 'Police' are not found in every society, and police organizations and personnel can have a variety of shifting forms. 'Policing', however is arguably a universal requirement of any social order, and may be carried out by a number of different processes and institutional arrangements.

To this we may add that 'police' is a relatively new concept whereas the concept of 'policing' has a much longer historical pedigree. Drawing further upon the work of Reiner (1994), it is possible to suggest that policing involves both 'the creation of systems of surveillance' and 'the threat of sanctions for discovered deviance' (Reiner, 1994) and may be carried out through a number of processes, of which the modern system of public police is but one example. Indeed, public police reflect 'a specialized body of people who are responsible for the use of legitimate force to safeguard security' (Reiner, 1994), and which has primarily developed in line with the growth of the modern state.

Reading the various contributions to *Policing Futures* it will become apparent that this volume is not just a collection of essays on the public police and its futures. Rather, this collection concerns itself with police and policing, including the plurality of organizations and processes associated with the latter. Moreover, it is concerned with policing *futures*, including analyses and speculation of the futures of policing, and the futures within which it may operate in the coming millennium. Indeed, the general theme of the book is that in the light of the fast-approaching twenty-first century, it is an appropriate time to review past and current developments and to consider future prospects.

The volume is structured around a number of general trends affecting policing at the end of the twentieth century. The early chapters, notably those by Brown, Campbell, McLaughlin and Murji and South, examine the nature, appropriateness and consequences of various reforms instigated during the late 1980s and 1990s in response to shortcomings surrounding the practices of the police. The middle chapters by Loveday and Hillyard explore the nature of policing in the light of increasing crime rates and declining levels of police effectiveness. The final two chapters by Johnston and Wall concentrate upon developments in policing occasioned by changes in the nature of late modern society. The final section of this introductory chapter very briefly sketches out the contents of each, and in doing so stresses the need to examine the past when considering future prospects.

CURRENT TRENDS AND FUTURE PROSPECTS

As indicated, a number of chapters examine recent changes and reforms in policing. For example, Jennifer Brown in Chapter 2 provides a critical assessment of equal opportunities legislation and the police organization, and argues that, if implemented fully, equal opportunities can make a positive contribution both to the police organization itself and the community it serves. The Sex Discrimination Act 1975 and the Race Relations Act 1976 first made it unlawful to discriminate on the grounds of sex, race and marriage in the field of employment

(Walklate, 1996). However, as Brown highlights, it was not until the publication of Home Office Circular 87/1989, *Equal Opportunities: Policies in the Police Service,* some fifteen years later, that any significant shift in organizational policy and practice was discernible. This Circular stated that all police forces should ensure that 'best use is made of the abilities of every member of the force', and that 'all members of the service are firmly opposed to discrimination within the service and in their professional dealings with the public' (Walklate, 1995, 1996). Additionally, Home Office Circular 87/1989 recommended the use of codes of practice issued by the Equal Opportunities Commission and the Commission for Racial Equality as guidelines in formulating policy and guidance.

Significantly, within a year of this directive, the most senior woman police officer at the time, Assistant Chief Constable Alison Halford of Merseyside, brought a charge of discrimination against her employers, which was to end acrimoniously but with an out-of-court settlement (Halford, 1994). One year earlier, in 1989, the Lesbian and Gay Police Officers Association was convened, while during 1991 the Black and Asian Police Officers Association was set up. More recently, in June 1995, Lancashire Police appointed Pauline Clegg as the first woman Chief Constable in England and Wales (McLaughlin, 1996).

Nevertheless, the extent to which equal opportunities Circular instruction has impacted across all spheres of policing is, for Brown, debatable. Through an audit of developments in the areas of gender, race and sexual orientation, she highlights the 'patchy' nature of equal opportunities practice within police forces across the United Kingdom. While progress can be identified, such as in the recruitment and training of police officers, and in the police response to incidents of rape, Brown argues that police organizational structures and occupational cultures, alongside community resistance, continue to pose major obstacles to securing change: 'it is apparent that despite progress in securing equal opportunities within police forces of England and Wales, much remains to be done, not only within the organization itself – structurally, culturally and individually – but also in the community it serves and from which it recruits its officers' (p. 35).

The use of Home Office Circular instruction has become widespread in instigating police reform, although the actual impact such advice can have, as Brown shows, is questionable. A further problem surrounding the use of Home Office Circular concerns the actual appropriateness of the advice and instruction offered. This issue, and its consequences for the formulation of policy in the area of police cautioning, is the central focus of the contribution by Elaine Campbell in Chapter 3.

On Tuesday 6 July 1993, the *Royal Commission on Criminal Justice* was published. The report contained 352 recommendations, one of which suggested that police cautioning be governed by statute (Home Office, 1993b: 82, para. 87). The recommendation was an attempt to iron out inconsistencies surrounding policy approaches and decision-making practices. However, for Campbell, far from being a solution to cautioning disparity, this recommendation is entirely inappropriate, not least because of the ineffectiveness of existing national standards as laid down by various Home Office Circular instruction. Indeed, the nature of the proposal, coupled with the failure to produce more radical alternatives, is a result, she argues, of an administrative and pragmatic relationship between research and policy formation within criminological and governmental circles.

Campbell develops her thesis twofold. First, she considers the historical and institutional connections surrounding research and policy on police cautioning, arguing that these links have continuously channelled analysis methodologically towards a characteristically empiricist style of research and away from more theoretically informed analyses; and politically towards reformist solutions to cautioning disparity, which has deflected attention away from more radical proposals to scrap the practice, or at least remove it from the control of the police. The trajectory of this approach, for Campbell, has meant an increasingly committed and ever-narrowing focus on the formal structures of cautioning practice.

Second, Campbell explores how this administrative framework has, by its very nature, failed to acknowledge structural, organizational and occupational limits to achieving satisfactory levels of uniformity. As a result the Circular advice offered may not be the most appropriate advice, but that which best suits the administrative framework within which it has been developed. In questioning the connection between research and policy, Campbell looks towards the future of police cautioning in two ways: first by suggesting the need for a clearing of the analytical debris of the past, and second by throwing open to more critical debate the political future of the disposition. Indeed it is precisely this need to consider the wider configuration of policing relations within which the practice is embedded which underpins her reservations surrounding the appropriateness of the proposed move to statute.

The contributions by Brown and Campbell highlight respectively the impact and appropriateness of reforms aimed at eradicating some of the problems associated with contemporary policing. A further attempt to eradicate the various shortcomings of the recent past of policing has been the injection of financial, managerial and organizational reform into the police organization through a process of inquiry, committee and report. This response, and the consequences of it for policing futures, is the focus of Chapters 4 and 5 by Eugene McLaughlin and Karim Murji and by Nigel South respectively.

The origins of this type of response can be dated to the election in 1979 of a Conservative administration, under the leadership of Margaret Thatcher, committed to rolling back the state and establishing an 'enterprise culture' in Britain whereby the state would purchase services from competing providers rather than providing services itself. It was a period in which there was a general commitment within the governing Conservative Party of the time to overhaul all public sector utilities by applying private sector management strategies and increasing competition through privatization. Therefore, as McLaughlin and Murji suggest in Chapter 4, it is no surprise that by the mid-1980s it was possible to identify several key features of a distinctively 'new public sector management model' emerging. This involved the creation of professional managers held accountable for tasks, resources and results; the setting of clear targets, measures and explicit costings; the introduction of performance measurement; an increasing emphasis on outputs and the creation of a competitive environment across many public sector bodies.

Initially it appeared as though the police would remain immune from this 'new public sector managerialism', despite a creeping influence upon other criminal justice and emergency services (McLaughlin and Muncie, 1994). However, as McLaughlin and Murji highlight, in the context of increasing crime rates and declining police–community relations, the police came under increasing scrutiny from Her Majesty's Inspectorate of Constabulary and from the Audit Commission. However, it was during the early 1990s that the government's 'managerialist' intentions could be seen most clearly, for example in the reform programme involving the *Inquiry into Police Responsibilities and Rewards* (Sheehy Inquiry) (Home Office, Northern Ireland Office and the Scottish Office, 1993); the White Paper on *Police Reform* (Home Office, 1993a); the Police and Magistrates' Courts Act 1994 and the Home Office *Review of Police Core and Ancillary Tasks* (the Posen Inquiry) (Home Office, 1995). As was the case throughout the public sector, the intention was reform through market and management solutions.

The worst aspects of this reform programme have been averted, for the time being at least, in part due to its successful resistance by the various police staff associations (Leishman, Loveday and Savage, 1996: 1). What is more, government–police relations appear to have improved; as indicated by the granting of concessions to the police in the form of new batons, pepper sprays and protective body armour; by the importation of 'Americanized' policies on law and order (see, for example, the implications of the Crime (Sentencing) Bill 1996); as a result of the Police Bill 1996; and due to what McLaughlin and Murji see as a re-emerging bipartisan agreement on the police in which both the Labour and Conservative parties have emphasized their commitment to increasing police funding, personnel and resources into the new millennium.

Nevertheless it remains the view of McLaughlin and Murji that 'the managerialized future has in many ways only just begun to take effect and looks set to last a long time' (p. 100). Certainly, one consequence has been a gradual expansion of private modes of policing (Jones and Newburn, 1995), alongside a blurring of policing across the public and private spheres (Johnston, 1992). Indeed, it appears that a plurality of policing systems will remain central to debates about policing in the foreseeable future. As Leishman, Loveday and Savage (1995: 221) succinctly argue:

> when we talk of 'policing' in the closing years of the twentieth century, we evoke not the simplistic image of a corps of functionaries with an uncontested monopoly over order maintenance and crime control, but rather a whole complex of personnel, techniques and technologies which . . . cross the sectoral and spatial divides between 'the public' and the 'private'.

Nigel South in Chapter 5 seeks to make some sense of these restructuring processes. In doing so, he argues that it is possible to witness new examples of private security clearly carrying out the role of private police, along with more general trends in surveillance and informal control. With regard to the former, he suggests the power and nature of private security has developed without concomitant public acknowledgment or understanding – witness the increasing role of private policing in airports, shopping malls and leisure arenas (Davis, 1992b), whilst with regard to the latter, South contends that 'privatized, "hybrid" (Johnston, 1992a) and informal and community forms are also deeply embedded in the fabric of late modern life' (p. 110) – witness the expansion of sophisticated technological surveillance techniques into everyday work, leisure and rest (see the contribution by Paddy Hillyard in Chapter 7).

The fundamental importance of a developing mixed social control economy alongside the commodification of legitimacy, for South, is that they raise enormous implications for the securing of rights and accountability, hitherto secured from the state:

> not only have the rules and expectations of the principle of 'legit-imacy' been changed, but so too have the possibilities for seeking remedy and redress when the rules work against citizens. . . . these changes mean that 'human rights' issues must be placed high on the agenda of responding to governmental erosion of respect for tradi-tional sources of state legitimacy. (p. 109)

Indeed, as changes continue, it is South's contention that violations of human rights atrocities and crimes against the environment will pose particular challenges for policing in general and the discipline of crimi-nology in particular in the coming millennium.

A further consequence of this reform process, according to McLaughlin and Murji, can be seen in trends variously associated with localization and centralization. With regard to the former, there is evidence of a decentralizing impulse across policing. For example, chief constables are now able to exercise greater managerial and operational autonomy over their own force areas. Local policing plans are drawn up in asso-ciation with police authorities, and chief officers experience greater levels of autonomy in exercising power within their area of command (Leishman, Cope and Starie, 1996). Moreover, the ideas associated with Herbert Goldstein (1990) and 'problem-orientated policing' have be-gun to establish themselves in British policing, albeit under different labels (Hough, 1996), while community policing is already central to much discourse on police and policing over recent years (Bennett, 1994). Most recently, talk of 'zero-tolerance policing' has highlighted a re-turn to local policing practice (Dennis, 1997).

Paradoxically, organizational changes variously point towards a more centralized, national and transnational policing structure. For example, Home Office Circular 'advice' and 'instruction' have increased in im-portance (see the contributions by Jennifer Brown in Chapter 2 and Elaine Campbell in Chapter 3), and quality assurance mechanisms and arrangements introduced under the Police and Magistrates' Courts Act 1994 have continued this centralization of command. Additionally, MI5 has become involved in the 'fight against crime', and the Police Bill 1996 detailed measures for a National Crime Squad for England and Wales operating alongside a remodelled National Criminal Intelligence Service, with powers to bug and forcibly enter private property placed on a statutory footing. Finally, European-wide law and order policies, including those surrounding policing and judicial cooperation and ex-tradition, continue to be introduced (McLaughlin and Murji, 1997).

The contrasting nature of these developments should be understood partly as a consequence of the twin functions of care and control performed by the police in late modern society (Stephens and Becker, 1994). Nevertheless, these various re-taskings and realignments have generated a variety of concerns and implications for policework. For example, a number of developments, most notably those of a centralizing nature, have led to a blurring of the boundaries of policework, causing grave concern over constitutional safeguards, forms of accountabilty and mechanisms of redress (McLaughlin and Murji, 1997). The contribution by Paddy Hillyard in Chapter 7 draws attention to many of these centralizing trends and their consequences through an analysis of policing Northern Ireland. However, preceding that, the contribution by Barry Loveday in Chapter 6 focuses upon the consequences of such developments for the police role and function at the end of the twentieth century. Indeed, as he argues, despite 'all of the management rhetoric, jargon and multiple performance measures, it is . . . clear that there is a continued uncertainty both as to what the police function is, and what it should be' (p. 125).

In recent years, the crime-fighting role of the police has become central to much discourse on the police task. The Audit Commission (1993) for example, argued that if suitably organized, resourced and targeted, the police can affect crime and detection rates; 'the ultimate price for the police is the development of a strategy in which the crime rate could be brought under control' (Audit Commission, 1993). Similarly, the White Paper on *Police Reform* (Home Office, 1993b) argued that 'the main job of the police is fighting crime' (1993: para. 2.3). Indeed, the resulting view from much discussion over the recent past is that effective policing is primarily about crime fighting, and anything which otherwise obstructs or impedes this core activity should be abandoned or hived off to the private sector (see the contributions by McLaughlin and Murji in Chapter 4 and Nigel South in Chapter 5).

However, for Loveday this focus upon 'crime fighting' demonstrates a naivety on the part of government and its agencies, and fails to acknowledge what he sees as the real problem affecting effective policing, namely the disengagement of the police from communities which may legitimately demand the most from them. For Loveday, the single most important factor which has disengaged residents is crime, linked as it is to income levels, unemployment rates and perceptions of deprivation (Box, 1987). Indeed, the growing inverse relationship between affluence, crime and victimization has meant that those most in need of a police service, including the poor and socially excluded, are the least likely to request a policing presence in their area. This is due to various inhibitory factors including the fear of reprisal, harassment and further victimization. However, as Loveday continues, the ability of the police to respond has coextensively declined during the same period, the result of a number of factors internal to the police organization. These include the size of the police bureaucracy and number of specialist departments; the abstraction rate occasioned by headquarters, illness, training and leave; management overheads; and the nature of shift patterns.

Further specialization, top-heavy management structures and larger force areas will only help further remove the police from its primary source of legitimation and effectiveness – the community. Indeed, to secure the amelioration of this crisis, and develop an effective policing role, he argues, the future orientation of policing must be community-based, an approach guided by recognition of the reality of crime and policing in late-modern society, although one that will necessarily increase demands on the visible presence of police by way of uniform patrol.

In Chapter 7, Paddy Hillyard identifies the policing task as one increasingly organized around the imperatives of social surveillance, 'fire brigade policing', and the use of sophisticated technologies, weaponry and hardware (Brake and Hale, 1992; Jefferson, 1990). While tensions between localized and centralized systems of policing are generally acknowledged, in focusing upon the situation in Northern Ireland, Hillyard's contribution not only raises further a number of pertinent issues surrounding the nature of the policing task, but also of the relationships between crime control, community and policing forms in modern (divided) society. Indeed, his overall aim is to highlight how 'forms of policing are a product of conflict, social divisions and the distribution of power in any particular society, and that these forms impact upon and radically affect both the economic and social structures of that society' (p. 163).

Hillyard begins his discussion with an analysis of the emergence and development of policing in Ireland, an emergence which not only predated the setting up of the state in 1921, but also the development of public policing methods in mainland Britain. In doing so, he is at pains to highlight how little has changed over the years in the style and method of policing, characterized by a security-led and surveillance-driven force backed up by a battery of extraordinary legislation. Indeed more recent developments in policing the province, including those associated with militarization, Ulsterization, professionalization and covertization are, for Hillyard, testament to the historical continuity surrounding the policing task within Northern Ireland.

Two themes emerge from Hillyard's analysis for policing futures. First, counter-intelligence and surveillance measures, routinely utilized across Northern Ireland, are now deeply embedded within the structure and operation of policing Britain, whether it be in the pursuit of drug trafficking, organized crime or public disorder. This can most clearly be seen in the increasing use of covert measures, such as informants (Dunningham and Norris, 1995; Audit Commission, 1993). Second, Hillyard's contribution highlights how policing strategies in Northern Ireland have created new employment opportunities within the control and security industries (Christie, 1993), a development which has not only helped maintain employment differentials within the province but which raises obvious problems for the reform process. As he argues: 'In such a context where thousands of people have a vested interest in the expansion of the industry, crime control in all its dimensions will become even more deeply embedded in the social structure of modern Britain' (p. 180).

One of the most enduring themes running throughout this volume is that the old certainties, embodied in the avuncular PC George Dixon, have been replaced by an altogether more uncertain and certainly more varied form of policing today. In reading the various chapters of *Policing Futures*, what is abundantly clear are the complexities surrounding the organization and operation of the police and policing. For some, these developments and complexities are the result of deep-rooted transformations taking place throughout society at the end of the twentieth century. Just as the nature of late modern society is constantly changing, so too are the agents and organizations empowered with its control and regulation. Indeed, as Reiner (1992b: 780) points out: 'policing now reflects the processes of pluralism, dissaggregation and fragmentation which have been seen as the hallmark of the postmodern'. These 'late modern' preoccupations and their consequences for policing and law enforcement are the focus of the final two chapters in this volume by Les Johnston and David Wall respectively.

One of today's major preoccupations, according to Johnston, is that of risk. Not only has it become a dominant focus of contemporary life, but people's increasing awareness of it has accompanied a growing industry capable of managing it. As he suggests, 'given the apparent ubiquity of risk, the existence of specialized technologies for dealing with it and the fact that disputes about the validity of those technologies are of growing significance, it is hardly surprising that conventional wisdom holds we live in a "risk society"' (p. 187).

It is Johnston's contention that over the recent past significant elements of the operational philosophy and practice of the public police have also been shaped by this concept. This can be seen not only in the development of methods of policing which are actuarial, proactive and anticipatory, but also in those founded on surveillance and information technology (see the contribution by Paddy Hillyard in Chapter 7). Moreover, it is an orientation, he argues, which is similar to that of the commercial security sector. Put crudely, society's preoccupation with risk, coupled with an increasing commodification of security, has produced a similarity of public and private sector policing philosophies and practices (see the contribution by Nigel South in Chapter 5).

This change in policing, however, is also reflected in the communities in which they operate. They are more diverse, temporary, pragmatic and divided: they offer changing spatial and sectoral boundaries: they are called 'global communities', 'contractual communities' and 'virtual communities'. As Johnston contends, they are no longer 'communities of collective sentiment' but more 'communities of risk'. It is within these worlds that the future of policing can be understood. Like Loveday, Johnston suggests the future lies in localized methods: 'Community policing – that form of government through community which is concerned with the provision of security – is likely to be dominant in the future' (p. 200). However, for Johnston it is unlikely to resemble what has nostalgically been associated with 'community policing'.

That the changing nature and complexities of late modern society are important in understanding policing futures is also the central theme of the contribution by David Wall in Chapter 9. Drawing upon Johnston's discussion of the diversity and pluralism of late modern society, Wall widens the analysis of policing futures through an exploration of the dilemmas and consequences for policing posed by developments in cyberspace, a socially constructed abstract world composed of 'virtual communities' in which the traditional boundaries of time and space are distantiated (Giddens, 1990), and where access is limited to individuals with knowledge and power.

While, for Wall, this development has produced innumerable benefits – 'cyberspace has now become an important site . . . where products are now manufactured, purchased and consumed' (p. 211) – it is also an area capable of redefining the boundaries of criminal activity. This can be seen in activities involving the appropriation of image and likeness, the theft of identity and the damage caused by hacking. Indeed, 'cyber-crime' respects little of the traditional conceptions and qualities of crime: it takes place in a virtual environment in which values are largely attached to ideas rather than traditional notions of physicality, agility and ability. However, for Wall, herein lies the problem: such developments are beginning to pose enormous problems as to its regulation and control.

It should come as no surprise therefore that Wall is critical of both the public police's appropriateness and capability as a policing agent in cyberspace. Not only does he suggest that the traditional policing model is inappropriate for the regulation of cyberspace, but also that 'the existing information suggests that extending the full jurisdiction of cyberspace to the public police would be counter-productive' (p. 228). At an occupational police level, problems relate variously to individual interest, ability and skill. At an organizational police level, Wall suggests more deep-rooted organizational fears of the unbounded world remain. Rather, Wall foresees the need for a more pluralistic approach to policing unbounded worlds, based upon the informal and *ad hoc* systems already in place. These would operate across different spheres including the formal and informal, the state and non-state, and the public and private.

CONCLUDING COMMENT

Between them, the various contributors to this volume provide a unique set of perspectives as to the present state and future of policing. To a degree, all accept that policing is undergoing a series of changes at the end of the twentieth century, with regard not only to its operation and organization, but also to its actual form and structure. Indeed for some, as conventional worlds expand rapidly into hitherto unknown territories, traditional conceptions of the 'police' and 'policing' are gradually being transformed by ever more uncertain modes and sophisticated methods of regulation and control.

That said, the various contributions do not purport to provide a definitive statement of policing change. However, what does unite them is an acceptance of the underlying assumption upon which this volume is predicated – that understanding the past is an important task in reconciling the present and anticipating future prospects. Indeed, collectively they do provide critical discussion of the more important themes affecting the police organization and methods of law enforcement at the end of the twentieth century. It is within this context that it is hoped *Policing Futures* will make some small contribution to wider debates about policing futures at the end of the twentieth century.

References

Audit Commission (1993) *Helping With Enquiries* (London: HMSO).

Becker, H. (1963) *Outsiders* (New York: Free Press).

Bennett, T. (1994) 'Recent developments in community policing', in M. Stephens and S. Becker (eds), *Police Force: Police Service* (London: Macmillan).

Bottomley, A. K. and Pease, K. (1986) *Crime and Punishment: Interpreting the Data* (Buckingham: Open University Press).

Box, S. (1987) *Recession, Crime and Punishment* (London: Macmillan).

Brake, M. and Hale, C. (1992) *Public Order and Private Lives* (London: Routledge).

Campbell, B. (1993) *Goliath: Britain's Dangerous Places* (London: Methuen).

Christie, N. (1993) *Crime Control as Industry: Towards Gulags Western Style* (London: Sage).

Cohen, S. (ed.) (1971) *Images of Deviance* (Harmondsworth: Penguin).

Davis, M. (1992a) *Beyond Blade Runner: Urban Control and the Ecology of Fear* (Amsterdam: Open Magazine).

Davis, M. (1992b) *City of Quartz: Excavating the Future in Los Angeles* (London: Verso).

Dennis, N. (ed.) (1997) *Zero Tolerance: Policing a Free Society* (London: IEA)

Downes, D. and Morgan, R. (1994) 'Hostages to fortune? The politics of law and order in post-war Britain', in M. Maguire, R. Morgan and R. Reiner (eds), *The Oxford Handbook of Criminology* (Oxford: Oxford University Press).

Dunningham, C. and Norris, C. (1995) 'The detective, the snout and the Audit Commission: the real costs in using informants', unpublished paper presented to the British Criminology Conference, University of Loughborough, July.

Eagleton, T. (1996) *The Illusions of Postmodernism* (Oxford: Blackwell).

Giddens, A. (1990) *The Consequences of Modernity* (Cambridge: Cambridge University Press).

Goldstein, H. (1990) *Problem Orientated Policing* (New York: McGraw-Hill).

Halford, A. (1994) *No Way Up The Greasy Pole* (London: Constable).

Hebenton, B. and Thomas, T. (1995) *Policing Europe: Co-operation, Conflict and Control* (London: Macmillan).

Home Office (1989) Circular 87/1989: *Equal Opportunities: Policies in the Police Service* (London: HMSO).

Home Office (1993a) *Police Reform: A Police Service for the Twenty First Century*, Cmnd 2281 (London: HMSO).

Home Office (1994) *Police and Magistrates' Courts Act* (London: HMSO).

Home Office (1995) *Review of Police Core and Ancillary Tasks*, Final Report (London: HMSO).

Home Office (1996) *Criminal Statistics, 1995* (London: HMSO).

Home Office, Northern Ireland Office and the Scottish Office (1993) *Inquiry into Police Responsibilities and Rewards*, Cmnd 2280 (London: HMSO).

Hough, M. (1996) 'The police patrol function: what research can tell us', in W. Salisbury, J. Mott and T. Newburn (eds), *Themes in Contemporary Policing* (London: Policy Studies Institute).

Hutton, W. (1996) *The State We're In* (London: Vintage).

Jefferson, T. (1990) *The Case Against Paramilitary Policing* (Buckingham: Open University Press).
Johnston, L. (1992) *The Rebirth of Private Policing* (London: Routledge).
Jones, T. and Newburn, T. (1995) 'How big is the private security sector?', *Policing and Society*, vol. 5, pp. 221–32.
Kinsey, R., Lea, J. and Young, J. (1986) *Losing the Fight Against Crime* (London: Basil Blackwell).
Lea, J. and Young, J. (1984) *What is to be Done About Law and Order?* (Harmondsworth: Penguin).
Leishman, F. Cope, S. and Starie, P. (1996) 'Reinventing and restructuring: towards a "new policing order"', in F. Leishman, B. Loveday and S. Savage (eds), *Core Issues in Policing* (London: Longman).
Leishman, F., Loveday, B. and Savage, S. (eds) (1996) *Core Issues in Policing* (London: Longman).
Lemert, E. (1967) *Human Deviance, Social Problems and Social Control* (Englewood Cliffs, New Jersey: Prentice Hall).
Lilly, R., Cullen, F. and Ball, J. R. (1995) *Criminological Theory: Context and Consequences* (London: Sage).
Loveday, B. (1996) 'Crime at the core?', in F. Leishman, B. Loveday and S. Savage (eds), *Core Issues in Policing* (London: Longman).
Lyotard, J. F. (1984) *The Postmodern Condition* (Manchester: Manchester University Press).
Maguire, M. (1994) 'Crime statistics patterns and trends: changing perceptions and their implications', in M. Maguire, R. Morgan and R. Reiner (eds), *The Oxford Handbook of Criminology* (Oxford: Oxford University Press).
McClintock, F. and Avison, N. H. (1968) *Crime in England and Wales* (London: Heinemann).
McLaughlin, E. (1996) 'Police, policing and policework', in E. McLaughlin and J. Muncie (eds), *Controlling Crime* (London and Buckingham: Sage in association with The Open University).
McLaughlin, E. and Muncie, J. (1994) 'Managing the criminal justice system', in J. Clarke, A. Cochrane and E. McLaughlin (eds), *Managing Social Policy* (London: Sage).
McLaughlin, E. and Muncie, J. (1996) *Controlling Crime* (London and Buckingham: Sage in association with The Open University).
McLaughlin, E. and Murji, K. (1997) 'Back to the future', *Criminal Justice Matters* vol. 26, Winter (London: ISTD).
McManus, M. (1995) *From Fate to Choice: Private Bobbies, Public Beats* (Aldershot: Avebury).
Mirrlees-Black, K., Mayhew, P. and Percy, A. (1996) *The 1996 British Crime Survey: England and Wales* (London: HMSO).
Morgan, R. and Newburn, T. (1997) *The Future of Policing* (Oxford: Oxford University Press).
Reiner, R. (1992a) *The Politics of the Police* (Brighton: Harvester Wheatsheaf).
Reiner, R. (1992b) 'Policing a postmodern society', *Modern Law Review*, vol. 55, no. 6, pp. 761–81
Reiner, R. (1992c) 'Police research in England and Wales: a critical review', in N. Morris and M. Tonry (eds), *Modern Policing* (Chicago, Ill.: Chicago University Press).

Reiner, R. (1994) 'Policing and the police', in M. Maguire, R. Morgan and R. Reiner (eds), *The Oxford Handbook of Criminology* (Oxford: Oxford University Press).

Rose, D. (1996) *In the Name of the Law: The Collapse of Criminal Justice* (London: Jonathan Cape).

Salisbury, W., Mott, J. and Newburn, T. (1996) *Themes in Contemporary Policing* (London: Policy Studies Institute).

Shearing, C. and Stenning, P. (eds) (1987) *Private Policing* (Beverly Hills California: Sage).

Sheptycki, J. W. E. (1995) 'Transnational policing and the makings of a postmodern state', *British Journal of Criminology*, vol. 35, no. 4.

Sheptycki, J. W. E. (1997) Folk devils and eurocops: reflections on policing Europe' in *Criminal Justice Matters*, No. 27, Spring.

South, N. (1988) *Policing for Profit* (London: Sage).

Stephens, M. and Becker, S. (eds) (1994) *Police Force: Police Service* (London: Macmillan).

Uglow, S. (1988) *Policing Liberal Society* (Oxford: Oxford University Press).

Walklate, S. (1995) *Gender and Crime* (Brighton: Harvester Wheatsheaf).

Walklate, S. (1996) 'Equal opportunities and the future of policing', in F. Leishman, B. Loveday and S. Savage (eds), *Core Issues in Policing* (London: Longman).

Young, J. (1971) 'The role of the police as amplifiers of deviance', in S. Cohen (ed.), *Images of Deviance* (Harmondsworth: Penguin).

2 Equal Opportunities and the Police in England and Wales: Past, Present and Future Possibilities
Jennifer Brown

INTRODUCTION

Since the 1980s, the police service in England and Wales has been subject to a number of pressures to change from an authoritarian, hierarchical and closed organization to one that is more managerially accountable and receptive to the policing needs of all the country's citizens (Weatheritt, 1994). One source of pressure, as Murji and McLaughlin discuss in their contribution to this volume, has been the new managerialism of the Conservative government of the 1980s and 1990s, which introduced business practices and market disciplines into the public sector, including the innovation of a battery of performance indicators within the police service (Savage and Charman, 1996). A second source of pressure has been the development of the quality of service initiative, driven by the Association of Chief Police Officers (ACPO) (Waters, 1996; see also Loveday, Chapter 6 in this volume). A third influence has been the introduction of equal opportunities policies within the police service (Walklate, 1996a, 1996b). It is this latter source of pressure which is the focus of this chapter, and in particular the progress achieved so far and possible future developments, although clearly it is difficult to assess the specific contribution made by equal opportunities without mention of other sources of change, especially as in some respects they may be antagonistic. For example, the quality of service approach implies a kind of gender and/or racial neutrality in which *all* are police officers, *some* of whom happen to be women or from ethnic minorities, whereas more radical equal opportunities policies operate on the basis of an *equal* but *different* philosophy (Holdaway, 1996: 186).

It is well documented that the police occupational culture underpinning working practices is action-orientated, hedonistic, but above all, male

(Fielding, 1994; Heidensohn, 1992; Holdaway, 1996; Reiner, 1993; Walklate, 1996b). It is this which has led Heidensohn (1992: 246) to speculate about the nature and impact of the police (and policing) if the gender balance were reversed. In doing so, Heidensohn suggests this less as a serious plan of action and more as a useful device allowing pertinent questions to be asked about the consequences for society if (white) men yielded their domination of policing. Similarly this chapter poses the question of how the police organization might be affected if the present minority presence of women, ethnic minorities and gay and lesbian officers were reversed. In doing so, the potential transformation of the police service as a result of the effective implementation of equal opportunities will be explored.

The chapter begins with an exploration of the *possible* benefits and the accompanying *need(s)* resulting from a culturally diverse police service. Following this, discussion centres upon the *actual* changes that have occurred in the police service with regard to equal opportunities (since the mid 1970s). From this equal opportunities audit of the proposed and actual changes implemented, it will be clear that progress has been patchy across police force areas. The final section concludes by discussing the way(s) a police organization which is more sensitive to equal opportunities *could* herald real changes in the nature and impact of policing, not only in operational styles and priorities but also in methods of management and mechanisms for controlling police conduct. However, in doing so, attention will focus upon the complexities surrounding policing and the real difficulties associated with securing equal opportunities in policework.

EQUAL OPPORTUNITY BENEFITS

The benefits of a culturally diverse police service have been outlined by, amongst others, the Commission for Racial Equality (CRE) (1996: 11). For the CRE, such benefits include: being able to recruit a better range of candidate; having a better understanding of the community; making optimal use of people's talents; permitting the police to become the employer of choice; winning the support of the community; and contributing to a just and stable society. The consequences of cultural diversity and gender balance, it is postulated, would have a transforming effect on police and policing. Braithwaite and Logan (1995) describe how the cultural diversity initiatives emanating from the 1964 Civil Rights legislation in the United States of America, required a change of policing philosophy through greater emphasis on community policing, proactivity rather than reactivity and greater multi-agency cooperation, while it is acknowledged also that greater feminizing influences on the police culture may help criminalize certain actions such as rape in marriage, wife-beating (Heidensohn, 1992: 248) and hate crimes against lesbians and homosexuals (Mason and Palmer, 1996: 100). Moreover, there is also a moral imperative accompanying a greater presence of women within the police service. It has been argued (Hunt, 1990:19) that policemen oppose the recruitment of women into the police because this would increase 'the risks of exposure and punishment' for rule bending or breaking, whilst police 'management oppose women in order to sustain organizational legitimacy, [and to] maintain the delicate balance between themselves and their subordinates'. A greater presence of women in policing is thus seen as desirable.

However, not only are there benefits associated with a more culturally diverse police force, there is also a very real transforming need. Hammer and Champy (1993) discuss at some length the changing nature of organizations in late modern society and the need to adapt to notions of customer power and the intensification of competition. They describe typical organizational pyramidal structures, characteristic of the police service, as being designed for centralized planning and control, and geared towards the achievement of tasks. Business re-engineering involves the search for new models of management that encourage less supervision of employees and delinearizing of processes in order to meet contemporary demands of quality, service, flexibility and low cost. That is, non-traditional styles and values are in demand, styles that incorporate boundary-spanning, handling conflict, problem-solving and stress reduction, and values that emphasize empathy, attachment and nurturing (Brandser, 1996): indeed styles and values more likely to typify women managers – it is acknowledged by many that male managers are more likely to think linearly, compete rather than cooperate and be task- rather than process-orientated (Stuart, 1994).

Thus, whilst there appears to be little difference between what motivates men and women to become managers (Alimo-Metcalfe, 1993) there is a suggestion of gender difference between management styles in general (Jago and Vroom, 1982), and in particular, the police (Price, 1974). Alimo-Metcalfe (1993), for example, suggests that women are more participative and make more use of group discussions than men while Martin (1993) shows that feminist values of mutuality, interdependence, self-determination and empowerment and feminist management practice based on these values have demonstrably transformed individuals as well as the organizations in which they work. Women have also been found to operate with different communicative styles. Stuart (1994) suggests that when a woman communicates a problem to a man, he is likely to try and solve it, while she may simply wish to explore alternatives. The man may then be frustrated by this apparent irrelevant diversion – into say issues about how people may respond to the various available options – instead of dealing purely with facts. Stuart goes on to demonstrate how research indicates that men focus on external issues and prefer to exchange hard information, whereas women talk to establish or reinforce a personal connection or exchange experience. In the workplace this means that women are more prepared to share power and information. For men information represents a way to accrue power and status.

From this discussion it is clear why there is a need for a greater presence of women within an organization, and how this can have a transforming effect. Moreover, such an analysis can be extended to include the diversity created by the incorporation into organizations of people of different ethnic backgrounds and sexual orientation. As Kandola and Fullerton (1994: 47) argue, such changes will help 'create a productive environment in which everybody feels valued, where their talents are being fully utilised and in which organisational goals are met'.

The objectives of equal opportunities policies are in general to achieve a better working environment for all staff in an organization, but which tend to be directed in the first instance to disadvantaged and/or minority groups. As can be discerned from the above, however, a longer-term objective remains the transformation of the organization itself as Colgan and Ledwith (1996: 1) argue: 'just by "being there" women inevitably bring new and different perspectives on employment issues and so become catalysts for change within their organisation'. A similar point is made by Holdaway (1996) with respect to black police officers: 'The tenor of the occupational culture will not be entirely changed by the raised consciousness of one group of minority ethnic officers but some features that sustain racialised relations could be reformed' (Holdaway, 1996: 199). The agenda is thus not simply adopting male models and masculinized values so that the women do it like the men, but rather 'to shape a new image of policing – one that does not just accommodate women [and ethnic minority officers] but which makes [them] a visible feature of the policing landscape' (Berry, 1996).

Given this brief excursion above, it can be suggested that the results of achieving gender equity and cultural diversity within the police could be to: first, change the emphasis of operational techniques, developing

social rather than physical skills and moving from a style dominated
by reactivity to one of proactivity; second, radicalize policing priorities,
defining new areas of concern such as sexual violence or hate crimes
to which resources are assigned as well as status to the officers involved; third, develop new methods of cooperative management; fourth,
develop new styles of communication both within the service itself
and with the communities served; and fifth, influence the probity of
police conduct. I will discuss these in greater detail in the last section
of the chapter. However, attention will now focus upon the progress
achieved in equal opportunities and the police of England and Wales
over the last three decades.

AN EQUAL OPPORTUNITIES AUDIT

The logic of an equal opportunities police service has been expressed
in a number of ways, as the following quotations indicate:

> A police force which fails to reflect the ethnic diversity of our so-
> ciety will never succeed in securing the full support of all its sec-
> tions. (Lord Scarman, 1981)

> Equal opportunities will result in better levels of service delivery
> from a well motivated and highly skilled work force. (Her Majesty's
> Inspectorate of Constabulary, 1992)

> Equal opportunities is not a requirement imposed on the [police]
> service but an expectation, indeed a demand, from people who serve
> within it. (Sir John Woodcock, Her Majesty's Chief Inspectorate of
> Constabulary, 1993)

> The causes of equality and fairness are innately and morally just . . .
> How will the public expect us to treat them if they gain the impres-
> sion that we cannot even treat each other fairly. (Sir Paul Condon,
> Metropolitan Police Commissioner, 1993)

> There is a problem in the way in which women officers are treated
> or mistreated. A clear statement was needed that such behaviour
> was intolerable and would be dealt with firmly. (John Hoddinott,
> Chief Constable, Hampshire Constabulary, 1993)

> Measures . . . targeted at lesbian and gay communities . . . are also
> part of a more general initiative to develop community safety strat-
> egies which would make society a safer place for all citizens. (Angela
> Mason and Anya Palmer, 1996)

The above extracts indicate a recognition of the need for both equal opportunities *within* the police service and *equity in the policing of all citizens*. The inference that may be drawn from them is that achieving equality will affect not only the police service's *modus vivendi* but also its *modus operandi*. The rhetoric, policies and procedures for equal opportunities are now in place within the police service (Walklate, 1996b; Heidensohn, 1992, 1994a). What follows is a review of progress made.

Gender

The Women's Advisory Council to the Los Angeles Police Commission (1993) defines gender equity as follows: 'the creation of a gender balanced department that fully integrates women into the ranks of officers and staff, values their contribution to policing and treats them fairly' (1993: 2). Gender balance is a reflection of the proportion of women's presence in the general workforce. In Britain women formed nearly half of the labour force by 1990 yet they represented little over 10 per cent of the police workforce (Anderson, Brown and Campbell, 1993; Heidensohn, 1994a). Prior to 1975 women officers were organized within separate departments having different pay and conditions. The Equal Pay Act (EPA) 1972 brought women's pay in line with men's and the Sex Discrimination Act (SDA) 1975 included the police within its provisions despite protestations by the various Police Staff Associations. At their annual conferences and in the letters pages of *Police Review*, Police Federation members argued that it was not appropriate to integrate women within the service, a number of examples of which can be found below:

> [Women] have been used to make up deficiencies in the strengths of the shifts. That such a situation should exist, where a young woman who might be a little dolly bird of nineteen [years] should perform street duty on her own on a Saturday night and be faced with goodness knows what. (Mr Davies, Gwent Constabulary, Police Federation Conference debate, 1976)

> What could be better than to bring in a distraught woman or child, the victim of an attack, and to take her along to the policewomen's department and be sure that the result would be an expert statement covering all points? This no longer occurs. We have young girls walking the streets who are expert in nothing. (Mr Chalton, Greater Manchester Police, Police Federation Conference debate, 1978)

> Let us keep the ladies in their proper place. Pay them the same and give them the same conditions but let them do the women's work

and relieve us of it. (Mr Fairfield, Warwickshire Police, Police Federation Conference debate, 1976)

One must consider the effect on a disciplined body of male persons under the command of a woman. By their very nature men found in the police service are of the strongest dominant type and this must cause disharmony. (Inspector J. Hugs, letter to *Police Review*, 22 August 1975)

Few women recruits join with the serious intention of making the police a full career. The reasons have nothing to do with sex discrimination, they are biological. In economic terms a vast expansion in the recruitment of policewomen is a waste of public money. (M. C. Pigg, article in *Police*, September 1974)

Such attitudes are not restricted to the Police Federation of England and Wales. Police unions have allowed their organizations to remain hostile and unresponsive to women, for example in restricting committee membership (McDermott and Rayment, 1996). Despite some initial changes following the SDA, women's roles within the police continued to remain limited in scope and excluded from a number of areas of duty including public order, firearms, dog handling and traffic departments (Heidensohn, 1992). Despite the effectiveness and dedication of women police officers during this period, there remained a prominent view at the time (which in some quarters continues to this day) that:

The police service should probably continue to have a preponderance of men, and not only for their strength and weight but also for their 'hard' image. One of the chief functions of the police service is to act as a boundary marker for society showing clearly what behaviour is tolerated. Although this leads to certain crudities in enforcement it is important that the police service does not drift into having a soft social therapy image, blurring 'right and wrong' as it might be if women (generally seen as less tough, hard-line and punitive than men) came to equal policemen in numbers. (Hilton, 1976: 1116)

Indeed, when Sandra Jones undertook her study of women officers in 'Medshire' (Jones, 1986) ten years after the SDA was first introduced, she found that the traditional patterns of deployment continued, and that policemen questioned the ability of policewomen to perform all duties. Interestingly, Jones also revealed that during the decade no police force had implemented an equal opportunities policy. To summarize, Jones's research painted a picture of systematic discriminatory treatment of women officers, their under-utilization in policing tasks and their under-representation within the rank structure.

It was not until Home Office Circular 87/1989 that chief officers of police were reminded of their commitment to equal opportunities within the police service. By the following year, 50 per cent of police forces in England and Wales had equal opportunities policies (Holdaway, 1991) and by the year 1993, all forces had produced written equal opportunities policies (Anderson, Brown and Campbell, 1993). However, despite a commitment to produce equal opportunities policies during this latter period, albeit at Home Office advice, their implementation across police force areas remained a serious point of contention, as did the consequences of the absence of policy. Indeed, a number of studies have provided evidence that sexual harassment, disregard for equal opportunities and differential deployment have continued throughout police forces in England and Wales. In 1992, Her Majesty's Inspectorate of Constabulary (1993b) reviewed the equal opportunities policies of twelve police forces in England and Wales and found 'blatant breaches' of policy (1993b: 5) and reported further that 'some chief officers and others [are] not committed to equal opportunity' (1993b: 15). Her Majesty's Inspectorate of Constabulary went on to argue that whilst there 'is evidence of change in what is known as the canteen culture . . . of predominantly white male values . . . There is the serious problem of sexual harassment of women, particularly police officers' (1993b: 15–16). Moreover, participants of a national survey of over two thousand officers conducted by Anderson, Brown and Campbell (1993) revealed the same pattern of differential deployment as had Jones (1986), and in addition drew attention to widespread sexual harassment within the police service, evidence of which can be seen in the quotations below from women police officers:

> Since working in the child protection unit I have found there to be no welfare support, stress counselling or anything else. My supervisors, who are all male, have no interest in how I am coping. They make suggestive remarks, ask how my marriage is, would I like to have affairs although married. Generally I found them to be sexist to such a degree I feel sure I will leave the police force because of it.

> As a result of declining a male officer's advances he then spread rumours that I was having an affair and made anonymous calls to my husband. (We knew because we taped the second call and recognized his voice). It ended with me being moved.

Nine out of ten policewomen in the survey reported hearing sexually explicit comments within their workplace with approximately one-third indicating that they found this created an unpleasant atmosphere. Over 60 per cent routinely had explicit sexualized comments made at their expense with nearly half reporting the experience as unpleasant.

However, despite the scale and nature of harassment revealed by the study it was also apparent that women were reluctant to use the available grievance procedures because of fear of further reprisals and/or victimization, a lack of sympathy, fear that complaints would be trivialized, and the thought of not being believed. The quotations below from policewomen highlight this point well:

> I went through the force grievance procedure. It was a waste of time. Many of the incidents were witnessed by PCs on the section but all denied witnessing the incidents, whereas the civilian witness backed up my story. It resulted in the person being counselled for 'man' management skills. When I was informed of the results of the inquiry, I was disgusted. The superintendent asked me 'what do you want? The man's head on a plate?'

> No one wishing to pursue a career in the police force would be so reckless as to complain to the Equal Opportunities Commission about sexual harassment – for example, Alison Halford. The attitude is, if you can't take the heat stay out of the kitchen. I don't agree with it but I want a career in the police.

Finally, the research conducted by Anderson, Brown and Campbell revealed a picture of policemen's attitudes towards sexual harassment steeped in traditional masculine values, again illustrated by the following comments elicited from respondents to the survey:

> I believe that most female officers are happy with the present situation and it will only worsen the situation by all this talk of sexual harassment.

> I believe that in an attempt to give women and ethnics ... a fair chance the thinking has now gone too far. In my opinion if you belong to the above gender or race you stand more of a chance in achieving your goals.

> I am a traditionalist. I still open doors for ladies and give up seats. I have no problems working with female officers but would like to see them treated as ladies. They are equal but I would not expect them to be put on the front line in a large scale violent incident. I accept that as my role. They earn their pay in other fields.

From the discussion above, it is clear that the implementation of equal opportunities policies has been slow and patchy, with differential deployment and sexual harassment remaining serious obstacles for change along with the 'masculine ethos' of policing and the ineffectiveness of current complaints procedures and mechanisms. Moreover, it is sensible to suggest that these examples are not isolated incidents but rather are representative of a sexist reality. Indeed, other reports into women and policing confirm this view. For example, an inspection conducted into the Merseyside Police revealed an underlying acceptance of certain racist and sexual banter (Her Majesty's Inspectorate of Constabulary, 1992: 7); an internal survey in Cleveland Police found 'widespread incidents of sexual harassment... involving uninvited derogatory and degrading jokes' (Her Majesty's Inspectorate of Constabulary, 1993a: 7); while in Warwickshire Constabulary an equal opportunities officer was not appointed due to financial constraints and the programme of equal opportunities seminars was suspended as a short-term money saving measure (Her Majesty's Inspectorate of Constabulary, 1995: 21). Furthermore the consultants Kinsley Lord (1994) reviewed the impact of equal opportunities policies in the Metropolitan Police. This revealed that most women and ethnic minority officers still believe that they are unfairly discriminated against; that many women feel that male colleagues still do not regard them as proper officers; and that officers believe equal opportunities policies are largely cosmetic. Indeed the consultants write 'women officers are still subject to behaviour they find unacceptable: the men can be very crude and basic. Generally our findings in the MPS mirror those of Jennifer Brown's study of the treatment of women in other police services nationally' (1994: 14). The most recent inspection of Her Majesty's Inspectorate of Constabulary (1996) presents a similarly depressing picture, despite acknowledging progress along the way. It reported that 'alongside praiseworthy examples of good practice, there is also scepticism, tokenism and indifference' (1996: 9); 'a worrying lack of faith in the grievance system' (1996: 9) as 'many people felt they would be victimized if they raised a grievance' (1996: 49); and 'evidence of continuing high levels of sexist and racist banter... Many women and ethnic minority staff felt that anyone who raised issues would be denigrated or dealt with inappropriately and most had developed coping mechanisms in order to continue with work which they valued highly' (1996: 9).

Clearly the conclusion that must be drawn from the above review of progress is that the occupational culture of the police remains hostile towards women (Young, 1991) and that women continue to find themselves under-represented at senior rank and within the whole range of police duties. Data, for example from the Police Staff College at Bramshill, reveal that although the absolute numbers of women eligible for accelerated promotion courses have steadily increased, their percentage share of higher rank has declined (Adler, personal communication). A similar picture emerges from a recent analysis of the Metropolitan Police, in which it is reported that there has been a 2 per cent reduction in the proportion of senior policewomen in two Metropolitan Police areas. Susan Davies, Head of Higher Training at the Police Staff College, responds to questions about the low selection levels of women for Bramshill courses by arguing:

> Often there are too few role models, and women officers become disheartened at their own failures and those of other women. We need to convince members of all minority groups that it is worth applying. Not to do so ('what's the point I would not stand a chance anyway') will only perpetuate the problem. (Davies, 1994: 26–9)

A parallel image emerges when analysing the presence of women in the full complement of policing roles (Brown and Funelle, 1993a). Over half (55 per cent) of all women constables serve in general patrol compared to 42 per cent of men. Even when it appears that women are at least proportionately represented, as in for example the Criminal Investigation Department, a more detailed analysis shows a within bias of assignment – nearly half the women detectives can be accounted for by child protection and vice work. Overall, it is clear problems remain, a point eloquently highlighted by Heidensohn (1994a) in a review of women in policing in the 1990s:

> Three main problems can be headlined as Discrimination, Discouragement and Deviance. . . . Research has continued to suggest that women officers feel discriminated and discouraged and that a major problem is the sexual harassment they experience from their male colleagues.
>
> Various recent examples have been given of this, from the detailed account in her career by Alison Halford, the vivid ethnography from Malcolm Young (former superintendent), as well as more serious allegations of rape. Behind this pattern of unprofessional behaviour seem to lie deep-seated assumptions about the macho nature of policing, that it is an unsuitable job for women. (Heidensohn, 1994a: 18–19)

Ethnic Minorities

Recent figures indicate that ethnic minorities make up about 6 per cent of the population of the United Kingdom but fewer than 2 per cent of the police personnel. Indeed the Commission for Racial Equality (1996) indicates that ethnic minority officers make up 1.7 per cent of all officers in England and Wales including the Metropolitan Police Service. However, such figures hide the differential deployment of ethnic minority officers and their differential rank and disposition (Anderson, Brown and Campbell, 1993). Analysis of the distribution of black and Asian officers within police forces in England and Wales (less the Metropolitan Police) has been the focus of a detailed study by Brown and Funelle (1993b), the findings of which can be seen in Tables 2.1 and 2.2.

Making use of the data gathered by Her Majesty's Inspectorate of Constabulary (1992), Brown and Funelle discovered that ethnic minority officers made up approximately 0.8 per cent of the police officer complement. Most, 78.5 per cent, served as uniform patrol constables, compared with 62 per cent of all women and 55 per cent of all white males who were serving at a similar rank and duty. Overall, the authors found that about 7 per cent of black and Asian officers held a supervisory post. When the figures are broken down by ethnicity and gender, then of all white males, 26 per cent held a senior rank, while only 8 per cent of all ethnic minority males held a supervisory position; equivalent rates for white women were 7 per cent and black women zero per cent. Whilst more recent figures do indicate a small increase in the percentage of ethnic minority officers, there still remain anomalies in their deployment and rank.

As with gender, there is a legal framework governing the fair treatment of people on ethnic and racial grounds. However, similarly to women, black officers experience discrimination and harassment within the police service (Smith, 1983). Indeed research findings indicate that Asian and black officers encounter difficulties of racial prejudice exhibited by *both* the public and their fellow police officers and that these difficulties are underestimated by senior officers (Holdaway, 1991, 1996).

In the light of such evidence, attempts to reverse the trend of discrimination and harassment have been implemented, although they have often not met the needs or the rights of ethnic minority officers. In 1976 the Home Office supported a national advertising recruitment campaign in the black and Asian press, although the view taken was that as immigrants became assimilated this would work its way into

Table 2.1   Rank and disposition of police men and women in the 42 police
             forces of England and Wales by ethnicity

	White men	White women	Ethnic minority men	Ethnic minority women
Chief Superintendent	374	6	0	0
Superintendent	1,196	18	4	0
Chief Inspector	1,671	39	0	0
Inspector	4,923	149	8	1
Sergeant	14,353	556	44	0
Constable	63,004	9,918	636	143
Total	85,521	10,686	692	144

Source: Her Majesty's Inspectorate of Constabulary, 1992 (Brown and Funelle, 1993b).

Table 2.2   Duties disposition of policemen and women in the 42 police
             forces of England and Wales by ethnicity

	White men	White women	Ethnic minority men	Ethnic minority women
Patrol	47,126	6,621	548	109
Security	1,670	154	4	0
Crime	11,829	1,368	76	16
Crime support	1,740	170	2	1
Community relations	1,541	314	3	5
Traffic	7,208	268	10	0
Traffic support	223	3	0	0
Other operations	5,453	420	30	5
Other support	4,290	563	12	5
Training	3,105	676	3	1
HQ management	1,336	129	4	2
Total	85,521	10,686	692	144

Source: Her Majesty's Inspectorate of Constabulary, 1992 (Brown and Funelle, 1993b).

police recruitment by a kind of natural osmosis (Holdaway, 1996). However, recruitment remained low, and as a result of additional concerns about the high attrition rate of black and Asian officers, a number of seminars were held at the University of Bristol during 1990 at which a wide range of issues were aired by serving officers including accounts of discrimination and racist treatment from colleagues (Hope, 1995).

Indeed, as Holdaway (1996) notes, despite Home Office advice, the numbers of police recruits from ethnic minorities has remained low and 'there are few signs that the general trend is likely to change dramatically' (Holdaway, 1996: 141). More recently the 1993 thematic inspection on equal opportunities described a police force that had fallen short on a proportionate representation of officers from ethnic minority communities and drew attention to the persistence of racist banter that turned officers away from careers in the police (Her Majesty's Inspectorate of Constabulary, 1993). In reviewing ethnic minorities and policing Holdaway notes that in the United Kingdom 'virtually no constabularies have taken a positive stance towards policies to deal with the *processes* of racialisation within constabularies' (1996: 175, emphasis added). Furthermore with respect to the recent quality of service initiative, Holdaway comments that 'neglecting all the academic work available to the police – ACPO proceeded with their management consultancy and published a policy document that will sustain the racialised prejudices and discrimination known to be present in the ranks' (1996: 186). This is because, argues Holdaway, ACPO failed to acknowledge the potency of team endeavour that seeks coherence and solidarity to the exclusion of difference (that is black and women officers).

It is in the context of the above and the very real ethnic minority experiences of policing that the Black and Asian Police Association (BAPA) was formed during 1993 following a major conference on Fairness and Community Justice organized by the Metropolitan Police. Amongst the aims of the BAPA is a commitment to attract more officers from ethnic minority backgrounds to enter and stay in the police service, not least because a wider base of recruitment will help to improve relations between police and minority communities (Hope, 1995). Indeed, there is some evidence to suggest that members of the various ethnic minority communities would like to see a greater recruitment of black and Asian officers (Brown and Campbell, 1994; Holdaway, 1996). Although it is still relatively 'new', Holdaway is optimistic about the positive influence that the Black and Asian Police Association will have within the police service 'because it will directly and uniquely articulate the voice(s) of black (and Asian) officers to senior ranks. In the longer term this impact will resound to challenge the rank and file' (1996: 193). That said, whilst the BAPA has the unreserved support of the Metropolitan Police Commissioner, the Police Federation was less forthcoming, believing that the Association is potentially divisive (Braithwaite and Logan, 1995), a viewpoint reminiscent of those previously discussed in relation to women officers.

In reviewing policing, ethnicity, race and equal opportunities, the conclusion, as with gender issues, must be that there remains a gap between policy and practice in that 'the rank and file can adapt the intentions of senior officers' directives' (Holdaway, 1996: 131). However, explanations and thus possible policy solutions are complex, as one respondent from Holdaway's 1991 study (reported in Holdaway, 1996) elaborates:

It wasn't just about blacks, it was about women who were beaten up, it was about women who were raped . . . it was about Irish people . . . I didn't really share the ideas. I really didn't.

The quotation above illustrates a whole set of interrelated attitudes and implications for the priorities and style of policing, an issue that will be developed in the last section.

Sexual Orientation

The lack of harmony between ethnic minority communities and the police and problems faced by black and Asian police officers is mirrored in the gay and lesbian community (Burke, 1995). Despite police equal opportunities policies including sexual orientation, the formation of the Lesbian and Gay Police Officers Association, and recruitment drives in the gay and lesbian press, studies of gay and lesbian officers (Burke, 1993) report that recruitment and acceptance remains difficult and 'coming out' highly problematic. For example, in 1995, Sussex Constabulary became the first police service in England and Wales to target gay recruitment by placing advertisements in the *Pink Paper*, a nationally distributed lesbian and gay newspaper. In the light of this development, a force spokesman was reported as saying 'we feel that the police force should be as representative of the community as possible and we do have quite a large gay community within our force area' (*Police Review*, 26 May 1995: 7). However, invited comments from Police Federation representatives once again reveal less tolerant attitudes:

[Homosexuality] is a completely unnatural thing and not a policy I would like to see adopted – recruiting people with unnatural tendencies.

There will be some who will be privately concerned. I don't think they will publicly express it because of the times we live in.

In contrast to equal opportunities surrounding gender and race, much less has been written about policing and sexual orientation, although some reviews can be found (Burke, 1993). Nevertheless, despite a lack of research and anecdotal evidence, it is possible to suggest that discrimination, discouragement and deviance continue to affect numerous officers across many force areas, and what research has been conducted tends to support this view. That is, there remains an identifiable 'gap' between policy provision and practice. One response currently receiving active interest in the United Kingdom regarding homophobia within police services is an initiative set up by the Ottawa Police in Canada, which involves the development of an Action Plan Project – a community-based hate-crime prevention programme. As Ottawa's Chief Police Officer Brian Ford has stated:

> We live in a dynamic, pluralistic society that should be free of persecution, hatred and bias. As a society, we should strongly reinforce our disapproval of violence and the promotion of hatred, especially when violence and hatred are based on race, religion, culture, gender, ethnicity, sexual orientation, or any other bias. (Pepper and Holland, 1995)

As part of a transformation evident in Canadian policing to a more community-based focus, the Ottawa police set up a Bias Crime Unit to respond to a range of harassment and violence towards particular community groups. It is hoped that interest continues overseas, and that similar developments follow suit in the UK.

THE TRANSFORMATION AGENDA: PROGRESS AND FUTURE PROSPECTS

From the above audit of equal opportunities, it is apparent that despite progress in securing change within police forces of England and Wales, much remains to be done, not only within the organization itself – structurally, culturally and individually – but also within the community it serves and from which it recruits its officers. Mention has already been made of possible ways forward and whilst these need further exploration, it is clear that benefits will arise as a result of the police being a more equal opportunities-sensitive organization. The final section of this chapter concludes by discussing the complexities of transforming equal opportunities in the police service as we approach the new millennium. In doing so, the discussion draws upon the work of Heidensohn noted previously, in which she speculated about the nature and consequences for the police if the gender balance were reversed and gender equity and cultural diversity within the police service were achieved.

Operational Style

It has been suggested that the domination and impact of the 'macho' culture (Fielding, 1994) of the police has contributed to some of the worst excesses associated with policing – the undue use of force and misconduct (Skolnick and Fyfe, 1993). Indeed, such views emerge whatever national police force is the focus. For example, in the United States of America, the Christopher Commission of 1991 enquiring into the style of policing in operation in the Los Angeles Police Department (LAPD) contended that pervasive gender bias contributed substantially to excessive force problems (Women's Advisory Council, 1993); the Fitzgerald Inquiry into the Queensland Police in Australia found a male-dominated culture that was rigid, unsympathetic, and had a disdain for due process (Finnane, 1990); while in the United Kingdom, the Scarman Report found evidence of racism and heavy-handed policing by mostly male officers which he suggested contributed much to the racial tensions and subsequent civil disturbance in Brixton (Scarman, 1981; see also Benyon, 1986).

In the light of the above, it is apparent that a more equal opportunities-sensitive police organization would help counteract the more blatant disregard for legal rules and construct a more inclusive rather than exclusive style of policing. Indeed, there have already been a number of positive developments over the recent past, although, as is often the case, with mixed results. The reasons for such disparities between rhetoric and reality are complex, but are associated with the nature and power of the cop canteen culture, with changes in the context within which policing operates and with changes in the nature and extent of public demand. Thus whilst a more equal opportunities-sensitive police organization may benefit areas such as police operational styles and priorities, and in some cases such benefits can already be identified, so too can reasons for their failure. Three examples are discussed below.

In Britain the maintenance of order has always been a focus for the police alongside a role to protect and reassure (Reiner, 1992). For example, Brown and Waters (1996) argue that these two roles oscillate as a kind of sine wave with one or the other being at the leading edge. Thus when in the 1970s and early 1980s major public disorder occurred in several urban centres of England and Wales including Bristol, Brixton and Toxteth, the police utilized new equipment and wore more protective gear in response. Such 'tooling up' became particularly apparent during the miners' strike of the mid-1980s when, for some commentators, the 'militarization' of the police was at its height (Green, 1990). While it is not the purpose of this chapter to discuss in detail changes in public order, it is of interest to note that women were *largely* excluded from such paramilitary activities, despite the results of much research, such as that by Price (1989) and Heidensohn (1994b), suggesting that women officers are less aggressive, better able to manage violent confrontations, and more pleasant and respectful to citizens. The exclusion of women, in spite of such qualities from many public order duties is remarkable, but understandable. Indeed as Price argues further, such findings have yet to influence men's formal policing style. However, it may have helped influence informal styles. For example, it is interesting to note that during the period of the miners' strike (approximately twelve months) there was no significant rise in crime or in outbreaks of public disorder in communities away from the conflict and whilst large numbers of male police officers were serving on the front (picket) line.

The 1980s also bore witness in the United Kingdom to the development of specialist command units and the deployment of specialist officers designed to assist in the policing of particular crimes such as domestic violence and racial attack. However, the effect of such measures has been less to support the victim and police the crime and more to remove the incident from the everyday operation of policing. It appears that despite new responsibilities, old prejudices and views prevail. Holdaway's (1996) analysis of the racialization of policing, for example, highlights how the specialization of community relations has actually made such issues 'distinctive and removed' from the responsibility of routine patrol work: 'Attention was deflected from an understanding of how patrol strategies or any other aspects of routine policing might have a detrimental effect on relationships between officers and black and Asian people' (Holdaway, 1996: 109). A similar conclusion is evident from evaluations of new approaches to policing domestic violence. Cromack (1995), for example, undertook an evaluation of Domestic Violence Units (DVUs) in one Humberside Constabulary division, looking in particular at the police's response to a proactive arrest policy. The study reported that male officers still thought it a waste of time to prepare documentation if the victim was uncertain as to whether to proceed; arrest of offenders was generally avoided; officers found it hard to comprehend why women stayed in violent relationships; and little awareness was demonstrated of how to monitor and follow up repeat victimization. The overall conclusion was that of 'an underlying police culture that tends towards the belief that domestic violence is a private family matter and more appropriately a subject for the civil law' (Cromack, 1995: 197).

A final example concerns current changes in policing styles. As a result of declining police–public relations evident in the 1980s, and anxious to restore the loss of public confidence, many chief constables have increasingly begun to emphasize the caring nature of the police's contemporary role. Indeed, many police forces throughout the country have substituted the word 'force' with 'service' in recognition of changes in policing orientation (Stephens and Becker, 1994). Moreover, such trends were formalized into the ACPO Quality of Service initiative, the aims of which are laid out in *Setting the Standards for Policing: Meeting Community Expectations,* in which equal opportunities is afforded a central place (Holdaway, 1996). The document explicitly states that there is a direct correlation between attitudes within the organization and officers' attitudes to members of the public.

Yet, as Holdaway (1996: 81) vividly describes, the potency of the rank and file informal culture, in which excitement and action predominate, subverts the more discerning approach to police work advocated by police managers, for example, the ability to influence operational styles away from the masculine stereotype which according to Fielding (1994: 55) 'is unlikely to find much room for expression within the social service aspects of policing'. This has been made even more difficult recently with the media highlighting the nature of crime, public worries about crimes of violence, and the public's and police's concerns over dangers facing officers (Her Majesty's Inspectorate of Constabulary, 1995). Her Majesty's Inspectorate of Constabulary report indicates that during the previous five years in England and Wales (excluding the Metropolitan Police), five officers had been killed and nearly 5000 seriously injured. It goes on to state that the number of serious assaults was at its peak in 1990 but has since decreased. Nevertheless, the response has led to a reconsideration of the use of force. There has been a renewed debate about arming the police (Sargent, Brown and Gourlay, 1994); there has been the use of long-handled or extendible batons in preference to the traditional truncheon; and in a number of police areas, the issue of rigid handcuffs and body armour and experiments with mace. As Brown and Waters (1996) comment: 'this display of these accoutrements of law enforcement represent an apparent move away from the constable armed only with his [or her] lawful powers and his [or her] use of discretion', and to which I would add the possibility of transforming the police. The results of a survey of personnel in one constabulary area illustrate this trend: 76 per cent of officers indicated they wanted more self-defence courses; 67 per cent wanted to be issued with body armour and pepper sprays; 38 per cent wanted more public order training and 32 per cent wanted to be armed (Brown, Evans, Chambers and Waters, 1996).

Policing Priorities

Recently there have been a number of changes in policing priorities, many of which have to some extent been informed by feminizing influences. Changes in policing racial violence (Neyroud, 1993), changes in the response to violent crime and female victims (Dobash and Dobash, 1992) and changes in attitudes towards gays and lesbians are well-documented (Burke, 1995). Yet, problems remain between policy advice, policy implementation and agency/individual practice which continue to hinder the transformation agenda. Francis and Matthews (1993) provide a recent review and evaluation of developments aimed at tackling racial attacks in England and Wales. Discussion here will focus upon the complexities surrounding the development of specialist crime units, such as Domestic Violence Units, and measures aimed towards the gay and lesbian communities.

For Jones, Newburn and Smith (1994) there has been an increasing interest since the 1980s within the criminal justice system of the problems surrounding women and violence, due in part to awareness-raising by the feminist movement, public attention provoked by the media, and the results of research. That said, as the authors also acknowledge, policy developments resulting from such interest have lagged behind other policing areas of concern. It was Home Office Circular 25/1983 which first drew attention to the need for the police to treat rape victims with tact and sympathy, following the screening of a 'fly on the wall' documentary about the Thames Valley Police during the 1980s, and in particular the portrayal of an oppressive police interview of a rape victim which resulted in much adverse media coverage. A report by the Women's National Commission examining violence against women stimulated Home Office Circular 69/1986. This emphasized the victim-centred approach to women suffering domestic violence and rape, and the Circular included a section on effective training for police officers in order 'to encourage the confidence and co-operation of victims'. The overriding concern of these circulars was to ensure the safety of victims, and in response, the police developed and implemented operational procedures that included the dedicated specialist units, staffed by specially trained officers.

In evaluating the impact of these various measures, Jones, Newburn and Smith (1994) examined four police forces which had implemented specialist units to deal with rape, sexual assault and domestic violence. Their findings make interesting reading. First, such developments were not considered policy priorities. Second, the units were mostly staffed by women, although usually line-managed by a male Detective Inspector. Moreover, while there had been improvements in training officers to deal with rape cases, Jones, Newburn and Smith indicate that there was less improvement for domestic violence. Indeed, the authors suggest that it was often the case that the role of women officers within the units was not properly appreciated. As they concluded their evaluation: 'although it appeared that some improvements in the ways that police deal with rape victims had been made, doubts were raised about the extent to which this new enlightened approach had extended' (1994: 131). It appeared that, on balance, police forces' policy changes had been greater in the area of rape than in that of domestic violence, and that, moreover, 'policy statements at the top of the organization do not necessarily reflect what is happening on the ground' (1994: 155).

Sheptycki (1991), Walker and McNicol (1994) and Cromack (1995) have looked more particularly at the work of DVUs in the light of Home Office Circular 60/1990 which encouraged greater use of arrest of the violent partner and linkages with other agencies to combat domestic violence. The research by Walker and McNicol (1994) concluded that whilst there was considerable praise for the officers staffing the DVUs by the victims, there was still limited understanding from patrol officers. DVU officers tended to advise women to leave the abuser and many abused women continued to experience the police as prejudiced and responding not to the realities of the case but to stereotypes in which violence is normalized as part of marital behaviour and that women contribute to their own abuse. Similarly Sheptycki (1991) analysed the working of DVUs in the Metropolitan Police District. His research provided evidence of the filtering out of cases by despatchers often because of beliefs that the complaint would be withdrawn. Moreover, in respect to the pro-arrest policy, Sheptycki suggests that 'what happens . . . is that the victim is asked whether or not she wishes to press charges. In most cases this is not what the victim wants and the case is dropped immediately or no crimed at a later date' (Sheptycki, 1991: 119).

It is in response to such findings that Walklate (1993) has argued that while there has been a change of direction in terms of policing policy, in reality the work of DVUs represents a further disempowerment of victims by transferring power to the police. Moreover as Glass (1995) points out, whilst the best DVUs offer help as well as evoking legal sanctions, too many 'just dole out tea and sympathy without offering advice or positive action. The effect of such units is to minimize and trivialize the seriousness of women's experience' (1995: 161). The complexities surrounding transforming priorities can be seen from this review. However, it is important to acknowledge that complexities not only surround the impact of such measures on communities or members of those communities, but also their status within the police and their role within police work – a point eloquently articulated by Walklate (1996a):

> how can policewomen take seriously, and encourage their predominantly male colleagues to take seriously, an area of work historically labelled as 'rubbish' work ... [this tension] foregrounds a potential area of contradiction between espoused policy commitments, especially with respect to equal opportunities and what appears to be ... deployment of policewomen in ... low status work. (Walklate, 1996a: 197)

A similar picture to that painted above can be seen with regard to policing and the gay and lesbian communities. In an analysis of the police relationship with gays and lesbians, Mason and Palmer (1996) note that some police forces have indicated that same-sex indecency, soliciting or procuring are not considered policing priorities, and fifteen police forces across England and Wales have set up local liaison groups. In Greater Manchester, for example, the Greater Manchester Police Authority, Manchester City Council and the Manchester Lesbian and Gay Police Initiative sponsored a national conference in November 1995 which culminated in a charter of good practice. This called for a recognition of homophobic hate crimes equivalent to racially motivated incidents and positive encouragement for victims to report attacks. However, in analysing the results of a survey of over 4000 lesbians, gays and bisexuals, Mason and Palmer (1996: 88) go on to suggest that whilst these new policies were beginning to have an effect there remained more complaints about the police than positive experiences.

The discussion above highlights some possible transformations in policing priorities resultant from a move towards a more equal opportunities-sensitive approach to police and policing. However, the discussion also highlights the problematic nature of the various obstacles in place, in particular that of the police occupational culture. That said, changes at the level of management may help dilute such constraining influences.

Cooperative Management

Research, especially that examining the occurrence of occupationally related stress in the police service, has continuously emphasized the recurring problem of management-induced stress (Brown and Campbell, 1994). Manolias (1983), for example, details poor management styles, systems and support as contributing to organizational stress. Police management has been characterized as hierarchical and as having a military-based culture obsessed with doing things right. It is as a result of these acknowledgements, along with the quality of service initiative and other external pressures, that the police have recently been in-volved in re-examining its management culture, and what is of interest is how many of the new management qualities that are presently being espoused look remarkably feminine. It is well-acknowledged that fe-male management is said to be facilitating, where subordinates are en-couraged to transform their own self-interest to the benefit of the group. Furthermore, women managers tend to look at the broader picture, ask questions and seek consensus; in other words, they are process-orien-tated. This view of management styles and qualities contrasts starkly with a male style which is linear, problem-orientated and task-focused (Stuart, 1994). This is in line with modern management techniques derived from re-engineering models, discussed earlier.

In response to the re-examination of management cultures, evalua-tion and assessment of how far these alternative management styles have impacted upon the police organization can be found in various stress studies (Brown, Cooper and Kirkcaldy, 1996; Alexander, Walker, Innes and Irving, 1993) and results of internal staff attitude surveys (Brown, Evans, Chambers and Waters, 1996). Most research examin-ing occupational stress in the police still find management style and systems as significant sources of stress. Whether those styles or sys-tems have responded to change and are experienced as different by the workforce may be inferred from the results of staff opinion surveys. For example, within the Hampshire Constabulary there have been a number of management innovations including: the appointment of a civilian HR professional; devolution of more responsibility to local area commanders; and the introduction of a policy planning unit and internal inspectorate. However, when a comparison of staff survey re-sults between 1992 and 1995 was conducted, there appeared little change in the opinions of police officers, that opportunities for promotion, training and career development had increased; indeed, civilian views were actually more negative across these dimensions in the later survey (Brown, Chambers, Evans and Waters, 1995).

Open Communication

It has been suggested that autocratic management often leads to a style of communication known as 'group think' (Janis, 1972), characterized by a preoccupation with the party line such that contrary information is distorted or ignored. Janis describes patterns typical of group think: illusion of vulnerability; *post hoc* rationalization; belief in the superior mentality of the leaders; stereotyping of the views of others; use of self-censorship; conformity; and suppression of doubt. Such a model of communication, in Janis's analysis, led to the Bay of Pigs policy débâcle of the Kennedy administration in the 1960s in the United States of America. However, it is also a style that could be applied to a police service which commentators have observed as a self-protecting, secretive culture often resistant to change (Reiner, 1992).

Recently, there has been some opening up of the communication process within the police service and between the police and the public. For example, women officers (albeit a few) have reached senior rank, and there have been developments such as regular surveys of public attitudes and customer satisfaction, although the latter perhaps owes more to government inspired citizen's charters and public sector accountability than to innovations originating within the police service itself. Moreover, as a consequence of the Police and Magistrates' Courts Act 1994, police authorities are experimenting with different ways to communicate and consult with local communities, such as policing priorities surveys. While it is still somewhat too early to indicate the impact of the few women officers who have reached senior rank to influence the style of communication, and there certainly remain telling stories of the inhibitory effect of the 'glass ceiling' (Taylor and McKenzie, 1994), there does seem to have been some openness surrounding public consultation with regard to communication.

Probity

Miscarriages of justice, apprehensions about the misconduct of officers more generally and ethical matters within the police service itself have caused considerable concern since the 1960s and the so-called 'golden

age of policing' (Finnane, 1990). However, such concerns have focused upon 'male' more than upon 'female' officers. Indeed, it has
been suggested that the massaging of crime statistics and anxieties over
supposed masonic interference with due process are archetypal male
activities (Young, 1991; Knight, 1985). The connection between probity, policing and equal opportunities issues was made recently by Sir
John Woodcock when serving as Her Majesty's Chief Inspector of
Constabulary. In discussing the early statement of values of policing
Sir John Woodcock states that these:

> were issued into a world in which domination by male, Anglo-Saxon
> and Protestant views was fully accepted. That value system has changed
> little during the subsequent one hundred and fifty years but, as a
> profession, we have not taken the opportunity to consider or state
> clearly what values our organisation now upholds. So in a multi-
> cultural society, with a changed role for men and women I believe
> that the [police] service now needs to make clear its ethical prin-
> ciples (Woodcock, 1993: 27).

In the light of recent research, however, it is difficult to establish whether
the greater presence of women and ethnic minority officers has improved the probity of the police service. Alley, Waugh and Ede (1996: 2)
in reviewing the literature on standards of conduct in the police force,
report some supportive evidence that as women see themselves as an
'outgroup' they feel less loyalty to the male majority and are in a
position to expose rule bending or breaking. 'In summary', the authors
argue, 'most previous research has reported that female police officers
tend to have higher personal ethical standards, generate fewer complaints and employ less aggressive policing styles than their male coun-
terparts' (Alley, Waugh and Ede, 1996: 4). However, in the light of
their own study which examined attitudes towards misbehaviour of officers
within the Queensland Police, Australia, the authors were less certain.
Police officers were asked to respond to a series of scenarios describing conduct which, if proven, would result in disciplinary action. Overall,
they found that women officers were no more likely than men to report a fellow officer's misconduct and that both men and women recruits showed a declining willingness to report misconduct once they
had experience in the field. The investigators themselves indicate a
weakness in their research design in that responding to hypothetical
scenarios may or may not relate to real-life behaviour. Moreover the
vignettes were very brief, indicating only general characteristics rather
than specific officers or incidents. That said, the study did show that

there was a slight but statistically non-significant tendency for women officers to initiate a complaint involving a fellow officer and that women were statistically significantly less likely to have complaints made about them than male officers. The conclusions by these researchers were that whilst women officers may not inherently be more ethical than men, there are still advantages in the employment of more women in that they are less likely to attract complaints, particularly those relating to the use of force, a conclusion similar to that reached by the Christopher Commission in relation to the Los Angeles Police which was discussed earlier.

CONCLUSION

There can be no doubt that reform is presently taking place in the police service. There are initiatives to police ethnic communities more sensitively; efforts to meet the needs of gays and lesbians; and policies which reflect society's concerns about violence against women. Brown and Neville (1996) discuss the role of equality policies in some of these developments and argue that the informal competitive behaviour inherent in the police culture actually maps on to the new managerialism of police reform. The potential of equality issues as transforming influences has not yet been realized. Notions that feminizing influences on the police, through equal opportunities policies, might lead to an organization having supportive management, open communication, and engaging in protective policing emphasizing social rather than physical skills are still somewhat embryonic. Indeed there are only trace elements of real structural change in the personnel composition of the police service in terms of numbers and diffusion of women, ethnic minority officers and those with alternative sexual orientation.

Changes within organizations are difficult to pinpoint. Colgan and Ledwith (1996) argue that equality initiatives have been a casualty within the very new managerialism of the public sector that was hoped to bring in devolved responsibility and empowerment of staff. For example, even in the National Health Service with a relatively well-resourced women's project, Colgan and Ledwith suggest that 'there is little sign so far of a change in the value system which sees the male career pattern as the norm: full time employment, long hours, high mobility and so on' (1996: 285). Similarly Kay (1993), in discussing women's progress within the Probation Service, suggests that reformist equal opportunities strategies themselves do little to improve the

representation of women, rather 'the service would be required to transform its organization so that women's values were recognized as worth-
while . . . and for women to develop alternative management styles'
(1993: 65). In acknowledging change, there is also the problem of
change in isolation. As Chan (1996) suggests, reformist policies within
the police service tend to be brought about by rule-tightening and/or
changes in the police occupational culture. Whilst these may be necessary
conditions in themselves they may be insufficient without some corresponding changes in the criminal justice and wider societal environments. As Chan goes on to argue, without these external shifts, police
practice 'may revert to old dispositions' (1996: 131).

Recently, Fiske (1990) outlined characteristics of organizations in
which discrimination and harassment were likely to occur. These included: minority groups constituting less than 20 per cent of the
workforce; a percentage of managers from minority groups in management lower than that in the workforce; uneven distribution of minorities in the full range of departments or specialism; the presence of
sexually explicit materials in the workforce; tolerance of obscene or
profane language in the workforce and workplace; and the lone presence of minorities in organizational locations. Interestingly, all of these
conditions still prevail in the police service, not only in the United
Kingdom but overseas also. As Holdaway (1996) acknowledges, the
police occupational culture has retained its traditional oppositional nature:
'Rather than placing a primary emphasis on positive and hopeful aspects of police work in which social order is preserved, people helped,
crime prevented and community bonds affirmed, its heart is a triumphant
defeat of what, by rank and file definitions, is not normal and taken
for granted' (1996: 156). The white male majority continues to remain
oppositional when working with women or black officers, thus diluting
the potential for change made possible through integration. Indeed, there
is evidence of a present backlash, with equality policies creating anti-
pathy, with harassment not only continuing but in some cases going
underground and becoming more pernicious (Her Majesty's Inspectorate
of Constabulary, 1996).

References

Alexander, D. A., Walker, L. G., Innes, G. and Irving, B. L. (1993) *Police
    Stress at Work* (Aberdeen: Scottish Cultural Press).
Alimo-Metcalfe, B. (1993) 'A woman's ceiling: a man's floor', *Health Service
    Journal*, 14 October, pp. 25–7.

Alley, A., Waugh, L. and Ede, A. (1996) 'Police culture, women police and attitudes towards misconduct', unpublished paper presented to the Australian Institute of Criminology's First Australasian Women Police Conference, Sydney, 29–31 July.

Anderson, R., Brown, J. and Campbell, E. A. (1993) *Aspects of Sex Discrimination in Police Forces in England and Wales* (London: Home Office Police Research Group).

Benyon, J. (1986) *A Tale of Failure: Race and Policing*, Policy Paper in Ethnic Relations No. 3 (Coventry: Centre for Research in Ethnic Relations, University of Warwick).

Berry, J. (1996). 'Making a difference: using training and development to feminize policing', unpublished paper presented to the Australian Institute of Criminology's First Australasian Women Police Conference, Sydney 29–31 July.

Braithwaite, J. and Logan, L. (1995) 'A report on the National Black Police Association twenty third annual education and training conference', unpublished mimeo, Orlando: Florida, 27 August–2 September.

Brandser, C. (1996) 'Women the new heroes of the business world', *Women in Management Review*, vol. 11, pp. 3–17.

Brown, J. and Campbell, E. (1994) *Stress and Policing* (Chichester: Wiley).

Brown, J. and Funelle, R. (1993a) *Rank and Role Disposition of Men and Women Police Officers in England and Wales* (Winchester: Hampshire Constabulary).

Brown, J. and Funelle, R. (1993b) *Rank and Role Disposition of Ethnic Minority Officers in England and Wales* (Winchester: Hampshire Constabulary).

Brown, J. and Neville, M. (1996) 'Arrest rate as a measure of police men and women's performance and competence', *Police Journal*, vol. LXIV, no. 4, pp. 299–307.

Brown, J. and Waters, I. (1996) 'Force versus service: a paradox in the policing of public order?', in D. Waddington and C. Critcher (eds), *Public Order Policing* (Aldershot: Avebury).

Brown, J., Cooper, C. and Kirkcaldy, B. (1996) 'Occupational stress among senior police officers', *British Journal of Psychology*, vol. 87, pp. 31–41.

Brown, J., Evans, A., Chambers, V. and Waters, I. (1996) *Internal Staff Survey: Report 162* (Winchester: Hampshire Constabulary).

Burke, M. (1993) *Coming out of the Blue* (London: Cassell).

Burke, M. (1995) 'Identities and disclosures: the case of lesbian and gay police officers', *The Psychologist*, vol. 8, pp. 543–7.

Chan, J. (1996) 'Changing police culture', *British Journal of Criminology*, vol. 36, no. 1, pp. 109–34.

Colgan, F. and Ledwith, S. (1996) 'Women as organisational change agents', in S. Ledwith and F. Colgan (eds), *Women in Organisations: Challenging Gender Politics* (London: Macmillan).

Commission for Racial Equality (1996) *Race and Equal Opportunities in the Police Service: A Programme for Action* (London: Commission for Racial Equality).

Cromack, V. (1995) 'The policing of domestic violence: an empirical study', *Policing and Society*, vol. 5, pp. 185–99.

Davies, S. (1994) 'Equality: to walk what we talk', *Policing Today*, vol. 1, no. 2, pp. 26–9.

Dobash, R. and Dobash, R. (1992) *Women, Violence and Social Change* (London: Routledge).

Fielding, N. (1994) 'Cop canteen culture', in T. Newburn and E. Stanko (eds), *Just Boys Doing Business: Men, Masculinities and Crime* (London: Routledge).

Finnane, M. (1990). 'Police corruption and police reform: the Fitzgerald Inquiry in Queensland, Australia', *Policing and Society*, vol. 1, pp. 59–171.

Fiske, S. (1990) *Expert Testimony Presented to Robinson vs Jacksonville Shipyards: US District Court Florida Division* (Ex: 482 U.S. 301).

Francis, P. and Matthews, R. (1993) *Tackling Racial Attacks* (Leicester: Centre for the Study of Public Order, University of Leicester).

Glass, D. (1995) *All My Fault: Why Women Don't Leave Abusive Men* (London: Virago).

Green, P. (1990) *The Enemy Without: Policing and Class Consciousness in the Miners' Strike* (Milton Keynes: Open University Press).

Hammer, M. and Champy, J. (1993) *Re-engineering the Corporation: A Manifesto for Business Resolution* (London: Nicholas Brealy Publishing).

Heidensohn, F. (1992) *Women in Control?* (Oxford: Clarendon Press).

Heidensohn, F. (1994a) 'Fairer cops?', *Criminal Justice Matters*, vol. 17, pp. 18–19.

Heidensohn, F. (1994b) 'Women can handle it out here: women officers in Britain and the USA and the policing of public order', *Policing and Society*, vol. 4, pp. 293–303.

Her Majesty's Inspectorate of Constabulary (1992) *A Report of HMIC [into the] Merseyside Police* (London: HMSO).

Her Majesty's Inspectorate of Constabulary (1993a) *A Report of HMIC [into the] Cleveland Police* (London: Home Office).

Her Majesty's Inspectorate of Constabulary (1993b) *Equal Opportunities in the Police Service* (London: Home Office).

Her Majesty's Inspectorate of Constabulary (1995) *Facing Violence: The Response of Provincial Police Forces* (London: Home Office).

Her Majesty's Inspectorate of Constabulary (1996) *Developing Diversity in the Police Service* (London: Home Office).

Hilton, J. (1976) 'Women in the police service', *Police Review*, 17 September, pp. 1116–70.

Holdaway, S. (1991) *Recruiting a Multi-Racial Police Force* (London: HMSO).

Holdaway, S. (1996) *The Racialisation of British Policing* (London: Macmillan).

Home Affairs Committee (1993) *Third Report: Domestic Violence* (London: HMSO).

Home Office (1983) Circular 25/1983 *Investigation of Offences of Rape* (London: Home Office).

Home Office (1986) Circular 69/1986 *Violence Against Women: Treatment of Victims of Rape and Domestic Violence* (London: Home Office).

Home Office (1989) Circular 87/1989 *Equal Opportunities: Policies in the Police Service in England and Wales* (London: Home Office).

Home Office (1990) Circular 60/1990 *Domestic Violence* (London: Home Office).

Hope, R. (1995) 'A force for change', *Criminal Justice Matters*, No. 17 Autumn pp. 17–19.

Howe, S. (1993) 'Inside outside: the Met and the gay community', *The Job*, Friday, 23 July, pp. 8–9.

Hunt, J. (1990) 'Logic of sexism amongst the police', *Women and Criminal Justice*, vol. 1, no. 2, pp. 3–30.

Jago, I. and Vroom, V. (1982) 'Sex differences in the incidence and evaluation of participative leader behaviour', *Journal of Applied Psychology*, vol. 67, pp. 776–83.

Janis, I. (1972) *Victims of Groupthink* (Boston, Mass.: Houghton Mifflin).

Jones, S. (1986) *Policewomen and Equality* (London: Macmillan).

Jones, T., Newburn, T. and Smith, D. J. (1994) *Democracy and Policing* (London: Policy Studies Institute).

Kandola, R. and Fullerton, J. (1994) 'Diversity: more than just an empty slogan', *Personnel Management*, November, pp. 46–50.

Kay, I. (1993) 'Judgements of worth: women's attitudes towards promotion', *Probation Journal*, vol. 40, pp. 60–7.

Kinsley Lord (1994) *Development of an Equal Opportunities Strategy [for] the Metropolitan Police Service* (London: Kinsley Lord Management Consultants).

Knight, S. (1985) *The Brotherhood: The Secret World of the Freemason* (London: Grafton).

Manolias, M. (1983) *A Preliminary Study of Stress in the Police Service* (London: Home Office Scientific Development Branch Human Factors Group).

Martin, P. Yancey (1993) 'Feminist practice in organizations: implications for management', in E. A. Fagenson (ed.), *Women in Management: Trends, Issues and Challenges in Managerial Diversity* (London: Sage).

Mason, A. and Palmer, A. (1996) *Queer Bashing: A National Survey of Hate Crimes Against Lesbians and Gay Men* (London: Stonewall).

McDermott, H. and Rayment, M. (1996) 'Women and police unions: equity on the horizon', unpublished paper presented to the Australian Institute of Criminology's First Australasian Women Police Conference, Sydney, 29–31 July.

Neyroud, P. (1993) 'Multi-agency approaches to racial harassment: the lessons of implementing RAG', in P. Francis and R. Matthews (eds), *Tackling Racial Attacks* (Leicester: Centre for the Study of Public Order, University of Leicester).

Pepper, D. and Holland, C. (1995) *Moving Towards Distant Horizons: The Public Summary of the Final Report of the Action Plan Project Funded by the Ottawa Police Services Board*, June 1993–March 1994.

Police Review (1995) 26 May.

Price, B. R. (1974) 'A study of leadership strength of female police executives', *Journal of Police Science and Administration*, vol. 2, pp. 219–26.

Price, B. R. (1989) 'Is policework changing as a result of women's contribution?', unpublished paper presented to the International Conference on Police Women, Netherlands, 19–23 March.

Reiner, R. (1992) *The Politics of the Police*, 2nd edn (Brighton: Harvester Wheatsheaf).

Sargent, S., Brown, J. and Gourlay, R. (1994) 'Who wants to carry a gun?', *Policing*, vol. 10, no. 4, pp. 242–52.

Savage, S. and Charman, S. (1996) 'Managing change', in F. Leishman, B. Loveday and S. Savage (eds), *Core Issues in Policing* (London: Longman).

Scarman, Lord (1981) *The Brixton Disorders: Report of the Inquiry*, 10–12 April 1981 (London: HMSO).

50   *Equal Opportunities and the Police*

Sheptycki, J. (1991) 'Innovations in the policing of domestic violence in London', *Policing and Society*, vol. 2, pp. 117–37.

Skolnick, J. and Fyfe, J. (1993) *Above the Law: Police and the Excessive Use of Force* (New York: Free Press).

Smith, D. (1983) *Police and People of London III: A Survey of Police Officers*, Report 620 (London: Policy Studies Institute).

Stephens, M. and Becker, S. (1994) *Police Force, Police Service* (London: Macmillan).

Stuart, C. (1994) 'Harmony in diversity', *Professional Management*, November, pp. 10–11.

Taylor, C. and McKenzie, I. (1994) 'The glass ceiling at the top of the greasy pole', *Policing*, vol. 10, pp. 260–7.

Walker, J. and McNicol, L. (1994) *Policing Domestic Violence: Protection, Prevention or Prudence?* (Newcastle: University of Newcastle Relate Centre for Family Studies).

Walklate, S. (1993) 'Policing by women, with women, for women?', *Policing*, vol. 9, pp. 101–15.

Walklate, S. (1996a) 'Equal opportunities and the future of policing', in F. Leishman, B. Loveday and S. Savage (eds), *Core Issues in Policing* (London: Longman).

Walklate, S. (1996b) *Gender and Crime* (Brighton: Harvester Wheatsheaf).

Waters, I. (1996) 'Quality of service: politics or paradigm shift', in F. Leishman, B. Loveday and S. Savage (eds), *Core Issues in Policing* (London: Longman).

Weatheritt, M. (1994) 'Measuring police performance: accounting or accountability?', in S. Spencer and R. Reiner (eds), *Accountable Policing* (London: Policy Studies Institute).

Women's Advisory Council to the Los Angeles Police Commission (1993) 'A blueprint for implementing gender equity in the Los Angeles Police Department', unpublished report.

Woodcock, Sir John. (1993) 'The values we uphold', *Police Review*, 1 January, pp. 26–7.

Young, M. (1991) *An Inside Job* (Oxford: Clarendon).

3 Two Futures for Police Cautioning

Elaine Campbell

INTRODUCTION

In 1993, the *Royal Commission on Criminal Justice* recommended that police cautioning be governed by statute. This recommendation reflected the failure of advice in successive Home Office Circulars to promote consistency across police force areas, in terms of both policy approaches and decision-making practices. Yet, despite this, given the ineffectiveness of existing national standards for cautioning, it is difficult to foresee the difference that a statutory approach will make, especially as there are definite structural, organizational and occupational limits to achieving a satisfactory level of uniformity.

However, it is precisely the failure to explore these limitations in almost five decades of research work which is responsible for the current political climate surrounding cautioning, and in particular recommendations for greater statutory control. With only two notable exceptions (Pratt, 1986; McConville, Sanders and Leng, 1991), successive research has constantly failed to understand the practice in a relational way. While it is one thing to select out cautioning policy and practice as a discrete analytical topic, it is quite another to ignore its embeddedness in a wide configuration of policing relations. It is in the light of the above that this chapter outlines the need for a sociological analysis of cautioning, and particularly of the possibilities such an approach might bring to the areas of cautioning research and practice. In doing so, this chapter addresses the future of police cautioning in two ways. First, by clearing the ground of the analytical debris of the past, it is hoped that the contours of *potential* research agendas show up in sharp relief; and second, it throws open to more critical debate the *political* future of cautioning.

The chapter begins with discussion of the problematic nature of police cautioning, including an analysis of its paradoxical function as diversion, and a broader consideration of its endemic geographical variability. It will be shown how, in the absence of theory, the vagaries of cautioning have been largely understood as a function of 'unfettered police discretion' in cautioning affairs. Following this, discussion suggests that political solutions have remained equally transparent, settling around the idea that the practice needs to be structured, regulated and controlled – culminating in governance by statute. In this way, both problem definition and its solution are formulated in conventionally legalistic ways. In highlighting current cautioning praxis, it will be suggested that such a perspective not only ignores the importance of context and process in understanding the nature of discretion in cautioning, but also obscures the need to appreciate discretionary actions from a sociological point of view. The final section of the chapter suggest that it is only through a sociological analysis that new ways of thinking can be explored. For example, it may be that the extent of police discretion in cautioning affairs is overstated; the idea that the practice is always-already[1] structurally overdetermined remains, at least, a theoretical possibility. I explore this possibility at the macro, mezzo, and micro levels of analysis, to show the difference that a sociological approach to the question of constraint and control might make.

CAUTIONING: PANACEA AND PARADOX

Diversion from formal prosecution in court is predominantly achieved by way of a police caution. In 1994, for indictable offences, 70 per cent of known offenders[2] under 18 years were cautioned; as were 36 per cent of young adult offenders (18 to 20 years); and 8 per cent of adult offenders (aged 21 and over). Two possible ways of interpreting such figures are as follows. From a 'managerial' point of view, it could be suggested that the disposal of cases at an early stage in the criminal process saves the time and resources involved in a full prosecution case.[3] At the same time, diversion at the pre-trial stage reduces the volume of cases to be tried at court, promoting greater efficiency in the trial process itself, and possibly reducing the downward pressure for prison places – the latter being reserved for only the most serious and violent offenders. A more humanitarian view would look towards the impact cautioning has on offenders, suggesting that early diversion reduces the stigmatizing and labelling effects resulting from formal processing and can help to minimize the development of criminal careers associated with a court conviction. However, it has been suggested that the principles of managerialism, with its emphasis on cost effectiveness and efficiency, and humanism, which looks to alleviate the worst effects of the criminal process, are potentially, if not actually, incompatible (Cohen, 1981: 229). Police cautioning, in theory at least, has the capacity to fuse these otherwise competing principles. Ditchfield's (1976) normative description of the practice makes the point well:

> The police caution is formally acknowledged as an alternative to prosecution. For indictable offences, it almost invariably takes the form of an oral warning by a senior, uniformed police officer about the offender's conduct, and about the possibility of future prosecution if a further offence is committed. A caution can only be administered if the offender admits his guilt, if the police are satisfied they have sufficient evidence to otherwise charge and prosecute, and if the complainant does not insist on a prosecution. As such, the caution is most often applicable to first offenders, and/or young, vulnerable and 'less serious' offenders. (Ditchfield, 1976: 1)

It is little wonder therefore, as Pratt (1986) argues, that the move to increase the usage of the practice in the 1970s, especially for juvenile offenders, commanded support across the ideological and political spectrums:

> Here at least, it might be thought, there are signs of progress that all can agree on, signs of a more humanitarian approach to our criminal justice system. Less formalism, less ritual, more speed, more efficiency, fewer lawyers ... the classical mixture for recipes of progress ... each measure of which leaves further behind some of the more barbaric relics of our past. (Pratt, 1986: 213)

The matter, however, does not rest there. As much as there exists a shared belief in the value of police cautioning (whether that value is conceptualized in economic, anti-professional, political or humanitarian terms), there is also a shared disbelief in its capacity to deliver the goods. For example, some analysts posit a 'net-widening' thesis.[4] In simple terms this evocative metaphor describes the tendency for cautioning to replace informal, screening mechanisms such as 'on-the-street' warnings; or indeed, to replace no further action (NFA) decisions made on those offences formally processed into the system (Ditchfield, 1976; Farrington and Bennett, 1981; Mott, 1983; Cohen, 1985; Giller and Tutt, 1987; Sanders, 1988; Wilkinson and Evans, 1990). Allied to this argument is the idea of 'denser nets'. This concept has been used to describe the relative intensity of different forms of 'enhanced' cautioning, which may include elements of reparation and mediation, or requirements to undertake intermediate treatment (Home Office, 1984; Cohen, 1979, 1985; Sanders, 1988; Evans and Wilkinson, 1990). Third, some authors argue that the relatively low visibility of the cautioning decision erodes opportunities for victims to make known their views about a case (Sanders, 1988; Davis, Boucherat and Watson, 1989). For example, Davis, Boucherat and Watson's (1989) study of the Northampton Juvenile Liaison Bureau, a multi-agency initiative, suggested that a serious weakness of the approach, whatever it achieved in terms of diverting juveniles from court, was its operation. As the authors argue:

> a closed system of justice . . . [and] administrative decision making by police and social workers cannot offer . . . a form of 'local tribunal', responsive to victim and offender perspectives, and reflecting neighbourhood justice norms. (Davis, Boucherat and Watson, 1989: 234)

Moreover, the idea is often put forward that police cautioning ignores compensatory principles (Sanders, 1988). Given the current resurgence of interest in the rights and role of the victim, how far these rights can be incorporated into the decision-making process, without compromising the legal rights of suspects, is left radically unclear (Ashworth, 1984). As Sanders (1988) notes, the dilemma of these competing interests can only lead to a diversionary process which is 'distorted by incompatible pressures, or stymied at birth' (1988: 518).

Notwithstanding the 'victim effect', some authors have also questioned the procedural propriety of the cautioning process, and suggest that the safeguarding of suspects' rights may be seriously at risk. For example, Laycock and Tarling (1985) found that a few police forces, rather than treat each case separately, responded uniformly to groups of offenders, and 'in line with the worst individual' (Home Office, 1984: 40). Sanders (1988) points out that cautions do not necessarily follow arrest and formal interview, two procedures which trigger rights to legal advice. Citing the frequent complaints of the Prosecuting Solicitors Society, and buttressed by his own research findings, Sanders further argues that even when guilt is 'self-evident' and admitted, police officers often fail to identify legal defences such as intent and intoxication; and, even worse, they refuse to accept their ignorance in these matters (Sanders, 1988: 516). There is also some dispute as to whether cautioning fulfils any meaningful crime-preventive function. Farrington and Bennett (1981) found that cautions were no more successful than court convictions in preventing recidivism; Mott (1983) claimed that for juvenile males cautioning was at least as effective as the more lenient court disposals, such as fines and discharges; while Westwood (1990, 1991), suggests that recidivism in an inner-city Bristol division for adults over 21 years of age was running at 77 per cent, although this fell (not too drastically) to 75 per cent following Avon and Somerset's revised approach to adult cautioning.

From the above review it can be suggested that for a number of authors, far from diverting offenders, police cautioning may make formal intervention more likely; it may increase the level and/or intensity of intervention; victims may not be consulted, or even informed, and certainly stand to gain little compensatory redress; the legal rights of suspects may be seriously undermined; and, after all that, there is no certainty that cautioning deters individuals from further offending.

Such concerns are troubling enough, but they are compounded when the persistence, over time, of variation in the use of the caution is inserted into the critical equation. The inconsistent patterning of police cautioning, both across and within police force areas, has captured academic attention for more than fifty years.[5] In this sense, the disparity argument predates those which bemoan the disposal's diversionary failings. While the aggregate use of the caution has increased for all age groups, there are persistently marked geographical variations in its use in terms of a number of offender characteristics – for example, age, sex, ethnicity, socioeconomic background and offending history; and in terms of types of offences committed (Landau, 1981; Fisher and Mawby, 1982; Landau and Nathan, 1983; Mott, 1983; Tutt and Giller, 1983; Home Office, 1984; Giller and Tutt, 1987; Evans and Wilkinson, 1990; Westwood, 1990, 1991; Wilkinson and Evans, 1990). Moreover, there is variability beyond this. For example, there are fluctuations over time in the cautioning rate for single forces – so that in 1993 Kent Constabulary cautioned 60 per cent of all persons found guilty or cautioned for indictable offences, while in 1994 the same constabulary cautioned 47 per cent (Home Office, 1994: 108). Equally, there is inconsistency over time, in the range between high and low cautioning forces – so that, in 1983, the range was 29 percentage points, while in 1994 it was 35 percentage points.[6]

This kind of data invites all kinds of interpretation. For example, it can be argued that the disparity is a product of extraneous factors such as crime patterns; the demographic features of different policing areas; local sentencing trends; rates of recidivism; legislative change; and levels of community involvement in policing affairs. All these features may affect the police propensity to caution, not only from one year to the next, but also within force areas and within police divisions. Similarly, the patterning can be attributed specifically to policing factors. For example, differences in force policy; variations in commitment to inter-agency diversion; varying availability of different forms of cautioning (informal caution, instant caution, formal caution, caution plus); diversity in attitudes to multiple cautions; variation in administrative arrangements for administering, recording and monitoring the practice; the predominance of different procedural processes, such as arrest and summons; and the ideological orientations of individual police decision-makers.

All of these features at one time or another have been suggested as determinants of variability. However, little in the way of reliable and valid evidence of any causal relationships has ever been established, and Bottomley and Pease's (1986) summary of the body of research work appears to reflect well the more general acquiescence to the circularity and sterility of explanatory models. As they conclude:

> No single factor is likely to account for all variation in police cautioning. Some can undoubtedly be laid at the door of differences in crime committed, some to the varying proportion of first offenders, and some perhaps to explicit policy choices, whether deliberately or incidentally impacting on the rate of cautioning. (Bottomley and Pease, 1986: 60)

The uneven patterning of the use of the caution, across both time and space, coupled with wide divergences in force approaches to policy and practice, suggest then that variability is not only an endemic feature of the disposition, but also beyond statistical explanation. From the discussion about it, it is clear that cautioning is not at all what it seems. It is neither diversionary (net-widening); nor is it non-interventionist (intensified forms of cautioning); it is unresponsive to victims; it undermines the protective rights of suspects; it may be ineffective at reducing recidivism; and it is simply unfair, both in terms of the relative rate of its use and the process through which it is delivered. If this was not bad enough, there is even doubt as to whether police cautioning really does represent an efficient and rational use of resources. Ditchfield (1976) for example, casts doubt on the cost benefits of increased cautioning. He suggests that greater usage of the disposition may not only cut off a source of revenue (from court fines and orders for costs), but may also increase the level of public expenditure by substituting the 'unpaid labour' of magistrates with more costly police administrative work. Although Ditchfield's assertions have never been empirically tested, they do remain a theoretical possibility. To all intents and purposes then, police cautioning has still to realize its full progressive potential. Yet for all this, the practice continues to function as the principal and only viable form of pre-trial diversion, albeit as a rather 'hit and miss process' (McConville and Sanders, 1992: 120) played out by a recalcitrant police organization.

REFORM, DISCRETION AND THE LEGAL PARADIGM

It could, of course, be argued that police cautioning be scrapped, or at least removed from the control of the police. Remarkably, there are few who have even considered the possibility. Patchett and McClean (1965) had hoped that the introduction of Family Councils as proposed in the White Paper *The Child, the Family and the Young Offender* 1965 would effectively remove the police power to caution for the under-sixteen age group at least (Patchett and McClean, 1965: 709–10).[7] More latterly, Sanders has called for diversionary discretion to be placed at the apex of the pre-trial system within the Crown Prosecution Service (Sanders, 1988: 525) although, as he also points out, for this to function fairly, a more radical shift to an inquisitorial system may be required. Expanding the range of alternatives to prosecution has also been suggested. Ashworth (1984), for example, discusses the role that fixed penalties might play in the diversion of offenders; while Sanders (1988) also considers the potential of introducing continental systems of conditional waivers. However, in reviewing some of the proposals put forward, two issues arise. First it is difficult to see how these different measures will avoid the same kinds of issues already discussed. Moreover, it is always possible that a different package of diversionary disposals might only replace old problems with new ones. As a result, it appears that we are left then with no alternative but to keep critical faith in a reformist agenda which seeks out ever more sophisticated ways of regulating, standardizing and controlling the practice as it currently functions – and this, according to most commentators is 'largely [as] a matter of unfettered police discretion' (Sanders, 1988: 513).

Sanders's comment both describes and explains the dilemmas of police cautioning; either way, the utility of 'unfettered discretion' to understanding the paradoxical situation sketched above remains an empirical question. Nevertheless, discursively, the link has been (and continues to be) made. In fact, the exercise of discretionary power and its control have provided both an *a priori* understanding of the contradictions of police cautioning and a political strategy for overcoming them. Even as problematic aspects of the practice were unfolding, the appropriate use of police discretion was already being called into question and ever since has seemed to serve as a kind of 'bucket theory' of observed cautioning discrepancies. While there may be no real problem with this, following *inter alia* Bankowski and Nelken (1981), Smith (1981), and Schneider (1992), there needs to be a degree of scepticism of the hitherto analytical approach to the discretionary question, particularly the political perspective that this approach promotes.

It was Davis's *Discretionary Justice: A Preliminary Inquiry* (1969) which stimulated, through legal reasoning, academic and political interest in the 'confining, structuring and checking' of discretionary power in the criminal process (1969: ch. 7). While this intellectual debt is rarely acknowledged in the literature, it does raise questions about the structure and regulation of cautioning discretion. Two main points can be raised about this. First, it is not altogether clear that the relevant, and *only* 'structures' have been identified and discussed. In order to stress this point it is necessary to reappraise the cautioning literature, in the light of those academic insights which converge on the idea that 'discretionary decisions are rarely as unfettered as they look', (Schneider, 1992: 79); and also those which conceptualize 'structure' in more holistic and flexible ways (Bankowski and Nelken, 1981; Smith, 1981; Schneider, 1992; Baldwin, 1995). Second, if it can be argued that 'unfettered discretion' is more apparent than real, and if cautioning discretion is always-already structurally overdetermined, then the reformist push to fix boundaries around free-wheeling aspects of cautioning practice must be considered as highly suspect, both politically and analytically.

The work by Davis (1969) collected together the analyses of a number of contemporary legal scholars, whose main aim was to explore the ambiguity and individualistic application of legal rules by judicial decision-makers.[8] As Hawkins (1992) suggests of Davis's work, it was a forceful critique of the extent of discretion formally allowed, and the manner of its exercise:

> Davis regarded discretion as the major source of injustice and confronted the basic question of how to reduce it ... [He] at once increased academic interest in discretion and re-directed conceptions of it away from the somewhat benevolent view then prevailing. (Hawkins, 1992: 16–17)

Although Davis was devoted to exposing the injustices which emerged from the exercise of discretionary power, his mission was more to remedy the improper use of such power. His contribution was therefore more political than it was analytical; according to Hawkins, Davis 'created a new vocabulary of reform by arguing for the "confining, structuring and checking" of discretionary power', (Hawkins, 1992: 17). Davis's work has faced a number of criticisms from a variety of quarters over the years, such as: its misplaced concern with individual rights, rather than social justice; its close association with the ideal of the 'rule of law'; its mechanical view of decision-making; its assumption that procedural justice will bring about substantive justice; and its unrealistic expectations of the practical potential of a rule-based approach (see, for example, Lacey, 1992; Baldwin, 1995). However, the critical point which needs to be stressed is that the perspective is founded on the assumption that to exercise discretion is to exercise free choice, albeit within effective (usually legal) limits (Davis, 1969: 4). From a jurist's vantage point, without legal limits, this 'freedom' remains unconstrained and unstructured, and choices will be made on the basis of individual, arbitrary and intuitive standards. Galligan (1990), for example, considers discretion as 'a sphere of autonomy within which one's decisions are in some degree a matter of personal judgement and assessment' (1990: 8). There is no room within this paradigm to consider how far individual 'free choice' may be always-already, collective, ordered, routinized and structured.[9]

However, from a social scientific standpoint, human agency is rarely, if ever, voluntary. Indeed, the whole enterprise is founded on the idea that all human behaviour is both structured and structuring – although how this may be so is understood in different theoretical ways. In the social world, legality is only one structure amongst 'a thousand limitations' (Schneider, 1992: 79); these do not evaporate conveniently when discretion is exercised. At the same time, discretionary decision-making is 'a continuing process, a subtle and shifting affair that is the result of substantial human interpretative work' (Baldwin, 1995: 25), and it cannot, therefore, be bracketed off from other forms of human action and interaction. Lacey (1992) eloquently makes the same point:

> The persistent difficulty, exemplified in the work of Davis himself, is that when lawyers open their minds to new areas of study, they do not necessarily also open their minds to the appropriateness (or lack of it) of applying conventional legal analysis and solutions to the newly discovered areas . . . Sociologists' recognition of discretion

as a crucially important and pervasive source of executive power has . . . led to an emphasis on the importance of context in understanding the nature of discretion. This acknowledgement of context-relativity has generated . . . an increasing concern to gather an appreciation of agents' own understandings of their discretionary actions . . . This interpretive, 'phenomenological', agent-centred approach has in turn generated insights relating to the existence among those who exercise discretion of 'operational ideologies', 'frames of relevance', or 'assumptive worlds' – systems of values and beliefs which allow agents to make sense of, to impose explanations on, and to order events in the world in which they are operating. (Lacey, 1992: 360–4)

Lacey is optimistic that the discipline of sociology will eventually 'rub off' on lawyers – 'if the dangers of the legal paradigm are to be averted, jurisprudential and legal approaches will clearly have to be modified in the light of the insights of social science' (1992: 380). However, the neat twist in this argument is that not all social scientific approaches to the question of discretion subscribe to phenomenology (or any other social theory for that matter). Cautioning research is a case (*par excellence*) in point. So far, this body of work has avoided any investigation of police cautioning as contextualized activity. Instead, research studies, and the policy recommendations which flow from them, reflect a peculiar fascination for what Baldwin dubs the 'Escort XR3i approach to processes' (Baldwin, 1995: 22); that is, following the legal paradigm, the focus has remained squarely on the structuring potential of rules and guidelines, statements of principle, policies, procedures, and the creation of administrative structures, *as if* the cautioning process 'can be improved by adding ever more legalistic trimmings and accessories' (1995: 22). The trajectory of this approach is worthy of brief review, since it demonstrates an increasingly committed and ever-narrowing focus on the formal structures of cautioning practice.

RESTRICTIVE PRACTICES AND OFFICIAL GUIDANCE

Even before the ink had dried on Davis's thesis, researchers were sketching out the potential for constructing a 'belt of restriction' around the practice. Often phrased in negative terms, authors of that decade complained that 'there has been little official guidance' (McClintock and

Avison, 1968: 155); or, 'there is no common policy' (Somerville, 1969: 480). In fact, for some, the very absence of direction from central government left the police as 'not wholly to blame for the situation' (Somerville, 1969: 483). There were more positive suggestions. For example, Somerville called for an inter-agency approach to juvenile cautioning, monitored through Her Majesty's Inspectorate of Constabulary; this, he argued, would standardize practice (1969: 481). McClintock and Avison argued for 'some serious discussion on the principles involved' (1968: 156); Steer proposed a number of procedural safeguards (1970: 57), and in particular, considered the importance of the incoming Children and Young Persons Act 1969 as a mechanism to 'reduce ideological differences between Chief Constables, and so lead to greater uniformity of practice' (1970: 19). By 1976, Nelken expressed concern with the extended use of the caution,[10] and saw this as the cue for urging the development of a framework for its proper governance. Citing Davis specifically, he proposed that the police themselves might formulate detailed, administrative rules, based on a clear identification of aims. Importantly, Nelken stressed that the structuring of police cautioning discretion could not be left to 'the necessarily episodic operation of judicial review' (1976: 368); yet, it was precisely this kind of mechanism which became the catalyst for a committed governmental response to cautioning matters.

The *Royal Commission on Criminal Procedure* (1981) (the Phillips Report), cited the vagaries of cautioning to illustrate inconsistency in prosecution practice generally; the need to reduce variation was seen as crucial to the fairness, accountability and efficiency of the system. Highlighted again by the All-Party Penal Affairs Group, in the same year, the issue was more thoroughly reviewed in a Consultative Document drawn up from the Report of the Working Group on Cautioning (Home Office, 1984; see also Laycock and Tarling, 1985). Falling some way short of advocating a rigid national policy, the government's preferred approach to achieving some semblance of uniform policy and practice has been by way of Circular exhortation. Three Home Office Circulars,[11] providing chief officers with detailed guidance on cautioning matters, have since been disseminated over the period 1985 to 1994 (Home Office Circulars 14/1985, 59/1990, 18/1994). The Circulars co-established national standards for cautioning which, it was argued, 'create a framework of general principles and practice within which forces should operate' (Home Office Circular 59/1990: para. 7). These 'standards' amount to the setting out of clear decisional criteria for cautioning; a clarification of the way in which cautions for different age groups should be administered; a recommendation that cautions should not only be carefully recorded (since they may be subsequently cited in court), but also monitored on a force-wide basis; a reiteration of the need for chief officers to produce force policy statements which reflect a clear and consistent stance on cautioning; and advice to maximize the inter-agency basis of cautioning at both the policy-making and the decision-making level.

In research terms, the Circulars certainly re-energized interest in the potential for confining cautioning discretion by way of guidelines (principles, criteria, procedures and policies). In fact, given the rash of positive commentary following the issuing of Home Office Circular 14/1985 (Cavadino, 1985; Kidner, 1985; Hullin, 1985),[12] it seemed that the panacea for containing the worst excesses of the disposition had all but arrived. Evaluation of Home Office Circular impact followed relatively swiftly. For example, while Giller and Tutt (1987) use secondary data to assess the impact of the first of these Circulars, the Home Office backed up its Circular advice by commissioning systematic research which has principally been undertaken by Evans and Wilkinson (see Evans and Wilkinson, 1990; Evans, 1991; Wilkinson and Evans, 1990). These researchers conclude that variations within forces are as great as variations between forces; information about cautioning is difficult to obtain due to the absence in many force areas of adequate recording systems; and furthermore, this inadequacy inhibits the effective monitoring of many force initiatives. These, in any event, may be rather oblique; 'initiative', it seems, may be nothing more than 'verbatim incorporation of the circular into force standing orders' (Evans and Wilkinson, 1990: 164). The Circular 14/1985 encouraged the development of multi-tiered decision-making structures (to accommodate the varied basis of decisions to informally warn; recommend no further action; administer instant cautions, deferred cautions, with and without consultation, and caution plus). However, this proliferation varied not only between forces, but within forces in the number of tiers used, and in the way they are used (Wilkinson and Evans, 1990: 176). All the indications from Evans's most recent study into the impact of Home Office Circular 59/1990 suggest that little progress has been made. Such findings are reminiscent of Stan Cohen's well-worn words: 'The reforms have been absorbed and integrated . . . it is business as usual' (Cohen, 1988: 216).

For some, the ineffectiveness of Home Office Circular advice adds weight to the long-running argument that police cautioning should be governed by statute (*Royal Commission on Criminal Procedure*, 1981;

Cavadino, 1985; Galligan, 1994). Indeed, the *Royal Commission on Criminal Justice* 1993 recommends such a move, and Commissioners suggest that the practice should be governed by regulations laid down in statute and based on the National Standards set out in Home Office Circular 59/1990 (*Royal Commission on Criminal Justice*, 1993: para. 57). However, given the negligible impact of successive Home Office Circulars, it is difficult to see the difference that governance by statute will make. Consider, for example, the impact of the Police and Criminal Evidence Act 1984 (PACE) on policing and police culture. For Reiner, PACE prescribes a set of changes in police powers, procedures and processes of accountability of unparalleled scope and importance (Reiner, 1992: 223). There are few who would disagree with this description; but PACE also exemplifies the equivocal nature of achieving reform through the use of rules. As Dixon's (1992) review of the impact of PACE suggests: 'It [PACE] makes us take seriously the clichéd insistence that rule change must be contextualised; and it poses critical questions about that context' (Dixon, 1992: 536).

It is precisely this concern to contextualize that underpins the difficulty with the move to statute. The organizational and occupational context of cautioning may set definite limits on the achievement of uniformity in police cautioning policy and practice. In other words, it is all very well creating elaborate legalistic frameworks to bring about standardized cautioning practice (or higher detection rates, faster response times, improved race relations and so on), but everyday policing will always conspire to handle things differently. This is not an act of deliberate subversion, as the 'unfettered discretion' thesis would seem to imply; rather, policing is always-already a disciplined, hierarchical, gendered organization which may be always-already structurally overdetermined. These structural features and their interrelationship with cautioning activity have simply not been explored. From Grunhut (1956) through to Evans (1991), successive researchers have failed to consider the wide configuration of policing relations within which the practice is embedded. Consequently, we have no understanding of the link between the social action of police officers involved in cautioning work and the social processes and structures which both condition that work and are outcomes of it. Criminal justice research is fascinated by policework – its organization, culture, practices and relationship to government, law, socioeconomic processes and democratic freedoms. We might have anticipated that elements of these debates would have, at some time, spilled over into cautioning analysis so that the meaning and nature of police cautioning could be examined in relation to the contingencies of policework. Instead, however, policing takes the form of an invisible background within which the caution is administered and recorded, but whose conditioning and/or constraining influence is left unexamined. The final section looks towards the possibilities afforded a sociological approach to the area of police cautioning.

FUTURES FOR CAUTIONING RESEARCH (AND PRACTICE)

The Macro-Structural Relations of Police Cautioning Work

We can appreciate the importance of the structural relations of cautioning by making a number of simple observations. As has been seen above, the point of departure for studies in the post-1985 period, and the sole frame of reference, has been the issuing of Home Office Circulars – the assumption being that any identified change in cautioning culture is a direct and unmediated function of Home Office Circular advice. Yet this only makes sense if Home Office Circular advice is dispensed in a political vacuum; otherwise it offers a very narrow foundation for claiming any shift in cautioning patterns and arrangements. Consider, for example, the sociopolitical context of the 1980s and early 1990s. The introduction of a wide variety of legislation over this period has had considerable impact on the institutional framework of criminal justice.[13] Quite apart from the 'creation' of a new criminal justice agency (the Crown Prosecution Service), legislative changes have reshaped the organizational responsibilities of the police service, the probation service and the prison sector. The comprehensive restructuring of almost every foundation principle, procedure, practice and process of criminal justice has inaugured massive organizational change throughout the entire system. Furthermore, even a cursory reflection on the substantive aspects of legal change recognizes that statutes often contain contradictory messages which inhibit a standardized and predictable pattern of organizational and interorganizational behaviour.

If we add to this the more recent shadow of the Sheehy Report (Home Office, Northern Ireland Office and Scottish Office, 1993), with its proposals to, *inter alia*, introduce local pay-bargaining and performance-related pay into police conditions of service; the report of the Royal Commission on Criminal Justice 1993, which seems to have prioritized the quest for efficiency in the criminal process at the expense of 'justice', (Field and Thomas, 1994); the introduction of the

Police and Magistrates' Court Act 1994, which reconstitutes the tripartite structure for the governance of the police, and arguably, tips
the balance towards greater central control (Newburn, 1995: 74–8);
the ongoing work of the Audit Commission (see Loveday, Chapter 6
in this volume) and the spectre of the Financial Management Initiative, both of which promote a social market approach to policing affairs, we are forced to conclude that policing is in a permanent state
of transition. It is easy to concur with the view that the criminal justice system is under stress (Stockdale and Casale, 1992), and policing,
in particular, finds little respite from an overdose of legality on the
one side, and a toxic injection of fiscal restructuring on the other. If
this was not enough to contend with, over the same period there have
been marked shifts in the direction and form of police relationships
with the private sector – 'load-shedding', compulsory competitive ten-
dering, contracting-out, service charging (Leishman, Cope and Stairie,
1996); with the community – the growth of Neighbourhood Watch,
participation in the Safer Cities Programme, the Five Towns Initiative,
and the Priority Estates Project (Gilling, 1996); with victims of crime
– the routinization of liaison with Victim Support, responsiveness to
Rape Crisis and Women's Aid, and the development of specialist teams
to deal with child abuse (Jones, Newburn and Smith, 1994). This rather
long description of the macro-structural world of policing fits neatly
with Grimshaw and Jeffersons's framework for understanding organized policework. They argue:

> We need to consider policing in terms of a combination of struc-
> tures . . . substantively . . . the importance of law, work and the com-
> munity . . . [and] the importance of attending to the relationship between
> the elements within a given social formation. (Grimshaw and Jefferson,
> 1987: 13–14)

Against this backcloth of organic legislation, the politico-ideologi-
cal shift to a fiscal model of criminal justice, the reinvention and restructuring of police working patterns and the development of a
heterogeneous, criminal justice community, it is difficult to see how a
single Home Office Circular can be expected to 'impact'. Yet this is
implicit to a literature which has isolated Circular advice from all other
structural influences on police activity, and then investigated the cautioning aspect of that activity from this limited premise. This has meant
that analysis has not only failed to engage with the political and material conditions of contemporary policing, but has failed to acknowledge these wider issues as relevant to the analysis of cautioning affairs.

At best 'structure' is consigned to the status of a passing remark;[14] or at worst, is reduced to a 'variable' which can be held constant rather than treated analytically. Consequently, research has never considered how structural shifts in the sociopolitical dimensions of policing interact with the cautioning approaches of different force areas; neither has it explored how proposed changes in cautioning practice are accommodated into a complex and multi-faceted policing task; equally, changes in the rate of cautioning have never been conceptualized in relation to the rate of change that occurs within police practice generally.

The Mezzo-Structural Relations of Police Cautioning Work

A second level of explanation and investigation focuses on what Harris and Webb (1987) dub the mezzo-level of analysis; that is, the form and nature of the structural relations which pertain *within* the policing organization. This includes cautioning research work which recognizes the structuring potential of police cautioning policy, but investigates the claim in an uncritical, unreflexive and non-sociological way. Evans and Wilkinson (1990) epitomize this position when they state: 'To assume that the Circular [14/1985], might affect cautioning rates is also to assume that significant changes in police force policy were implemented following its issue' (Evans and Wilkinson, 1990: 164).

There was no caveat to this comment and it exemplifies what Grimshaw and Jefferson (1987) refer to as a 'machine' model approach to police policy relations. It is a perspective which subscribes to the mechanistic notion that Home Office Circular advice, police policy and cautioning practice simply coincide; policy is regarded unproblematically as a set of 'super-relevant' instructions or guidelines which inform practice; moreover, any failure to achieve this can be explained as a breakdown of communication or understanding – as a blockage in the 'machine'. There are a number of problems with this view, not least the narrow understanding of 'policy' which it implies. Nevertheless it characterizes the post-1985 policy focus of cautioning research.[15] There is no attempt within this focus to raise questions about what, in fact, constitutes 'policy' – this is simply reduced to 'text'. For example, Evans and Wilkinson are quite happy to canvas the idea that 'cautioning policy is mainly confined to standing orders' (1990: 164); while Laycock and Tarling amass data on 'policy' by requesting chief officers to submit 'copies of force standing orders and any other relevant policy documents' (1985: 84). This would seem to side-step any questioning of what is meant by 'policy', even though the definitional issue is central to social scientific approaches to policy analysis (see, for example, Heclo, 1972; Jenkins, 1978). Two variants on the definitional question seem to me to offer different but equally effective ways of investigating the complex phenomenon of 'policy'. Grimshaw and Jefferson (1987), for example, go to great lengths to define what they understand as 'policy'. This is not the place to argue the merits (or otherwise) of Grimshaw and Jefferson's definition;[16] the main point is that the definitional exercise enabled the authors to distinguish 'policy' from other managerial mechanisms of control. To establish some conceptual clarity about the matter, the authors compare and contrast the form and nature of 'policy' with that of advice, command, supervision, discipline, deployment and training – all of which 'structure' police practice in general. This enables them to go on to be analytically and empirically specific in their examination of the policy aspects of operational policing (*inter alia*, racist incidents, attacks on council workers, stop and search practices) – but at the same time, they remain alert to the idea that the policy structure is but one element of a web of interconnected mezzo-structural influences on practice.

However, a second variant of policy definition rejects the view altogether that 'policy' can be treated as an artefact. Ham and Hill (1984) remind us of the prolonged debate on the issue:

> The definitional problems posed by the concept of policy suggest that it is difficult to treat it as a very specific and concrete phenomenon. They also imply that it is hard to identify particular occasions when policy is made. Policy will often continue to evolve within what is conventionally described as the implementation phase, rather than the policy-making phase of the policy process. (Ham and Hill, 1984: 11–12).

Here the emphasis is on process, and outcomes can only be understood as constituted by this process. In cautioning research, the social relations of the cautioning policy process remain something of a mystery – at worst, these relationships are taken as self-evident, at best, they are drawn into research discussion (rather than analysis), as speculative explanations of endemic 'policy failure'. Laycock and Tarling (1985), for example, confidently state that 'the differential treatment of juveniles and adults is obviously due to policy considerations' (1985: 90) – but the reader is left to guess at how this difference is socially organized. On the other hand, Westwood's (1990) apologia for the 'falling into disuse' of Avon and Somerset's adult cautioning policy offers some important clues to the mezzo-social relations of cautioning affairs. For example, he considers that changes, and the reasons for them, must be widely broadcast across all ranks; second, he proposes the nomination of a senior officer to act as a responsible facilitator – 'and this officer should be able to answer the queries which naturally arise when something of a major departure from previous practice is undertaken' (Westwood, 1990: 392); third, he argues that decision-making should be devolved to inspectors, with sergeants and constables being encouraged to bring forward any relevant factors in the case. These suggestions conform, roughly, to Grimshaw and Jefferson's identification of training, supervision and deployment as structural influences of mezzo-level police practice (in this instance, police cautioning work). The great pity is that these valuable insights are only introduced retrospectively, as recommendations for improving subsequent practice. This seems to gloss over an important analytical point – questions of training, supervision and deployment, (recording methods, administrative arrangements, information systems, and so on) are always-already settled. Far from being 'outside the scope of the research', these structural features of the cautioning process are conditions of understanding police cautioning work as situated activity. From this sociological standpoint, how cautioning officers signal, discuss, decide, mediate and routinize 'policy' change would be more clearly understood.

The Micro-Structural Relations of Police Cautioning Work

The corollary to this argument is that the beliefs, attitudes and activities of cautioning officers would move to centre-stage of the analysis. The pivotal role of decision-makers is not lost within the cautioning literature. In some ways, the studies which concentrate on cautioning decisions reflect the best of what the literature has to offer, in as much as there is a real attempt to consider the role of human agency. However, studies characteristically tend to operate with an underdeveloped concept of structure. This can be demonstrated by looking at the way that decisional criteria have been examined. Here, we find splendid attempts to 'discover' the legal and extra-legal considerations brought to bear on cautioning decisions. Steer (1970) identifies these factors as the complainant's wishes, the role of the victim in the commission of the offence, the sufficiency of the evidence, the circumstances of the offender, and a range of other criteria, such as the social (rather than legal) acceptability of the offending behaviour, triviality of the offence, or where offences are 'technical' matters. Fisher and Mawby (1982) cover more or less the same ground, but focus upon the kinds of criteria which underpin decision-making in juvenile cases. Despite the promise of these studies, the objective was only ever to demonstrate how far these legal and extra-legal factors determined cautioning decisions, with the ultimate goal of finding some sort of explanation for cautioning variation between different categories of offenders. Of course, studies of this kind are never quite exhausted – Landau (1981) and Landau and Nathan (1983), for example, extend the range of extra-legal factors by considering ethnicity; more imaginatively, Fraser and George (1992) examine attitudinal criteria and look at the kinds of disposals made by 'cannabis-friendly' (and unfriendly) officers in drug offence cases. More crucially, I would argue that the drawing-up of these kinds of factorial lists buys into legalistic rather than sociological discourses on discretionary decision-making. The point is succinctly made by Baldwin (1995):

> Such an approach pays too little attention to the problematic nature of the information upon which the decision is based, to the judgements involved in defining issues as relevant and to the ways in which cases or policies proceed through the organisational handling system. 'Facts of the case' are thus treated as some taken-for-granted reality rather than as the results of complex processes in which reality is socially constructed and reconstructed. (Baldwin, 1995: 25)

It seems, then, that the same kind of decontextualized approach which permeates research work conducted at the macro and mezzo level of analysis may be equally characteristic of investigations into micro-level activity. For example, both Steer (1970) and Fisher and Mawby (1982) read off decision-making criteria from the text contained in case files. These criteria are then grouped in appropriate ways. Fisher and Mawby describe the process thus:

> We may distinguish three types of information contained on the PROS 60 form – identifiers, behavioural and personal. Identifiers are pieces of information which tell us the basic characteristics of the juvenile . . . Behavioural data refer to the offence situation . . . Finally, the form included personal details. (1992: 66)

This content analysis of files allows the researchers first to show the frequency and distribution of identifying, behavioural and personal criteria across the sample; and second, to cross-tabulate these criteria with disposal decisions. We arrive then at a variety of claims – for example, age and previous record are highly correlated with the decision to caution (Fisher and Mawby, 1982: 68); there is also a higher chance of a caution if the offence is committed in a particular area, if the juvenile's family owns its accommodation, if he/she is not a latch-key child, or if he/she is white (Landau and Nathan, 1983: 133). Alternatively, Mott (1983) argued that 'as the great majority of first offenders of both sexes are cautioned, the concern about whether or not the police take account of family circumstances or welfare considerations in their decision-making is largely irrelevant' (1983: 260). This seems to confirm what we may have suspected all along, but it does not get us very far down the road of understanding why or how some criteria are included in reports and others omitted. Neither does it offer an understanding of how report-writers ascribe meaning, value and motive to the actions of others, or how they do so within a structural framework of cultural norms (such as the need to reconstruct the situational dynamics of police action),[17] organizational requirements (such as the need to justify an arrest) or record-keeping styles (such as the need to 'stick to the facts'). These kinds of sociological questions have been buried alive in the cautioning literature. For example, Wilkinson and Evans (1990) complain of difficulty in 'discovering' the meaning of significant harm, substantial damage, or property of substantial value. In a later study, Evans (1991) proposes the idea of 'getting behind the labels' – but a methodology which treats the text of police reports as a transparent representation of 'cautionable' or 'chargeable' incidents does not have the epistemological wherewithal to achieve this. We should favour, as does Young,

> a mode of reading inflected by attention to context and the condition of the text's existence as a social and discursive practice constituted by certain institutional frames and directed to bring about certain effects. (1990: 158)

Even without a post-structuralist questioning of the 'text', the aggregate patterning of discretionary decisions suggests that some kind of ordered process is at work (police officers do, after all, claim to be working in a rational and disciplined way!). As Baumgartner (1992) points out, questions of age, sex, education, ethnicity and respectability influence discretion in predictable ways – throughout the legal process they tend to have similar effects, and to impose remarkable uniformity on the ways in which officials dispose of their cases. As she suggests:

> While governmental laws may not structure the realm of discretion, then social laws do, and, while discretionary outcomes may not *formally* predictable, they are instead *sociologically* so. (1992: 130, emphasis in original)

CONCLUSION

Baumgartner (1992) confirms the thesis explored in this chapter. Understanding the nature of discretion from a sociological point of view does not amount to a new direction in academic work. However, in the context of cautioning research it would represent something of a radical departure from existing frames of analysis. It has not been the business of this chapter to account for the lack of sociological ambition in cautioning work, although the institutional connection of Home Office funding springs to mind. Arguably, the original investment in the concept of discretion was, at best, an expedient move; it certainly established a residual category into which unexplained and unacceptable aspects of cautioning practice could be conveniently deposited. But this exemplifies what Smith (1981: 60) refers to as treating discretion as a resource for, rather than a topic of, investigation. Even though we may readily agree that individual officers make decisions by reference to criteria which are 'personal to themselves' (Patchett and McClean, 1965: 707); or that the police are pretty much 'left to their own devices' (Somerville, 1969: 481), we are given no insight to the kinds of devices which are available, how they are marshalled, or how they are used. As Smith, citing Bittner, suggests:

> [t]he meaning of [discretion] and of all the terms and determinations that are subsumed under it, must be discovered by studying their use in real scenes of action by persons whose competence to use them is socially sanctioned. (Bittner, 1973: 270, cited in Smith, 1981: 60)

Cautioning authors, in any other field of inquiry, contribute greatly to theoretical understandings of the criminal process; yet, within the confines of their cautioning work, critical questioning has been suspended in favour of a non-reflexive and legalistic stance. The analytical weakness of this approach always stood to benefit from an incorporation of the many insights provided by police studies which do examine the community–police interface (Shapland and Vagg, 1988); the decisional momentum of the pre-trial process (McConville *et al.*, 1991); police decision-making processes (Manning and Hawkins, 1989; Kemp, Norris and Fielding, 1992); police policy-making (Grimshaw and Jefferson, 1987); the work of chief constables (Reiner, 1991); police culture (Holdaway, 1983; Young, 1991); and the role of the victim in the criminal process (Shapland *et al.*, 1985). Thus, the meaning and nature of cautioning practice, and its disparity, have never been understood within a wider theoretically informed framework of policing and policing relations.

Political urgency underlies the need to re-examine the received wisdom of the cautioning literature. In terms of praxis, the policy recommendations yielded by research and animated by successive governments have not, as we have seen, diluted decades of disquiet with cautioning matters. Statutory cautioning represents a last-ditch attempt to regulate and confine the worst excesses of the cautioning disposition, beyond which lies a political void. It may be that *less* control and *less* structure may be desirable. Indeed, Evans and Wilkinson (1990:173) ponder the vexed question of what would constitute acceptable variability in cautioning activity. Implicitly, this accepts the view that there *are* definite limits to the extent to which police cautioning can be standardized, controlled and regulated, both in terms of policy and practice. However, this remains both a hypothetical and an empirical question, the response to which may lead us towards a different sense of the possible. The boundaries of possibility are both the outcome *and* condition of human agency. A committed series of projects, which take as their point of departure the situated activity of police cautioning, can only stimulate theoretically informed debate on the political future of the disposition.

Notes

1. Always-already is a term borrowed from Alison Young (1990), who has used it throughout her book *Femininity in Dissent*, to convey the idea of 'pre-existence', 'preconstruction', and/or 'pre-determination'. In this instance, it is being suggested that the world of policing is already highly structured on a number of levels: 'new', procedural or policy structures cannot be created or imposed outside the world of existing structures, but are 'always-already' embedded in them.
2. Known offenders in this context are those found guilty at court or cautioned (Home Office, 1995: 14–27).
3. In 1996 the cost of administering a police caution is estimated at £51.00, compared with £2094 for bringing a full prosecution case to summary trial (Paling, 1996). On this kind of comparison, the cost benefits of cautioning over charge and prosecution are both clear and substantial. This equation does not, of course assume that cautioned offences will always merit full prosecution in the courts.
4. Persuasive evidence of the occurrence of net-widening (Cohen, 1979, 1985) has not been forthcoming. Ditchfield (1976) claimed to have identified the phenomenon; Farrington and Bennett (1981) tentatively confirmed the existence of net-widening in the Metropolitan Police District. However, after careful review of competing claims, Wilkinson and Evans (1990) concluded that 'there can be no statistical test of the net-widening thesis

by measuring the extent to which informal street warnings or NFA decisions have been replaced by formal cautions' (Wilkinson and Evans, 1990:
173). Indeed I am inclined to agree with McMahon's (1990) view that
net-widening is a politically loaded metaphor rather than an accurate reflection of an empirically verifiable state of affairs. As she notes, 'arguments about the occurrence of quantitative forms of net-widening often
underlie, and always reinforce, critical arguments about the increasingly
sinister nature of penal control' (McMahon, 1990: 124).

5. See for example Bagot, J. H. (1941) 'Juvenile Delinquency' cited in
M. Grunhut (1956) *Juvenile Offenders Before the Courts* (Oxford: Oxford
University Press); McClintock, F. H. and Avison, N. H. (1968) *Crime in
England and Wales* (London: Heinemann); Ditchfield, J. A. (1976) *Police
Cautioning in England and Wales*, Home Office Research Study No. 37
(London: HMSO); Laycock, G. and Tarling, G. (1985) 'Police force cau-
tioning policy and practice' in *The Howard Journal*, vol. 24, no. 2, pp.
81–92; Evans, R. and Wilkinson, C. (1990) 'Variations in police cautioning policy and practice in England and Wales', in *The Howard Journal*,
vol. 29, no. 3, pp. 155–76.

6. In 1983 the Metropolitan Police cautioned only 9 per cent of all persons
found guilty or cautioned for indictable offences; in the same year, Suf-
folk cautioned 38 per cent. In 1994, South Wales cautioned 21 per cent
of all persons found guilty or cautioned for indictable offences, while
Surrey cautioned 56 per cent. It is worth noting that in 1981 the Metropolitan Police did not caution a single adult offender (aged 21 and over),
and only 11 persons aged 17 to 20 (Laycock and Tarling, 1995: 85).

7. The poorly argued proposals for the abolition of Juvenile Courts and the
introduction of Family Councils as their replacement encountered fierce
opposition from a number of groups, including: the Magistrates' Association, lawyers, and the Probation Service. The proposals were withdrawn
in due course. Martin *et al.* (1981) argue that the successor White Paper
Children in Trouble (1968), which was also criticized by the same groups,
was nevertheless able to muster sufficient support to find its way into the
watershed legislation Children and Young Persons Act 1969. Much of the
resistance, they suggest, was blunted by the Act's retention of the juvenile court system (Martin *et al.*, 1981: 7). See also Morris *et al.*, (1980).

8. See for example, Allen, F. A. (1959) 'Legal values and the rehabilitative
ideal', in *The Journal of Criminal Law, Criminology and Police Science*,
vol. 50, pp. 226–32; Nonet, P. (1969) *Administrative Justice* (New York:
Russell Sage Foundation); Reich, C. (1963) 'Midnight welfare searches
and the Social Security Act', in *Yale Law Review*, vol. 74, pp. 1347–60;
Reich, C. (1964) 'The new property', in *Yale Law Journal*, vol. 73, pp.
733–87; Reich, C. (1965) 'Individual rights and social welfare: the emerging
issues', *Yale Law Journal*, vol. 74, pp. 1245–57; Reich, C. (1966) 'The
law of the planned society', *Yale Law Journal*, vol. 75, pp. 1227–70. All
cited in Hawkins, K. (ed.) (1992) *The Uses of Discretion* (Oxford: Clarendon
Press) p. 17, note 6.

9. It is perhaps misleading to refer to *the*, or *a* legal paradigm. While Davis
is generally acknowledged as a major contributor to legal perspectives on
discretion, his thesis is only one among many approaches developed by

legal scholars. See also, for example, Dworkin (1977); Nonet and Selznick (1978); Galligan (1990).

10. Over the period 1960 to 1974, the number of cautions recorded for all offenders (indictable and non-indictable offences) rose from 71,703 to 136,509. For the juvenile age groups, the percentage rise in cautions was especially marked. For example, in 1960, 33 per cent of known offenders aged 10 to 13 were cautioned – by 1974 the percentage had risen to 66.2 per cent; in 1960, 21.2 per cent of known offenders aged 14 to 16 were cautioned; by 1974 the percentage had risen to 36.1 per cent. An important caveat to this substantial rise in juvenile cautioning is that for adults (17 years and over) where the percentage use of the caution actually decreased – from 9.4 per cent in 1960 to 5 per cent in 1974 (aged 17 to 20); and from 8.9 per cent in 1960 to 5.2 per cent in 1974 (21 years and over) (Ditchfield, 1976: 6–7).

11. It is important to acknowledge that Section 5 of the Children and Young Persons Act 1969 made consultation between the police and social services a statutory requirement before the decision to prosecute any child or young person. The section, along with a number of others, was never implemented. Equally, an earlier Home Office Circular, Circular 70/1978, *The Citing of Police Cautions in the Juvenile Court*, clarified the administrative and procedural aspects of juvenile cautioning. The circular also detailed the criteria required for consistent decision-making in juvenile cases. These criteria were developed and expanded in the later Home Office Circular 14/1985.

12. Bottomley (1985) remained unconvinced that Home Office Circular 14/1985 would bring about consistency in cautioning practice. Importantly he did not doubt the capacity of Circular advice generally to impact on cautioning arrangements; rather, he argued that the Circular's identification of cautioning principles lacked clarity, and was sufficiently imprecise to allow (even encourage) wide interpretational latitude.

13. Significant 'new' legislation includes the Mental Health Act 1983; Police and Criminal Evidence Act 1984; Prosecution of Offences Act 1985; Children Act 1989; Criminal Justice Acts 1989, 1991, 1993; Bail (Amendment) Act 1993; Criminal Justice and Public Order Act 1994; Police and Magistrates' Court Act 1994.

14. Tucked away in *Police Review*, Tutt (1985) outlines the importance of macro-structural relations of cautioning affairs. For example, he observes the demise of elaborate decision-making structures in some force areas, especially for juvenile offenders, and their replacement by instant cautioning procedures. He suggests that this may reflect wider demands of cost efficiency, and/or a return to non-specialist decision-making as part of the renewed emphasis on beat policing:

> The cost efficiency and manpower arguments have raised a fundamental question mark over the appropriateness of elaborate decision-making structures for juvenile offenders. [Furthermore] the need to place officers back on the beat in volume and to give them effective decision-making power . . . means that specialist departments . . . quite apart from being costly, can be seen to be contrary to the very ethos which is sought to be created. (Tutt, 1985: 1268)

These comments emerged from Tutt's inspection of the survey's findings. Unable to tease out the relationship between cost efficiency, community policing and decision-making arrangements from the data, his comments were ventured in a spirit of recommendation for further research – so far, there have been no takers.

15. The main contribution of the Working Group on Cautioning (1984) was to indicate the wide variation in expressed policy choices, and to describe the effect of these differences on cautioning practice. In highlighting some of the administrative, procedural and practical aspects of these variations, the study provided enough scope for the Working Group to eschew uniformity in the cautioning rate and advocate a policy-centered solution to the inconsistency problem. More cynically, the former solution was unlikely to be either achievable or manipulative.

16. For information, Grimshaw and Jefferson define policy as 'an authoritarian statement signifying a settled practice on any matter relevant to the duties of the Chief Constable' (Jefferson and Grimshaw, 1987: 204).

17. Evans (1991) discusses the hostile attitudes of some officers towards the use of the caution. He comments on:

> The widespread belief among the lower ranks of the police that a caution is a 'let off', an inadequate response to criminality and an insufficient reward for the efforts of officers who have sufficiently established the case for the prosecution. (1991: 599)

Moreover, these attitudes are not necessarily confirmed to the lower ranks, but may serve as a cultural resource for officers directly engaging in cautioning activity. Davis, Boucherat and Watson (1989), in their analysis of the diversionary work of the Northampton Juvenile Liaison Bureau (JLB), suggest that:

> As far as police members of the JLB were concerned, their discomfort with a policy based on the disutility of prosecution was reflected in a tendency, once away from the Bureau, to become policemen again, albeit of a notably 'soft' variety. (1989: 230)

References

Ashworth, A. (1984) 'Prosecution, police and public – a guide to good gatekeeping?', *The Howard Journal*, vol. 23, no 2 (June) pp. 65–87.

Baldwin, R. (1995) *Rules and Government* (Oxford: Oxford University Press).

Bankowski, Z. and Nelken, D. (1981) 'Discretion as a social problem', in M. Adler and S. Asquith (eds) *Discretion and Welfare* (London: Heinemann) pp. 247–68.

Baumgartner, M. P. (1992) 'The myth of discretion', in K. Hawkins (ed.), *The Uses of Discretion* (Oxford: Clarendon Press) pp. 129–62.

Bottomley, A. K. (1985) 'Guide-lines on cautioning – identifying the principles', *Justice of the Peace*, 18 May, pp. 311–12.

Bottomley, A. K. and Pease, K. (1986) *Crime and Punishment: Interpreting the Data* (Milton Keynes: Open University Press).

Cavadino, P. (1985) 'Two cheers for cautioning circular', *Justice of the Peace*, 18 May, pp. 310–11.

Cohen, S. (1979) The punitive city: notes on the dispersal of control', *Contemporary Crisis*, vol. 3, no. 4, pp. 341–63.

Cohen, S. (1981) 'Footprints in the sand: a further report on criminology and the sociology of deviance in Britain', in M. Fitzgerald *et al.* (eds), *Crime and Society* (London: Routledge).

Cohen, S. (1985) *Visions of Social Control: Crime, Punishment and Classification* (Oxford: Polity Press in association with Basil Blackwell).

Cohen, S. (1988) *Against Criminology* (New Brunswick, NJ: Transaction Books).

Davis, G., Boucherat, J. and Watson, D. (1989) 'Pre-court decision making in Juvenile Justice', *British Journal of Criminology*, vol. 29, no. 3, pp. 219–35.

Davis, K. C. (1969) *Discretionary Justice: A Preliminary Inquiry* (Baton Rouge: Louisiana State University Press).

Ditchfield, J. A. (1976) *Police Cautioning in England and Wales*, Home Office Research Study No. 37 (London: HMSO).

Dixon, D. (1992) 'Legal regulation and policing practice', *Social and Legal Studies*, vol. 1, pp. 515–41.

Dworkin, R. M. (1977) *Taking Rights Seriously* (Cambridge, Mass.: Harvard University Press).

Evans, R. (1991) 'Police cautioning and the young adult offender', *Criminal Law Review*: 598–609.

Evans, R. and Wilkinson, C. (1990) 'Variations in police cautioning policy and practice in England and Wales', *The Howard Journal*, vol. 29, no. 3 (August) pp. 155–76.

Farrington, D. P. and Bennett, T. (1981) 'Police cautioning of juveniles in London', *British Journal of Criminology*, vol. 21, no. 2 (April) pp. 123–35.

Field, S. and Thomas, P. A. (eds) (1994) *Justice and Efficiency? The Royal Commission on Criminal Justice* (Oxford: Blackwell).

Fisher, C. J. and Mawby, R. I. (1982) 'Juvenile delinquency and police discretion in an inner city area', *British Journal of Criminology*, vol. 22, no. 1 (January) pp. 63–75.

Fraser, A. and George, M. (1992) 'Cautions for cannabis', *Policing*, vol. 8, no. 1: pp. 88–103.

Galligan, D. J. (1990) *Discretionary Powers: A Legal Study of Official Discretion*, 2nd edn (Oxford: Clarendon Press).

Galligan, D. J. (1994) 'Regulating pre-trial decisions', in N. Lacey (ed.), *A Reader on Criminal Justice* (Oxford: Oxford University Press).

Giller, H. and Tutt, N. (1987) 'Police cautioning of juveniles: the continuing practice of diversity', *Criminal Law Review*, pp. 367–74.

Gilling, D. (1996) 'Policing, crime prevention and partnerships', in F. Leishman, B. Loveday and S. Savage (eds), *Core Issues in Policing* (London: Longman) pp. 101–13.

Grimshaw, R. and Jefferson, T. (1987) *Interpreting Policework* (London: Allen & Unwin).

Grunhut, M. (1956) *Juvenile Offenders Before the Courts* (Oxford: Clarendon Press).

Ham, C. and Hill, M. (1984) *The Policy Process in the Modern Capitalist State*, 1st edn (Hemel Hempstead: Harvester Wheatsheaf).

Harris, R. and Webb, D. (1987) *Welfare, Power and Juvenile Justice* (London: Tavistock).

Hawkins, K. (ed.) (1992) *The Uses of Discretion* (Oxford: Clarendon Press).

Heclo, H. (1972) 'Review article: policy analysis', *British Journal of Political Science*, vol. 2.

Holdaway, S. (1983) *Inside the British Police* (Oxford: Basil Blackwell).

Home Office (1978) Circular 70/1978: *The Cautioning of Offenders* (London: HMSO).

Home Office (1984) *Cautioning By The Police: A Consultative Document* (London: HMSO).

Home Office (1985) Circular 14/1985: *The Cautioning of Offenders* (London: HMSO).

Home Office (1990) Circular 59/1990: *The Cautioning of Offenders* (London: HMSO).

Home Office (1994) Circular 18/1994: *The Cautioning of Offenders* (London: HMSO).

Home Office (1994) *Criminal Statistics* (London: HMSO).

Home Office (1995) *Digest 3: Information on the Criminal Justice System in England and Wales* (London: HMSO).

Home Office, Northern Ireland Office and Scottish Office (1993) *Inquiry Into Police Responsibilities and Rewards: The Sheehy Report*, Vol. I: Appendixes Vol. II, Cmnd 2280I:II (London: HMSO).

Hullin, R. P. (1985) 'The cautioning of juvenile offenders', *Justice of the Peace*, 18 May, p. 312.

Jenkins, W. I. (1978) *Policy Analysis* (London: Martin Robertson).

Jones, T., Newburn, T. and Smith, D. J. (1994) *Democracy and Policing* (London: Policy Studies Institute).

Kemp, C., Norris, C. and Fielding, N. (1992) *Negotiating Nothing: Police Decision Making in Disputes* (Aldershot: Avebury).

Kidner, D. H. (1985) 'Cautioning', *Justice of the Peace*, 18 May, pp. 308–9.

Lacey, N. (1992) 'The jurisprudence of discretion: escaping the legal paradigm', in K. Hawkins (ed.), *The Uses of Discretion* (Oxford: Clarendon Press) pp. 361–88.

Landau, S. F. (1981) 'Juveniles and the police', *British Journal of Criminology*, vol. 21, no. 1 (January) pp. 27–46.

Landau, S. F. and Nathan, G. (1983) 'Selecting delinquents for cautioning in the London Metropolitan Area', *British Journal of Criminology*, vol. 23, no. 2 (April) pp. 128–49.

Laycock, G. and Tarling, R. (1985) 'Police force cautioning: policy and practice', *The Howard Journal*, vol. 24, no. 2 (May) pp. 81–92.

Leishman, F., Cope, S. and Starie, P. (1996) 'Reinventing and restructuring: towards a new policing order', in F. Leishman, B. Loveday and S. Savage (eds), *Core Issues in Policing* (London: Longman) 9–25.

Manning, P. K. and Hawkins, K. (1989) 'Police decision making', in M. Weatheritt (ed.), *Police Research: Some Future Prospects* (Aldershot: Avebury in association with the Police Foundation).

Martin, F. M., Sanford, J. F. and Murray, K. (1981) *Children Out of Court* (Edinburgh: Scottish Academic Press).

McClintock, F. H. and Avison, N. H. (1968) *Crime in England and Wales* (London: Heinemann).

McConville, M. and Sanders, A. (1992) 'Fairness and the CPS', *New Law Journal*, 31 January, pp. 120–2.

McConville, M. Leng, R. and Sanders, A. (1991) *Constructing the Case for the Prosecution* (London: Routledge).

McMahon, M. (1990) 'Net widening: vagaries in the use of a concept', *British Journal of Criminology*, vol. 30 (Spring) pp. 121–49.

Morris, A., Giller, H., Szwed, E. and Geach, H. (1980) *Justice for Children* (London: Macmillan).

Mott, J. (1983) 'Police decisions for dealing with juvenile offenders', *British Journal of Criminology*, vol. 23, no. 3 (July) pp. 249–62.

Nelken, D. (1976) 'Extending the use of police cautions: a critical appraisal', *Criminal Law Review*, pp. 360–73.

Newburn, T. (1995) *Crime and Criminal Justice Policy* (London: Longman).

Nonet, P. and Selznick, P. (1978) *Law and Society in Transition: Toward Responsive Law* (New York: Harper & Row).

Paling, Her Honour Judge Helen (1996) 'Risk: a sentencer's perspective', verbal presentation at The National Association of Probation Officers Annual Conference, Otterburn, May 1996.

Patchett, K. W. and McClean, J. D. (1965) 'Decision-making in juvenile cases', *Criminal Law Review*, pp. 699–710.

Pratt, J. (1986) 'Diversion from the juvenile court: a history of inflation and a critique of progress', *British Journal of Criminology*, vol. 26, no. 3 (July) pp. 212–33.

Reiner, R. (1991) *Chief Constables* (Oxford: Oxford University Press).

Reiner, R. (1992) *The Politics of the Police*, 2nd edn (Hemel Hempstead: Harvester Wheatsheaf).

Royal Commission on Criminal Justice (1993) The Runciman Report, Cmnd 2263 (London: HMSO).

Royal Commission on Criminal Procedure (1981) Final Report, Cmnd 8092 (London: HMSO).

Sanders, A. (1988) 'The limits to diversion from prosecution', *British Journal of Criminology*, vol. 28, no. 4 (Autumn) pp. 513–32.

Schneider, C. (1992) 'Discretion and rules: a lawyer's view' in K. Hawkins (ed.), *The Uses of Discretion* (Oxford: Clarendon Press) pp. 47–88.

Shapland, J. and Vagg, J. (1988) *Policing by the Public* (London: Routledge).

Shapland, J., Willmore, J. and Duff, P. (1985) *Victims and the Criminal Justice System* (Aldershot: Gower).

Smith, G. (1981) 'Discretionary decision-making in social work', in M. Adler and S. Asquith (eds), *Discretion and Welfare* (London: Heinemann) pp. 47–68.

Somerville, J. G. (1969) 'A study of the preventive aspect of police work with juveniles', *Criminal Law Review*, pp. 407–14, 472–84.

Steer, D. (1970) 'Police Cautions: A Study in the Exercise of Police Discretion', Occasional Paper No. 2, Penal Research Unit (Oxford: Basil Blackwell).

Stockdale, E. and Casale, S. (eds) (1992) *Criminal Justice Under Stress* (London: Blackstone).

Tutt, N. (1985) 'Proper juvenile cautions', *Police Review*, vol. 93 (January–July) pp. 1267–9.

Tutt, N. and Giller, H. (1983) 'Police cautioning of juveniles: the practice of diversity', *Criminal Law Review*, pp. 587–95.

Westwood, D. (1990) 'Adult cautioning', *Policing*, vol. 16 (Spring) pp. 383–98.

Westwood, D. (1991) 'The effects of Home Office guide-lines on the cautioning of offenders', *Criminal Law Review*, pp. 591–7.

Wilkinson, C. and Evans, R. (1990) 'Police cautioning of juveniles: the im-. pact of Home Office Circular 14/1985', *Criminal Law Review*, pp. 165–76.

Young, A. (1990) *Femininity in Dissent* (London: Routledge).

Young, M. (1991) *An Inside Job* (Oxford: Clarendon Press).

4 The Future Lasts a Long Time: Public Policework and the Managerialist Paradox

Eugene McLaughlin and Karim Murji

[If you could pass one law what would it be?]
A law outlawing the whole phoney, corrupting, double-talk of Thatcherite-inspired 'new managerial speak'. (Stuart Hall, 1996)

INTRODUCTION: UNSETTLED TIMES

The 1990s have the appearance of being the worst and best of times for the British police. The organization has made a sustained effort to climb back up the U-shaped curve of political legitimacy after the disastrous period of the late 1980s and early 1990s when it was exposed to searching scrutiny by the Audit Commission, the Sheehy Inquiry, internal Home Office reviews and sections of the media. The largely successful campaign by police staff associations to neutralize the reforming thrust of the proposals emanating from these scrutinies seemed to mark some sort of watershed in their relationship with the previous Conservative government and in part contributed to the reconstruction of a bipartisan consensus on the police with the main political parties emphasizing their commitment to increasing police numbers and resources. Furthermore, in 1996 the Home Secretary agreed to the police having long-handled batons and CS gas, while police criticisms of the Crown Prosecution Service, the judiciary, the laws of evidence and so-called 'revolving door' cautioning policies for juveniles also registered as a cause for concern with leading politicians. This however is only part of the story. During the same time period the police continued to claim that they were being pulled in conflicting directions and 'overrun' by the demands made upon them, that morale was declining, that traditional patrolling was under threat from cost-cutting and that they felt unprotected and unsupported in the war against violent crime. Also during this period league tables comparing police performance were published, national objectives for the police were set by the Home Secretary and critical public discussion of police performance by official bodies continued. Thus, even after their 'victory' in 1993–94 over government proposals for radical reform, the police continued to be beset by a 'gnawing', edgy feeling that all was not right.

These are therefore fascinating as well as impossible times at which to be considering the possible futures of public policework. Fascinating in that the current period has undoubtedly gone beyond the old certainties and securities, but also impossible because, at the time of writing, there is no way of predicting the shape or form in which the manifold contingencies and risks that will affect the future of public policework will play themselves out. What seems undeniable is that the police organization is experiencing sustained and far-reaching strain and that this looks likely to continue for the foreseeable future. At the heart of that tortuous process is the profound pressure on the management, organizational culture and decision-making processes of the police bureaucracy, the sources of which are of both long-term and more recent origin. The former, which we do not consider here, include tentative attempts by the Home Office dating from 1967 to introduce planning, programming and budgetary systems, designed to measure the relationship between police resources and outputs (see Home Office, 1967; Martin and Wilson, 1969; Weatheritt, 1986; Oliver, 1987; Horton and Smith, 1988). The more recent source can be traced to the election of a radical Conservative government in 1979. This chapter details how the current state of affairs came about and analyses how it may play itself out.

BACK TO THE FUTURE

The Conservative administration came to power in 1979 with the aim of rolling back the state in order to establish an 'enterprise culture' in Britain. Among its many strands this entailed the curbing of state expenditure, the privatization of public utilities, the cutting of 'red tape', reducing the power of trade unions, the restoration of 'incentives' and, at least rhetorically, the demolition of the postwar Keynesian–Beveridgite settlement. At the level of the state the underlying monetarist ideology of the New Right envisaged a slimmed-down (if not minimalist) public sector, based on the beliefs that first, most decisions were best left to self-reliant individuals, families and private enterprise, and second, that the state, as an unproductive burden on individuals and businesses, had to reduce its share of gross national product (GNP) in order for the country to remain globally competitive. Hence, concerted efforts would be made to replace the state's role as a provider of multiple public services with one where it became the purchaser of services from competing providers. Market mechanisms would be used to enforce efficiency and economy on providers, as they too had to be 'lean and fit' to survive in a competitive world. The terms 'the contract state' or the 'entrepreneurial state' have sometimes been used to describe the thrust and direction of the Conservatives' reform process (Kirkpatrick and Martinez-Lucio, 1996). However, in line with a considerable body of work (Hood, 1991; Hoggett, 1991; Wilding, 1993; Pollitt, 1993; Clarke, Cochrane and McLaughlin, 1994; Stewart and Walsh, 1992), we take the view that what has occurred is better conceived of as a 'new managerialist' approach to the bureaucratic stasis that was seen to characterize the public sector. Managerialism does not preclude outright privatization, indeed it *drives* essentially private sector ideas into the heart of the old public sector, but it does provide a sharper focus for understanding the contradictory processes of change and their mixed outcomes.

Deprivileging the Public Sector

In 1979 Michael Heseltine, the new Secretary of State for the Environment, declared that: 'Efficient management is the key to national revival . . . and the management ethos must run through our national life – public and private companies, the civil service, nationalized industries, local government, the national health service' (Heseltine, 1980). Heseltine's statement signalled the beginning of the long road to renewal that a neo-Conservative government was about to unleash on the public sector in Britain. As Peter Hennessy (1989) has detailed, at the time little attention was paid by public commentators to this managerial rallying call. It was dismissed as anti-statist rhetoric, wishful thinking, a passing fad, or the utterances of a new minister who had failed to realize or recognize that private sector *managerial* ideas could not be applied to public sector *administration*. The new minister would soon realize, according to 'old Whitehall hands' that this sector was founded on a bureau-professional culture and set of ground rules that were inherently *different* and separate from the private sector in purpose, rationale and configuration.

Four main forms of reasoning underpinned this belief in public sector difference. First, public institutions are complex, omnicompetent bureaucracies primarily concerned with the recurrent dilemmas and risks associated with determining and meeting the 'public need'. Decision-making is governed by principles such as equity, eligibility, fairness, universality and due process. Public institutions have statutory duties and responsibilities that *must* be fulfilled. Consequently they have little operational control over their working environment. They also, at certain moments, have to exercise coercive powers – they are legally empowered to order, inspect, enforce, monitor, intervene and regulate. Such powers and capacities make notions such as 'the customer' or 'the consumer' or 'the market' inapplicable or inappropriate to such institutions. Second, patterns of funding are determined and budgets allocated through the political process rather than being customer-generated. There is also the fiscal reality of unavoidable built-in costs. Third, lines of accountability are much more diffuse and broader than the relatively straightforward ones, based on profit and loss margins, that characterize the private sector. Fourth, staffing issues are multidimensional in nature. Public institutions must attract individuals who are motivated by the values of service rather than financial considerations. The institutional ethos must be integrative rather than competitive in nature, inculcating integrity, propriety, good sense and must compliment professional codes of conduct. Conditions of service have to be standardized into hierarchically graded levels of professional, administrative and clerical expertise. Pay scales have to be unified and progressive in nature, and dependent on grading and length of service. Formally specified rules and principles define individual duties and responsibilities. Individual progress within the bureaucracy must be premised on an uninterrupted career structure. For these reasons the public sector is inherently 'different' from the private sector (see Bekke, Perry and Toonen, 1996).

The solidity and weightiness of these seemingly well-established assumptions and set of arrangements may have led proponents of the public sector model to dismiss Heseltine's statement as just another example of a minister who did not yet understand the ways of public service. However, the Conservatives came to power with the ideological conviction that the postwar settlement about the nature and functioning of the public sector was ripe for root and branch reform. They saw the institutions of the social(ist) democratic state in a condition of bureaucratic sclerosis: over-extended, cumbersome, inflexible, unaccountable, unresponsive, inefficient, riddled with illogicalities and staffed by arrogant and complacent professionals who jealously guarded their autonomy and sought to enhance their budgets at every opportunity. The Conservative government was equally convinced that the means to transforming this state of affairs was through the application of free market and public choice principles and private sector managerial ideas. The public sector would be subjected to radical restructuring. While certain parts of it could be easily turned around, others would have to undergo a process of 'constructive destruction'.

Managerial reform of the public sector has not by any means proved to be straightforward. It has been marked by unevenness, partial, ragged-edged progress in certain areas, collective challenges, messy compromises, near chaotic outcomes and spectacular climb-downs. But at a generic level it is possible to identify several key features of a distinctively new public sector management model. At its core, we would argue, is a complex of discursive nostrums and procedures which force public institutions to reconceptualize the financing and delivery of their services in ways which will in turn trigger and drive further transformations:

1. The creation or appointment of professional/real managers to be held accountable for (i) specified tasks, (ii) the resources they consume and (iii) results. Good managers are defined as those who can use existing resources imaginatively and extract maximum value from them. They learn, out of necessity, how to do more with less.

2. All aspects concerned with the formulation and delivery of public services are operationally managerialized and become more business-like.

3. The setting of clear, measurable standards and targets.

4. The explicit costing of all activities, choices and priorities.

5. The development of performance indicators to enable the measurement and evaluation of efficiency and the publication of 'league tables' showing comparative performance against these indicators.

6. Increased emphasis on 'outputs' and results rather than processes. Organizations are to be turned 'outwards' rather than being concerned primarily with internal 'ways and wherefores'. In other words, organizations and managers must be concerned with what Newman and Clarke (1994) have termed 'doing the right thing' rather than 'doing the thing right'.

7. Hyper-rationalization of the purpose, range and scope of organizations through the identification of 'core competencies', the shedding or externalization of peripheral or illogical activities and 'market testing' against competitive providers.

8. Learning to operate in a competitive environment characterized by full or quasi-market relations, service contracts, agency status, the separation of finance from provision, a split between providers and purchasers of services, client–contractor relationships and customer service.
9. The reconfiguration of the recipients and beneficiaries of public services as customers and consumers.
10. The de-rigidification, shake-up and overhauling of the working culture of public organizations to improve productivity. This involves the individualization of rewards, flexibility on staffing and pay issues and the establishment of short-term or renewable contracts. Promotion should be dependent on ability and the quality of work rather than (i) age and experience ('Buggin's turn'), or (ii) being 'one of us'. This also involves the creation of new appraisal systems and new incentive packages including performance-related pay.
11. Fragmentation of the monolithic model in which the state is seen as the locus of all activities in favour of flexible, local and more responsive organizational configurations.

During the 1980s the impact of the new managerial broom became clearer in a host of areas in the public sector. New managerialism became a key means through which the state sector was to be reconstructed along 'business-like' lines, so that management was guided by objectives and organizations became customer-focused. In the process the traditional distinction between public and private was undermined as a set of essentially private sector values were brought into the centre of organizational and managerial thinking in the public sector. In this chapter it is argued that new managerialism is best understood therefore as an attempt to displace and realign notions of power within a given institutional setting. It seeks to disperse, localize and individualize certain aspects of power and responsibility and in the same moment to consolidate and centralize others. The resultant disaggregation and reconfiguration produce highly unstable multi-form relations of power and reframed responsibilities.

A Force Apart: The Political Privileging of the Police

During the 1980s the traditional public sector model and its assumption of 'difference' creaked and buckled under the Conservative government's various reform programmes. Over time a host of policy and legislative changes across the state sector have substantially destabilized it (see Clarke, Cochrane and McLaughlin, 1994). The criminal justice system itself experienced some of the consequences of the new competitive enterprise culture as first the probation and prison services and then the courts were gradually subjected to variants of the managerial solution (Jones, 1993; Spencer, 1993; McLaughlin and Muncie, 1994). Even the armed forces were heard to complain as pressure for economy and effectiveness bore down on them. But the police, probably alone among the emergency services (as the fire brigade and ambulance services also felt the impact of managerialism), appeared to stand alone and apart from all of the reform and reconfiguration going on around them. The police, it seemed, were unique, they were what could be called 'doubly different', first because of their place *within* the public sector, and second because, in terms of their unique constitutional position, they were also *different from* the rest of the public sector.

The reasons for this state of affairs are fairly well established. During the 1980s the police negotiated a considerable degree of autonomy from the rest of the public sector in Britain. In 1978 the Edmund–Davies committee recommended a new pay formula for the police (Committee of Inquiry into the Police, 1978). In 1979 the Conservatives were elected on a manifesto which promised to spend 'more on fighting crime while we economize elsewhere' (Conservative Party, 1979: 19) and implemented immediately and in full the Edmund–Davies pay award that the outgoing Labour government had intended to fulfil in stages. Because police pay was linked to average, as opposed to basic, earnings the police moved well ahead of other public sector workers in the course of the decade. Between 1979 and 1982 a constable's pay increased by 41 per cent in real terms. The trend has continued on much the same trajectory: in the period from 1986/7 to 1993/4 expenditure on the police increased by 41 per cent in real terms (Home Office, 1995b). Police officers were also the recipients of generous pension arrangements and personal allowances, particularly in relation to housing, that were not available to other sections of the public sector. Necessary funding was also made available to ensure a 23 per cent increase in the number of uniformed officers and a 15 per cent increase in the number of civilians.

It does not require a conspiracy theory to see that these developments were closely related to the political context and interests of the government during the early and mid-1980s. The police were able to depend on the unquestioning support of the Conservatives whenever concerns were raised by Labour-run police authorities about controversial police tactics in Britain's inner cities, during the anti-police riots of 1980, 1981 and 1985, and the industrial disputes of the 1980s, most notably, the newspaper industry disputes at Warrington and Wapping and the 1984–85 coal dispute. The police were also granted increased legal powers under the Police and Criminal Evidence Act 1984 and the Public Order Act 1986, as well as increased technological hardware to combat the 'vandals, pickets and muggers' (see Hillyard and Percy-Smith, 1987; McCabe and Wallington, 1988; Ewing and Gearty, 1990). Given the degree of government patronage the police seemingly enjoyed and the ongoing 'war against crime', it is not surprising that they were perceived as being virtually immune from the fiscal restrictions and ideological assault to which the rest of the public sector was being subjected. The police's 'most favoured' status was due not only to the need to contain recalcitrant trade unions and troublesome inner city populations. Their apparent immunity can also be linked to the government's need for an emergency back-up when it tackled other public sector workers in sensitive areas, for example, ambulance workers, fire fighters and prison officers. Since police officers are legally barred from striking they could be relied upon to step into the breach if workers in the other emergency services did exercise their right to strike. Certain police representatives periodically reminded the government of this reality and seemed confident that their strategic position as frontline guardians of the 'authoritarian state' would guarantee the continuation of their privileged, 'feather-bedded' existence.

Versions of the 'authoritarian state' view of the 1980s are relatively well-known and, in broad outline, attract a wide measure of agreement from a variety of commentators (see Scraton, 1985; Reiner, 1985; Waddington, 1991; Davies, 1992; Leishman and Savage, 1993). However, a closer re-examination of the 1980s and rereading of key 'moments' reveals a gradual and complex process of increasing 'under the counter' governmental scrutiny of virtually every aspect of public policework. This can in retrospect be seen as laying the ground for the comprehensive 'surface shredding' reviews and critiques of police organization and management that emerged in 1993.

FROZEN WARNINGS: THE DECONSTRUCTION OF POLICEWORK

During the 1980s a considerable amount of detailed research and critical commentary from a variety of sources placed virtually every aspect of policing under the spotlight. First there were a number of Home Office reports that questioned one of the cornerstones of police culture: that they were crime fighters (Clarke and Mayhew, 1980; Clarke and Hough, 1984; Morris and Heal, 1981). This research effectively debunked and demythologized the 'reality' of policing as it was portrayed by the police; it presented a picture of policework which differed considerably from the public image. For example it indicated that, contrary to police and media characterization, law enforcement and crime-related work accounted for a relatively small proportion of police time and that most calls were related to the '24-hour social service' side of policing. It questioned whether increased expenditure on the police would have any significant impact on levels of crime and disorder. More specifically, the research indicated the following: most of what police officers actually do spend their time on is not visible to police managers; patrolling levels had little or no effect on crime clear-up rates; there was no obvious link between particular detective methods and the solving of crimes; and that detection rates were an inadequate measure of police effectiveness. These conclusions, as Horton and Smith (1988) have argued, when combined with rising crime rates and falling detection rates, raised fundamental questions about the purpose of policing, about what constituted effectiveness in the police force, and about how efficiency could be measured and value for money obtained. The construction of crime statistics was also highlighted by the first British Crime Survey in 1982. This indicated for the first time how much crime actually took place and how little of it was, in some cases, reported to or recorded by the police (see Hough and Mayhew, 1983).

Second, the glare of attention on the police and police management was enhanced by other reports from the early 1980s. Lord Scarman's report into the 1981 Brixton riots was critical of police training, disciplinary procedures, the lack of effective supervisory/managerial structures, the lack of monitoring of effectiveness and the failure to realize that the support of the community was necessary in the fight against crime. Crucially Scarman opened a 'Pandora's box' by stating that he saw no reason why local communities could not be consulted about the type of policing appropriate to their own neighbourhoods (Scarman, 1982). The Policy Studies Institute (PSI) research published in 1983 received considerable publicity because the researchers stated that confidence in the police was 'dangerously low' among some sections of the community and expressed serious concern about certain police practices. The PSI also presented stark evidence of the 'cult of masculinity',

and the racism and sexism that pervaded the 'canteen culture'. Like
Home Office research, it also contained a picture of what the police
actually spent their time doing that differed considerably from the picture of crime fighting that informed the public representation of
policework. Much less publicized however was the picture painted by
the PSI of the police organization's management structures. The researchers argued that the nature of the organization and the style of
management not only condoned bad practices but encouraged malpractice. They said that the existing force structure was too centralized
and inflexible with an overly long chain of command. An authoritarian
management style was identified which led to evasion of responsibility
and 'enormous inertia' at all levels of the organization (Smith and
Gray, 1985). The PSI report argued for a 'more positive approach to
management' based upon consultative, simplified and devolved management arrangements; managerial information systems; clearly defined
force tasks, objectives and responsibilities; indicators for assessing the
performance of officers; incentives for good officers and effective sanctions
to deal with the 'rotten apples'.

Third, during a concerted campaign to enhance police accountability,
concern about key aspects of policework was raised by the Labour-
controlled Metropolitan Police Authorities during the 1980s. Their research units investigated local police policies, practices and outcomes
and unearthed a very different perspective to the one conveyed in the
glossy, anodyne annual reports presented by the Commissioner of the
Metropolitan Police and other chief constables. They too pointed to
ineffective policework, inappropriate deployment of resources, under-
reporting of crime, especially by women and working-class people,
and considerable alienation amongst certain sections of local communities,
particularly among the young and ethnic minorities (McLaughlin, 1994).

Counting Coppers

So even in the earliest days of the new golden relationship between
the police and the Conservative government, a number of searching
questions were being asked about organizational practices and management capabilities. The key problem was that there was no means of
inputting these research findings into policing practices. Traditionally,
the operational independence constitutionally accorded to chief police
officers allowed them to ignore critical research findings, whether they
emanated from the Home Office or elsewhere. If necessary senior officers
could define those who asked difficult questions as being politically

motivated. However if the 'political' critics could be easily brushed aside it proved much harder to deal with the fiscal and budgetary concerns that underlay the government's 'value for money' Financial Management Initiative (FMI) launched in 1982. This aimed at improving the efficiency, effectiveness and accountability of government departments (see Treasury, 1983; Fry, 1988). Each department was required to: have a clear view of their objectives; produce means to assess and measure outputs on performance in relation to those objectives; and have well-defined managerial responsibility for making the best use of their resources. In addition, 'where practicable, performance indicators and output measures will be developed which can be used to assess success in achievement of objectives . . . The question departments will address is "where is the money going *and* what are we getting for it?"' (House of Commons, 1982: paras 13 and 15).

These were uncomfortable 'reality check' questions for a central government department that was normally exempted from review and evaluation exercises. As the provider of 51 per cent of police expenditure the Home Office was required to focus on the police as part of its response to the FMI. Home Office Circular 114/1983, *Manpower, Effectiveness and Efficiency in the Police Service* (Home Office, 1983), was issued, declaring the need for a period of consolidation rather than continued growth in police expenditure. In its call for the more efficient and effective use of existing resources it also sought to introduce 'a highly specific language of rational management into the process of determining policy priorities' (Weatheritt, 1986: 111). In future, police forces and police authorities requesting more personnel would have to demonstrate that existing resources were being used and managed to best advantage, that they had the means of assessing the extent to which objectives and priorities were being achieved and that there was a specified reason for the requested increase. It also attempted to promote a more questioning style of management and encouraged thinking about what constituted 'good practice' (see also Horton and Smith, 1988; Sinclair and Miller, 1984).

Weatheritt argues that the need to account for itself *vis-à-vis* the police forced the Home Office to realize that it needed systematic knowledge concerning how police resources were allocated, what results any extra funding would deliver, how the performance of the 43 forces in England and Wales compared, and the efficient use of public resources.

In seeking this information and in taking a direct interest in what the products of policing are, the Home Office has been drawn into a new set of relationships with forces and has signalled very clearly its interest in what forces do and how well they do it: in other words with operational priorities. (Weatheritt, 1986: 104)

The difficulty that the Home Office had in getting to grips with the police in the 1980s was twofold. First, in a rerun of some of the problems that it had encountered in the 1970s, it was necessary to find practical mechanisms to define and measure effectiveness and efficiency. The doctrine of constabulary independence, the unusually high degree of discretion at the lowest levels of the organization and the low visibility of policework made the measurement of routine police activities highly problematic. The second problem was the political positioning of the police as mentioned above. In particular, when the coal dispute started in 1984, all financial considerations were subordinated to the political need to provide the police with the resources and the manpower required to defeat the miners. Then there were further serious urban and industrial disturbances in 1985 and 1986. In a period of continuing public disorder and seeming social crisis, questions about the efficiency and effectiveness of the police in relation to 'mundane' crime matters (and even the evidence of an escalating crime wave) were sidelined. In addition any intention to cut police expenditure was put on hold, as overtime bills and the costs of acquiring public order equipment escalated. Any overt fiscal 'assault' upon the police during this period would also have been seen as ideologically giving ground to left-wing critics of the police who were demanding that the political accountability of the police be strengthened. Ironically then, these disputes can in retrospect be seen as the 'saving' or 'making' of the police at this time, without which the FMI and Home Office Circular 114/1983 may have begun to take greater effect. None the less it is clear that the sacrosanct 'double difference' of policework was already being scrutinized by the underlying fiscal and ideological imperatives of the government's managerialist reform programme.

By the late 1980s it was clear that the police had successfully 'managed' public disorder and the 'troublesome' Metropolitan Police Authorities had been abolished. This should have heralded a new golden age for the police. In 1987 the then Home Secretary Douglas Hurd told senior officers that 'there is now a need for a period of stability and consolidation' (Hurd, 1987: 4). However for a number of reasons this was not to be. New instruments and discourses had been found to fiscally scrutinize the police which would take account of the legally mandated operational autonomy of chief officers. First, Home Office

Circular 114/1983 had allocated Her Majesty's Inspectorate of Constabulary a key role in the pursuance of Home Office aims because, under the Police Act 1964, the HMI has statutory responsibility for reporting on police efficiency and identifying and disseminating good practice. The resultant 'focused inspections' and Home Office Circulars 105/1988, 106/1988 and 35/1989 compelled the different forces, for the first time, to think about their activities, budgets, establishment levels, civilianization, and to produce quantifiable evidence of effectiveness. Because the Home Office now required information to be broken down into nationally agreed functional categories, as opposed to administrative ones, these detailed inspections produced more comprehensive information about resource use and the performance of different forces.

Second, two other levers were applied in a sort of 'pincer' movement in the late 1980s. In 1988 the first Audit Commission research paper on the organization of policing was released. Because of its 'non-political' remit (evaluating the management of local government activities in terms of economy, efficiency and effectiveness) the Audit Commission proved to be a much more searching scrutinizer of police practices than the more easily dismissable 'politically inspired' opponents of the early and mid-1980s. Since the promotion of 'better management' sounds neutral, it is difficult for anyone to quibble with it (Garrett, 1986; Pollitt, 1993). The Audit Commission was clearly managerialist in orientation and provided the government with a means of reforming the organization of policing without seeming to touch the sensitive matter of operational independence. But in directing its gaze to the management of the police the Audit Commission in fact trampled all over the 'operational independence' of chief police officers, thereby exposing its questionable organizational, though not legal, status. Successive Audit Commission reports proposed the need for rethinking the financing of policing; how budgets were allocated; the manner in which police activities were costed; and the organization, rank structure and salary scales of provincial police forces (Audit Commission, 1990a, 1990b, 1991a, 1991b). The Commission's managerialism brought to the fore the need for decentralized, flexible and streamlined managerial structures; clearly stated priorities and objectives; and output-based quantifiable performance indicators covering key operational functions in order to facilitate inter-force comparisons. The language of the market was also introduced as the Commission discussed the needs of 'customers', and methods for delivering a value-for-money service. In later reports the Commission has moved 'deeper' into the heart of policing by advocating more effective methods of managing crime investigations and patrolling (Audit Commission, 1993, 1996a). A reading between the lines of these reports reveals an organization riven by conflicts of interest and self-serving rhetorics, which led the former head of the Audit Commission to declare that, 'of all the public services the police are most over ripe for reform' (Davies, 1992).

Alongside the Audit Commission's work, the Home Affairs Select Committee's deliberations on policing under the chairmanship of Sir John Wheeler began to enter the public domain. The committee started from the premise that policing was 'big business', in terms of budget and personnel, but that police forces were insufficiently business-like in structure and functioning. Unlike the Audit Commission, it confronted the constitutional position of the police. Wheeler argued that the policing needs of the 1990s and beyond, including the advent of the European Union and the emergence of transnational crime networks and markets, necessitated rationalization. In order to compensate for what he described as 'glaring deficiencies, incompetent use of resources and blinding incompetence' (*The Independent*, 26 July 1990), existing forces should be merged, police authorities should be replaced by a small board of appointed directors and a national policing policy committee consisting of regional chief officers and Home Office representatives be established. Government dissatisfaction with police performance was also highlighted by Mrs Thatcher's call in February 1990 for a direct entry 'officer class' to impose a set of standards and values into the police (see Wheatcroft, 1991; Savage and Leishman, 1993). Thus the need for radical reform was being clearly signalled from a number of sources and the political time frame which senior police officers would be given to put their 'own house in order' was limited.

A FORCE OR A SERVICE?

There is evidence that senior officers, in the aftermath of the FMI and the resultant Home Office directive, were forced to pay more attention to the new managerial discourse and to positively respond to certain Audit Commission inquiries. Senior officers were well-aware that they had little management control over the rank and file and were not adverse to suggestions that would enable them to manage more effectively and indeed give formal recognition to their managerial role. There had already been more attention paid to issues of recruitment, training, supervision and policing skills (interrogation, procedural issues and paperwork) in the aftermath of the Scarman Report, the Police and Criminal Evidence Act 1984 and the establishment of the Crown Prosecution Service (Morgan, 1987). Sir Kenneth Newman was at the forefront of such moves including the issuing of *The Principles of Policing and Guidance for Professional Behaviour* (Newman, 1987), which stressed the need for good conduct and respecting citizen's rights. However, his top-down management style failed to carry the rank and file with him. His successor at the Metropolitan Police, Sir Peter Imbert, and the Inspectorate of Constabulary took the lead in advocating further change in order to preserve the organization. In 1989, following an inquiry by the public relations firm Wolff Olins into the image and presentational style of the police, the Plus Programme – the prototype police 'mission statement' – was unveiled, stressing the need for radical organizational and cultural change, including devolved responsibility to divisional level; strategic management; the setting and monitoring of identifiable standards of service; efficient and cost-effective service delivery; indicators to measure customer satisfaction; identifying and disseminating good practice and specified managerial responsibilities (Wolff Olins, 1988; Metropolitan Police, 1989). Through the encouragement of a consultative managerial philosophy every effort was made to carry the rank and file with the changes and to ensure their active participation. In the 1989 annual report the Inspectorate argued that the police should 'recognize the need for a theoretical, ethical and completely professional base on which the practical policing strategy of the future can be developed'.

In 1989, in an unprecedented collaboration, the first ever operational review of policing was carried out internally by the three staff associations (Joint Consultative Committee, 1990). As a result the first 'quality of service' corporate statement *Setting the Standards for Policing: Meeting Community Expectations* (Association of Chief Police Officers (ACPO), 1990) was issued. It acknowledged that there was public concern about 'poor performance and failures that range from incivility and aggressiveness to corruption'. To counter this concern the statement committed the organization to producing a strategic management framework and a matrix of performance indicators to facilitate identifying, implementing and monitoring the quality of service as well as improving standards of service delivery. This formally signalled the intention of senior officers to move from a police *force* to a police *service*. Managerial roles and responsibilities would be specified at every level to deliver the new service. There would be clearly identified mechanisms for monitoring and evaluating organizational performance, and more consultation and opinion surveys to identify different customer priorities. The attitudes and standards of behaviour of officers would be monitored more tightly and in the context of a Statement of Ethical Principles (Woodcock, 1993; *Police Review,* 11 December 1992; McLaughlin and Murji, 1993). The document also acknowledged that the resultant information would have to be collated centrally because of the need to record 'the process of organizational change and the effect of those changes on and by indicators of public satisfaction'. Some senior police managers began to make noises to the rank and file that there would have to be changes to the archaic shift system, the inflexible rank structure and the promotion system. These managers made it clear that they would welcome the freedom to introduce incentives and the power to remove corrupt and ineffective officers (*The Times*, 24 November 1988).

Around the same time, a bifurcation in policing strategies became apparent. ACPO agreed to the nationalization of certain functions whilst pushing localized and flexible sectoral or problem-solving policing, an elaboration of an earlier dynamic (policing by objectives) and experiments to improve the efficiency and effectiveness of service delivery and community relations (Weatheritt, 1989). Thus, as we have argued elsewhere, ACPO's strategy during this period can be seen as a twin-track one which emphasized a community police *service* at the local level and a police *force* at the national and international level (Murji and Cutler, 1990; McLaughlin, 1992). The wish to keep their options open and avoid being 'boxed in' also led police representatives to warn that although they were willing to reform the organization, there were limits to the changes they would countenance. They made it clear that they would resist attempts to make the organization comparable to a business. Sir Peter Imbert warned that a 'non-profit making, caring public service could not be judged by economic criteria used by ICI and Marks and Spencers' (*The Independent*, 5 March 1990). He also proclaimed that British society would be wary of a police service that was 'too efficient, too effective, too sophisticated' (quoted in Judge, 1990: 43). Throughout 1990, Alan Eastwood of the Police Federation complained about the government's restrictions on law and order expenditure which since 1983 had resulted in what he described as 'no-growth' budgets: 'It is our view that a policy of putting financial considerations above all others now threatens the ability of the police service to play its fundamental and unique role to the full' (*The Guardian*, 5 October 1990). The Federation also claimed that the Treasury was pressing for market testing and the privatization of police tasks.

TIGHTENING THE SCREW

Hence a contradictory picture was established by the late 1980s. Some police managers had begun to embrace, in an *ad hoc* manner, aspects of managerialism and acknowledged the need to reform the culture, image and content of policework, mainly by recasting policing as a service to meet the needs of local communities and as a force to combat drug traffickers, terrorists and international criminal gangs. These measures, combined with a deep-seated belief in the essential 'double difference' of policework, were probably thought to be enough to fend off the critics and lead to a period of calm. But pressure upon the police continued to bite because, in the context of successive scandals such as the miscarriages of justice, the exposure of normalized corruption in the West Midlands Serious Crime Squad and the dramatic cases of senior officers such as John Stalker and Alison Halford, key sections of the media, most notably *The Economist* and *The Independent*, pieced together and published a fractal image of the police as a cocooned public institution that embodied many, if not all, of the characteristics that the New Right was ideologically opposed to:

1. Enormous differences between the 43 police forces in terms of policies and practices on the one hand with, on the other hand, unnecessary duplication of effort.
2. Inflexible, quasi-military hierarchical structures.
3. A 'pass the parcel' approach to taking responsibility.
4. A powerful workforce with cast-iron job security, ring-fenced pay and pension agreements and restrictive working practices.
5. An ever-increasing budget with non-existent checks and balances.
6. A cynical and over-defensive occupational culture that was deeply resistant to change.
7. A non-existent appraisal system and ineffective disciplinary procedures.
8. Hopelessly blurred lines of fiscal responsibility and public accountability.
9. Evidence from opinion polls that the organization had forfeited the trust and respect of certain sections of the public and was also not responding to the fears and needs of 'middle England'.
10. An inadequate range of targets against which to measure and judge police performance.

There is no doubt that by the early 1990s the force fields erected by the police to deflect criticism had been severely dented. Indeed some were on the verge of collapse. What remained unclear was the extent to which the post-Thatcher Conservative government would explicitly 'take on' the police and thus expose the last veneer of the 'special relationship'. In the run-up to the 1992 General Election, rumours began to circulate that a re-elected Conservative government would reform the procedures and practices of the last 'closed shop' in the public sector. For example, the government had already fired a shot across the police bow in June 1991 when it announced that the organization would fall within the scope of John Major's Citizen's Charter. To reinforce the image of police officers as public servants and make them more responsive to customers the organization would be expected to develop a framework of targets and objectives. This at the time controversial move contributed to an intensification of police attacks on the Conservatives' record on law and order, while at the same time increasingly friendly overtures were being made towards the Labour Party. In 1991 the three police staff associations released a nine-point policing agenda denying that money had been lavished on the police, stressing that the police could not be held responsible for the increases in crime, claiming that the organization had been subject to unfair criticisms and demanding that the next government should commit itself to making law and order a priority.

To the consternation of some senior police officers the Conservatives were re-elected. In 1992 the new Home Secretary, Kenneth Clarke, announced that reform would be necessary to win back the confidence of 'middle England'. A three-pronged strategy emerged out of this. First Clarke announced the establishment of an inquiry to examine the rank structure, remuneration framework and the terms and conditions of service of police officers. What became known as the Sheehy Inquiry was augmented in July 1992 by an internal Home Office review of the tripartite structure of police governance and in December 1992 by a Home Office survey of core and ancillary police tasks. Overall, these reviews signalled the government's intention to subject the police, like the rest of the public sector, to the disciplines, rationales and discourses of new managerialism (McLaughlin and Murji, 1995a).

The Sheehy report was explicitly geared towards realizing more efficient and cost-effective management of existing resources. It proposed: the simplification and streamlining of the rank structure; fixed-term appointments to end the 'jobs for life' culture; a new flexible pay matrix premised upon the principle of performance-related pay; the abolition of allowances and overtime and a revision of pension entitlements (Sheehy, 1993). The White Paper recommended that radically restructured police authorities should become free-standing bodies, independent of local government. The new authorities and chief constables would be responsible for producing, in the context of Home Office national objectives, a local policing plan outlining their objectives and priorities as well as details of the budget, expenditure levels and measurable outcomes. The White Paper also argued for a reform of the funding formula through the reallocation of budgetary responsibilities and establishment controls (Home Office, 1993).

The Police and Magistrates' Courts Act 1994 contained less than the full reform package, because of the successful lobbying campaign by the police and, to a lesser extent, local authorities against the Sheehy and White Paper proposals (McLaughlin and Murji, 1995b, 1996; Leishman, Cope and Starie, 1995). None the less, the partial reforms introduced by the Act served to further the managerial nexus within policing. The Act establishes a set of strategic relationships: the Home Secretary, by order, determines nationally key objectives for policing, sets performance targets, issues codes of practice, orders inspections and requests reports. Locally, through the need to produce an annual local policing plan, police authorities have been brought into a new formal relationship with their chief officers. By allocating authorities the power to devise fixed-term contracts and performance-related pay for senior officers, police authorities have been empowered with a degree of managerial control over chief officers. In turn, chief constables have been given greater flexibility. Because central government determines the budget there is no longer a need for the system where the Home Office used to set establishment levels and had to approve increases. Rather, the responsibility for how many officers to employ rests with individual authorities and chief constables. Chief constables also have greater day-to-day financial control and their management responsibility is extended to civilian staff. In other words the reforms have placed greater managerial responsibility on police authorities and chief constables to control and manage their resources and personnel to best effect. Thus, overall the Act seeks to make explicit the priorities, targets and performance criteria for each police force, as well as the resources available, the ways in which they are to be allocated and, through the annual report, an assessment of the extent to which the local policing plan has been realized. It comes as near as has been possible to date to establishing a framework for more 'business-like' police forces, with clear measures of inputs and outputs.

CONCLUSION: ENDLESS PRESSURES

The managerial solution is however far from complete. To some extent this is true for many areas of the public sector but, focusing on the police alone and looking back at the model of new managerialism outlined at the outset, it can be seen that some aspects of it have been met. A doctrine of professional management has been taken seriously by many senior officers. The operation of the police in a more business-like manner has been enhanced by the Police and Magistrates' Courts Act and with it has come a clearer idea of what the police are being asked to do. Thus league tables are already here (Audit Commission, 1996b). Other elements of the model, however, have been stunted by the police's rearguard action. So, there has been inadequate rationalization of policework partly because of the limited outcome of the review of core and ancillary tasks (Home Office, 1995a) and there is an incomplete competitive environment. Hierarchies based on rank rather than competence continue to exist in some form, while new appraisal and incentive systems are still being contested within the organization. The ability of chief police officers and police authorities to manage within their budgets remains to be seen.

It is for these reasons that we are confronted with a contradictory and confusing picture in the late 1990s. The police have ridden a roller-coaster of political fortune but, as that image suggests, the ride will always be an uncertain, tension-filled one. While, on the one hand, there continues to be deep resistance to managerialization, on the other hand, at many levels within the organization, the impact of various forms of managerialism have already been felt deeply. The ways in which these tensions will be played out remain to be seen. But for the police the more worrying consequence of managerial discourses is that they have questioned and indeed debunked and demystified hitherto 'sacred' and hidden aspects of organizational culture, practice and performance. Thus many commentators, from a variety of perspectives, within and without the police, can announce that the 'golden days' of the 'sacred' status of the British police officer are at an end (Woodcock, 1992; Reiner, 1992; McLaughlin and Murji, 1995a), that the 'past' cannot be remade (though some might doubt whether it ever existed in anything more than the imagination) and that it is time to concentrate on mundane realities. But even this is highly problematic because, in 'unravelling' policing, managerial discourses have served to open up different and very contradictory conceptions of the purpose, organization and delivery of policework. As we have seen, senior police officers have desperately 'flipped' between *service* and *force* orientations, in an attempt to resist being pinned down to either. But new managerialism has undoubtedly interrupted and to a degree transcended this relatively comfortable dichotomy by introducing a more 'business-like' conception of policing. Unlike the former two, this is the most uncomfortable position for police officers and managers because both 'force' and 'service' aspects of policework can be subjected to 'business-like' imperatives. A managerialized future does not offer any 'public' sector organization the security and stability that may have existed in the 'golden age' of the Keynesian welfare state. Because efficiency is a direction and not a terminus we can never arrive at the ideal 'lean, fit' efficient organization. Management can only ever be 'better', not 'perfect'. Thus there is set in motion a potentially ceaseless dynamic for multidimensional organizational transformation. Managerialization, therefore, has had and will continue to have a profound impact upon the police at an organizational level. This in turn will play through to the cultural 'mind set' of the police though not in a direct, unmediated and uncontested manner. We can expect to see much continual wailing as the pains of various rebirthings and concurrent resistances work their way through the organization. The managerialized future has in many ways only just begun to take effect and looks set to last a long time.

References

Association of Chief Police Officers (1990) *Setting the Standards for Policing* (London, Scotland Yard: Association of Chief Police Officers).

Audit Commission (1990a) *Effective Policing: Performance Review in Police Forces*, Paper No. 10 (London: HMSO).

Audit Commission (1990b) *Footing the Bill: Financing Provincial Police Forces*, Paper No. 6 (London: HMSO).

Audit Commission (1991a) *Reviewing the Organization of Provincial Police Forces*, Paper No. 9 (London: HMSO).

Audit Commission (1991b) *Pounds and Coppers: Financial Delegation in Provincial Police Forces* (London: HMSO).

Audit Commission (1993) *Helping with Enquiries: Tackling Crime Effectively* (London: HMSO).

Audit Commission (1996a) *Streetwise: Effective Police Patrol* (London: HMSO).

Audit Commission (1996b) *Local Authority Performance Indicators, Vol 3. Police and Fire Services* (London: HMSO).

Bekke, H., Perry, J. and Toonen, T. (eds) (1996) *Civil Service Systems in Comparative Perspective* (Bloomington, Ind.: Indiana University Press).

Clarke, R. and Hough, M. (1984) *Crime and Police Effectiveness* (London: HMSO).

Clarke, R. and Mayhew, P. (eds) (1980) *Designing Out Crime* (London: HMSO).
Clarke, J., Cochrane, A. and McLaughlin, E. (eds) (1994) *Managing Social Policy* (London: Sage).
Committee of Inquiry into the Police (1978) *Report on Negotiations, Machinery and Pay* (Reports I and II), Cmnd 7283 (London: HMSO).
Conservative Party (1979) *Conservative Manifesto* (London: Conservative Central Office).
Davies, H. (1992) *Fighting Leviathan: Building Social Markets That Work* (London: Social Market Foundation).
Ewing, K. and Gearty, C. (1990) *Freedom Under Thatcher* (Oxford: Oxford University Press).
Fry, G. (1988) 'The Thatcher government, the Financial Management Initiative and the "New Civil Service"', *Public Administration*, vol. 66, no. 1.
Garrett, J. (1986) 'Developing state audit in Britain', *Public Administration*, vol. 64, no. 3.
Hall, S. (1996) *New Statesman*, 9 February.
Hennessy, P. (1989) *Whitehall* (London: Fontana).
Heseltine, M. (1980) 'Ministers and management in Whitehall', *Management Services in Government*, vol. 35.
Hillyard, P. and Percy-Smith, J. (1987) *The Coercive State* (London: Pinter).
Hoggett, P. (1991) 'A New Management in the Public Sector?' *Policy and Politics*, vol. 19, no. 4.
Home Office (1967) *Police Manpower, Equipment and Efficiency* (London: HMSO).
Home Office (1983) Circular 114/1983 *Manpower, Effectiveness and Efficiency in the Police Service*, November. (London: Home Office).
Home Office (1993) *Police Reform: A Police Service for the 21st Century*, Cmnd 2281 (London: HMSO).
Home Office (1995a) *Review of Police Core and Ancillary Tasks*, Final Report (London: HMSO).
Home Office (1995b) *Digest 3: Information on the Criminal Justice System in England and Wales* (London: Home Office).
Hood, C. (1991) 'A public management for all seasons?', *Public Administration*, vol. 69, no. 1.
Horton, C. and Smith, D. (1988) *Evaluating Policework* (London: Policy Studies Institute).
Hough, M. and Mayhew, P. (1983) *The British Crime Survey* (London: Home Office).
House of Commons (1982) *Efficiency and Effectiveness in the Civil Service*, Report of the Treasury and Civil Service Select Committee (London: HMSO).
Hurd, D. (1987) Unpublished address to the Police Foundation, 30 July.
Joint Consultative Committee (1990) *Operational Policing Review* (Surbiton: Police Federation).
Jones, C. (1993) 'Auditing criminal justice', *British Journal of Criminology*, vol. 33, no. 2.
Judge, A. (1990) 'A force under fire', *Police*, June.
Kirkpatrick, I. and Martinez-Lucio, M. (1996) 'The contract state and the future of public management', *Public Administration*, vol. 74, no. 1.
Leishman, F. and Savage, S. (1993) 'The police service', in D. Farnham and S. Horton (eds), *Managing the New Public Services* (London: Macmillan).

Leishman, F. Cope, S. and Starie, P. (1995) 'Reforming the police in Britain', *International Journal of Public Sector Management*, vol. 8, no. 4.

Martin, J. and Wilson, G. (1969) *The Police: A Study of Manpower* (London: Heinemann).

McCabe, S. and Wallington, P. with Alderson, J., Gotsin, L. and Mason, G. (1988) *The Police, Public Order and Civil Liberties* (London: Routledge).

McLaughlin, E. (1992) 'The democratic deficit: European Union and the accountability of the British police', *British Journal of Criminology*, vol. 32, no. 4.

McLaughlin, E. (1994) *Community Policing and Accountability* (Aldershot: Avebury).

McLaughlin, E. and Muncie, J. (1994) 'Managing the criminal justice system', in J. Clarke, A. Cochrane, and E. McLaughlin (eds), *Managing Social Policy* (London: Sage).

McLaughlin, E. and Murji, K. (1993) 'Controlling the Bill', *Critical Social Policy*, no. 37.

McLaughlin, E. and Murji, K. (1995a) 'The end of public policing? Police reform and the new managerialism', in L. Noaks, M. Levi, and M. Maguire (eds), *Contemporary Issues in Criminology* (Cardiff: University of Wales Press).

McLaughlin, E. and Murji, K. (1995b) 'Resistance through representation: the police campaign against the Sheehy Inquiry', unpublished paper presented at the British Criminology Conference, Loughborough University, July.

McLaughlin, E. and Murji, K. (1996) 'Times change: new formations and representations of police accountability', in C. Critcher and D. Waddington (eds), *Policing Public Order: Theoretical and Practical Issues* (Aldershot: Avebury).

Metropolitan Police (1989) *The Plus Programme: Making it Happen* (London: Metropolitan Police).

Morgan, R. (1987) 'Police accountability: developing the local infrastructure', *British Journal of Criminology*, vol. 27, no. 1.

Morris, P. and Heal, K. (1981) *Crime Control and the Police* (London: Home Office).

Murji, K. and Cutler, D. (1990) 'From a force to a service? The police, racial attacks and equal opportunities', *Critical Social Policy*, no. 29.

Newman, J. and Clarke, J. (1994) 'Going about our business? The managerialisation of public services', in J. Clarke, A. Cochrane and E. McLaughlin (eds), *Managing Social Policy* (London: Sage).

Newman, K. (1985) *The Principles of Policing and Guidance for Professional Behaviour* (London: Metropolitan Police).

Oliver, I. (1987) *Police, Government and Accountability* (London: Macmillan).

Pollitt, C. (1993) *Managerialism and the Public Services*, 2nd edn (Oxford: Blackwell).

Reiner, R. (1985) *The Politics of the Police* (Brighton: Harvester Wheatsheaf).

Reiner, R. (1992) '*Fin de siècle blues*: the police face the millennium', *Political Quarterly*, vol. 63, no. 1.

Savage, S. and Leishman, F. (1993) 'Officers or managers?', *International Journal of Public Sector Management*, vol. 6, no. 5.

Scarman, Lord (1982) *The Scarman Report: The Brixton Disorders, 10–12 April 1981* (London: Penguin).

Scraton, P. (1985) *The State of the Police* (London: Pluto).

Sheehy, Sir P. (1993) *Inquiry into Police Responsibilities and Rewards*, Cmnd 2280 (London: HMSO).

Sinclair, I. and Miller, C. (1984) *Measuring Police Effectiveness and Efficiency* (London: HMSO).

Smith, D. J. and Gray, J. (1985) *Police and People in London* (Aldershot: Gower).

Spencer, J. (1993) 'The criminal justice system and the politics of scrutiny', *Social Policy and Administration*, vol. 27, no. 1.

Stewart, J. and Walsh, K. (1992) 'Change in the management of public services', *Public Administration*, vol. 70, no. 3.

Treasury (1983) *Financial Management in Government Departments*, Cmnd 9058 (London: HMSO).

Waddington, P. A. J. (1991) *The Strong Arm of the Law* (Oxford: Clarendon Press).

Weatheritt, M. (1986) *Innovations in Policing* (London: Police Foundation).

Weatheritt, M. (ed.) (1989) *Police Research: Some Future Prospects* (Aldershot: Gower).

Wheatcroft, G. (1991) 'Why the armed forces outclass the police', *Sunday Telegraph*, 11 March.

Wilding, P. (1993) 'The public sector in the 1980s', in N. Manning and R. Page (eds), *Social Policy Review no. 4* (Canterbury: Social Policy Association).

Wolff Olins (1988) *A Force for Change: A Report on the Corporate Identity of the Metropolitan Police* (London: New Scotland Yard).

Woodcock, Sir J. (1992) 'Why we need a revolution', *Police Review*, 16 October.

Woodcock, Sir J. (1993) 'The values we uphold', *Police Review*, 1 January.

5 Control, Crime and 'End of Century Criminology'
Nigel South

INTRODUCTION

Late modern society exhibits profound tensions and competing tendencies at several levels (Giddens, 1990). Cultural critics have described
this at great length in debates around post-modernity (Jameson, 1984;
Lyotard, 1984), but in more concrete arenas – for example, practices
of policing, the politics of criminal justice provision and the social
regulation of populations – there are also significant fragmentations,
diversifications and new concerns. This chapter examines various features of such developments and also addresses some implications for
two key themes: legitimacy and human rights. The chapter proceeds
by moving from a discussion of policing and the privatization of criminal justice, through developments in surveillance and security, before
finally moving to the European and global levels. In doing so it will
highlight; first, some questions about the legitimacy of contemporary
control systems; second, the importance of human rights; and third,
the neglected significance of crimes against the environment and the
future state of the planet. The chapter's central concern is with some
issues that will (or should) influence policing and control, as well as
the broader field of criminology, as we approach the year 2000 and
beyond.

ON POLICING AND THE PRIVATIZATION OF CRIMINAL JUSTICE

By the end of a century characterized in terms of progress and modernity, when it might have been supposed that the contemporary organization of policing, legitimated and delivered by the state, would have
been unchallenged, there is in fact an increasing pluralization of policing forms. Whilst some state systems of surveillance, data banks, and
operational agencies of control move toward centralized locations and
directions (Marx and Reichman, 1984; Dandeker, 1990; Lyon, 1994;

Goodwin and Humphreys, 1982; Christie, 1993), at the same time – in both the West and now the East – there has emerged a continuum of control, a division of policing labour (South, 1984, 1994a) and an extension of traditional reliance on informal resolution of control and conflict problems (Ellickson, 1991; Black and Baumgartner, 1980; Baumgartner, 1988; Greenberg *et al.*, 1985). In short, much of the activity of the agents and agencies on this continuum of control takes place *outside* the state domain, being private or informal, with priorities largely dictated by profit, self-interest or community/mutual benefits (South, 1988, 1994b). Globally, societies variously differing in composition, government and politics may be characterized as embracing a 'mixed economy of control'.

The Modern 'Mixed Economy of Control'

In a paper reviewing trends shaping the state of British policing in the 1990s, Johnston (1992b: 15) outlined the consequences for public and private policing of the ideology of the 'free economy and strong state' which the British government has held to during the 1980s and into the 1990s. As Johnston observes, this formula is:

> Above all else, an attempt to encapsulate the changing relations between the state (public) sphere and the market (private) sphere in late-twentieth century capitalism . . . however, it is apparent that that formula fails to grasp some of the complexity of those changing relations. In particular, a situation is occurring in which the range of the public sphere is coming to be distorted by encroachments of the private sphere and vice versa . . . What is becoming apparent is that the boundaries between the public and private spheres are . . . becoming less and less tangible. (Johnston, 1992b:15) [cf. Cohen, 1985; South, 1988]

It is probable that this increasing public/private *permeability* is a characteristic of most western (and increasingly eastern) social economies (see Matthews (1995) on the weakness of this divide in the first place; and South (1987 1989b) on the historical balance of public/ private policing initiatives). Certainly in terms of policing, the common experience of most western countries has been that as public police forces have met changing patterns of service demand and set new priorities (including 'civilizing' more and more tasks to release police officers for operational duties), at the same time the private sector of policing has continually made incursions into the former 'public' sector.

One common view of this trend is that as the public policing services have had to direct scarce resources toward 'new' as well as traditional but worsening crime problems (such as increases in property and violent crimes, plus terrorism, drug trafficking and international fraud), they have left behind them spaces to be 'colonized' by 'payment-for-protection' services. This 'colonization' view is, in some respects, quite convincing, as is the other popular explanation that it has been a 'fiscal crisis of the state' which has stimulated the commercial provision of private policing services – simply because they are cheaper (see for example Spitzer and Scull, 1977). However, by themselves, these propositions are too simplistic and inadequate (Shearing and Stenning, 1981, 1983; South, 1984; Johnston, 1992a; Matthews, 1995). Rather the elaboration of more adequate theoretical perspectives might build upon the insights of the explanations noted above, but also discuss the process of the 'commodification of security' (Spitzer, 1987) in material and social–psychological senses; relatedly, the relationship between what Narr (1992) calls 'the anxiety market' and the 'selling' of security services; and finally, the influence of post- or late modern conditions on centralizing versus decentralizing tendencies in modern policing (McLaughlin, 1992; Shearing, 1992; Sheptycki, 1995).

The postwar emergence of the private security sector is a significant 'quiet revolution' (Stenning and Shearing, 1980) in policing. To define this sector, among its characteristics are the following. The modern private security sector embraces a variety of surveillance and reporting tasks aiming to ensure the efficient use of resources, the maximum productivity of employees' labour time, the prevention of theft, and the maintenance of buildings and equipment in secure and safe conditions (Shearing and Stenning, 1981, 1983; South, 1987a, 1988; for two topical reports on recent examples of such activities see: on Russia, Specter (1994); on the United States of America, Schultz (1994)). The significance of private security as a supplement to, and indeed substitute for, public police has now been well-noted in various studies, as well as the popular media. What is worth noting in the late 1990s is that, while some commentators (including myself in the past (South, 1988)) have argued that the term 'private *security*' is more applicable than the term 'private *police*', it increasingly appears that perhaps the latter term is now more appropriate. Interestingly, this may also be the view of representatives of the security industry.[1]

PRIVATE SECURITY POWERS – THE PRIVATIZATION OF LEGAL POWERS AND THE LEGITIMATE USE OF FORCE?[2]

What is the changing nature of private policing? In part, this is a question about legal powers and legitimacy. In the UK, it has generally been claimed that there is no cause for concern about the 'powers' of private security personnel simply because they have none. Or at least, no more than the ordinary citizen (unless authorized by some form of statute). If ever this was an adequate reassurance, it is surely no longer so. Ordinary citizens are in fact routinely in positions where private security personnel may search them (airport security[3]), exclude them (shopping malls), place them under surveillance (CCTV), evict them (nightclubs) and so on. Further, it is unlikely that members of the general public appreciate the basis of powers for a 'citizen's arrest' (under section 24 of the Police and Criminal Evidence Act 1984), nor the provision whereupon a court acquittal can allow the 'arrested' person to bring subsequent legal proceedings for 'unlawful arrest'. Indeed, it remains doubtful that the public understand very much at all about the legal basis for the powers of private security personnel (Flynn, in preparation; South, 1988; Scott and McPherson, 1971: 272); or about what kind of 'official' or moral authority the wearing of a uniform is supposed to bestow (South, 1988: 53, note 1; 124). As Flynn (in preparation: 215) observes:

> Tracing the legal authority of private policing is not easy. The private sector is not dependent upon the state for its authority and private security staff do not have to adhere to the same procedural restraints as the public police. The power of private security personnel derives principally from their being legal 'agents' of those who control and own private property (Sarre, 1994: 169). By contrast, public police power is generally found in the various law enforcement statutes, common law, rules and regulations.

Flynn (in preparation: 216) gives the example of the private policing of fox-hunt meetings as one example of the extension of 'power' conferred upon private agents.[4] As agents appointed by the landowner, private security personnel can evict trespassers. This is not a power which the public police can exercise unless a criminal offence is taking place. Private agents can employ 'necessary' and 'reasonable' force to carry out their task – the definition of 'necessary' and 'reasonable' obviously being widely open to interpretation. In 1996 this matter was highlighted in news coverage of the protests against a road bypass scheme at Newbury, in the south of England. Only a few media commentators picked up on the significant question of who is *actually* physically and forcefully removing the protesters (although the same question has also applied to a number of recent anti-motorway protests). The answer is not the public police, who are almost invariably bystanders, but private security personnel, hired by the sheriff's office and/or road-building contractors, and provided with a 'uniform' of distinctive jacket and helmets. While these 'front-line' private security personnel are involved in what might be called 'conflict policing', at the periphery of the encounters stand employees from private detective agencies, taking photographs of the protesters, the injured and injuring, for possible use in subsequent court cases – what might obviously be described as 'surveillance policing'.

Why is this emergent shift from private security to private police of significance? Because it raises the fundamental question of the *legitimacy* of policing in society.

Privatization, Legitimacy and Human Rights

In *Policing for Profit* (South, 1988: 1), Stan Cohen's (1985) observation concerning the prospects for privatization in relation to policing and criminal justice services was noted: 'For the state to give up here', wrote Cohen, 'would be to undercut its very claim to legitimacy.' Whatever irony Cohen might or might not have intended here, the use of this quote aimed to highlight the fact that already, from the 1970s and early 1980s onwards, there actually were clear signs of real and possible privatization in relation to both policing and other dimensions of the criminal justice system (see Cohen, 1985). Cohen was, in one way, quite right to point to the problematic challenge that privatization of criminal justice agencies *ought* to pose for the legitimacy of the state. However perhaps he was wrong about how 'the state' – in the case here the government of the United Kingdom – might respond to such a legitimacy issue. Contrary to the assumptions of some 'grand' sociological theories, this matter has proved to be less a signifier of 'legitimation crisis' than something to be treated as a minor, technical matter of 'contractual interpretation'! Indeed, Cohen was perhaps fundamentally wrong if he assumed (though probably he did not) that the traditional legitimacy of liberal democracy (Mann, 1970) was what mattered to the new Conservative ideologues or their supporting voters. The fundamental question that then arises here is whether sociological and criminological appeals to classical Weberian notions of legitimacy and the control of force still hold. In some respects they do, in others they do not. Concomitantly, all of this means that not only have the rules and expectations of the principle of 'legitimacy' been changed, but so too have the possibilities for seeking remedy and redress when the rules work against citizens. It shall be argued later that, among other implications, these changes mean that 'human rights' issues must be placed high on the agenda of responding to governmental erosion of respect for traditional sources of state legitimacy.[5]

The Use of Force: From 'State Monopoly' to Market Subcontracting

The state's reliance on a 'mixed social control economy' of informal and formal, private and public surveillance and enforcement agents, raises interesting and important questions about matters of account-ability, legitimacy and civil rights: in other words, questions about the nature of the authority, status and powers which are formally given to private agents; and about what lines (if any) can be drawn between their 'non-state' authority and their activities as permitted and/or con-tracted by the state. Central to these considerations is Max Weber's contention that 'the claim of the modern state to monopolise the use of force is as essential to it as is its character of compulsory jurisdic-tion and continuous operation' (Weber, 1978: 56). Given increasing evidence of the privatization of the 'legitimate' use of force, the ques-tion is whether Weber's proposition retains any validity.

One simple resolution of this matter is to argue that Weber's argu-ment might once have been true but is now outdated and has been overtaken by the capacity of the market to do a better job than the state. In Britain this would be the view of Conservative policy ad-visers (see for example, the influential Adam Smith Institute's Omega Report on Criminal Justice, 1984), perhaps especially during the mid-1980s period when the Thatcherite programme of privatization and deregulation was being formulated.[6] More subtly, Ryan and Ward (1989), in their critique of prison privatization, have argued that 'the monopoly claimed by the state . . . is over the power to *define* the legitimate use of force . . . This power does not necessarily depend on the State *owning* the means of force or employing the individuals who use it' (Ryan and Ward, 1989: 69; emphasis added). The implications of this post-Weberian recognition of the realities of the modern mixed economy of policing will be returned to later, when considering further issues of legitimacy and human rights.

ON SURVEILLANCE AND CONTROL

It is easy to overlook and take for granted just how much the physical and social environments we inhabit 'police' us (albeit with mixed results[7]). Closed-circuit television (CCTV) watches our movements and actions, aspiring to protect us and our property or to lead to our punishment if we do wrong.[8] Buildings and public and private spaces are designed with security and surveillance considerations in mind – perhaps sometimes oversecuring the built environment to the detriment of its liveability (South, 1987a). Individuals also police each other, complying with expectations, responding to disapproval, and reporting the deviations of others. The public do much to 'police the public' (Shapland and Vagg, 1988), whilst the police are increasingly reliant on 'good citizen' witnesses and criminal informants to provide the information necessary to help 'clear up' crime (Greer and South, 1997).

In the reality of everyday life, as well as on TV soap operas, 'Neighbours' are prone to have personal, property and territorial disputes but generally rely on non-legal strategies of conflict resolution rather than turning to the police and law (Baumgartner, 1988; Ellickson, 1991). Individuals also police themselves by following the directions of those who would order lives and relationships to the built environment, submitting to those static policing devices better known as 'signs'. These tell us what is and what is not allowed, where it may or may not be conducted, how old an individual must be to do some things (for example, buy alcohol), how young an individual must be to do others (for example, play in a children's playground), and so on. Thus, as well as state-sponsored forms of control, other privatized, 'hybrid' (Johnston, 1992a) and informal and community forms are also deeply embedded in the fabric of late modern life (South, 1994b).

In the late modern city, the interfaces between architecture, planned (that is 'approved') pathways and human action, are becoming ever more entwined. Should individuals be disturbed by this? Well, if they are among the privileged of society perhaps not (except by troubled consciences if they comprehend the emerging forms of social segregation); but if they are among the undesirables to be excluded from these planned pathways, then the answer is 'yes'. This is particularly so if we consider Mike Davis's (1992) explorations of 'urban control and the ecology of fear' in post-riot, increasingly militarized, Los Angeles. Here, a twin strategy of segregation and surveillance has made its impact on the city, not least by creating 'a city within a city'. After the Watts 'race riots' of the 1960s and fears of further conflicts, the city's redevelopment agency began to physically segregate the new core business areas from the ghetto communities: palisades, concrete pillars and freeway walls were built, traditional pedestrian connections between poor district and new business district were removed, 'foot traffic in the new financial district was elevated above the street on pedways whose access was controlled by the security systems of individual skyscrapers'. All of this has, as Davis (1992: 4) observes, 'ominous racial undertones'. Similarly, the extensive and comprehensive surveillance of all these areas 'constitutes' what Davis calls

> a virtual *scanscape* – a space of protective visibility that increasingly defines where white-collar office workers and middle-class tourists feel safe . . . Inevitably the workplace or shopping mall video camera will become linked with home security systems, personal 'panic buttons', car alarms, cellular phones and the like, in a seamless continuity of surveillance over daily routine. Indeed, yuppies' lifestyles may soon be defined by the ability to afford *electronic guardian angels* to watch over them. (Davis, 1992: 5; emphasis in original)

The question of 'who is doing all this surveillance?' is important; but so too is the other fundamental question – 'what is all this for?' The primary 'public good' justifications for increased surveillance are 'crime prevention' and 'public safety'. These propositions sound agreeable and are difficult to argue with until examined in terms of a *broad* notion of 'public good'. For example, the use of CCTV to direct private guards to remove 'undesirable youths' from a shopping mall may be justified. However, the broader questions of *where these youths are displaced to* and *what they will do there* usually remain unasked. In the present 'hard' crime prevention climate, it simply doesn't matter – if these *are* troublesome youths, they are now someone else's problem and thus 'someone else' can take up the options the market offers – that is, more CCTV, more private patrols, and more entry security.

Now, having safely walked the streets and done the shopping (always with someone to watch over us), let's go to work. Here, in the information society inner city, the electronic service sector is increasingly a mass employer, from the low-level rationalized employment in the McDonaldized world of delivering consumables to the mass-information-processing world of computer operators (Ritzer, 1993; Lyon, 1994). For the McDonalds worker, the tyranny of the factory clock (Thompson, 1967) is replaced by the rational plan adhered to by a computerized kitchen (Ritzer, 1993); for the office worker, the technology on the desk may represent the new 'networked panopticon'.

Here, 'time and motion' philosophy meets security and surveillance.[9]

In Hagerstown, Maryland, United States of America, the post-industrial workplace is reflected in, for example, the 'controlled environment' of Electronic Banking System Inc. (EBS) (Schultz, 1994). Here 'cameras help deter would-be thieves. Tight security also reassures visiting clients . . . But tight observation also helps EBS monitor productivity and weed out workers who don't keep up. "There's multiple uses" [the manager] says of surveillance. His desk is covered with computer printouts recording the precise toll of key-strokes tapped by each data entry worker. He also keeps a day to day tally of errors.' The 'security and surveillance mentality' extends further and further into the routines of everyday life (South, 1987b).

To take another example, in the near future, new satellite systems will ease mobile communications, but the police are concerned about how this will aid organized crime. A solution is to build in the capacity for surveillance. However, the builders of the technology are not public utilities but private international consortia and they demand a price for their services (*Statewatch*, 1995: 1). In the information age, the *security* of phone calls made via privatized communications systems, versus *surveillance access* to them, may simply become just another commodity for sale in the emerging, international public/private security market (South, 1994a).

Security technology can, obviously, bring many crime prevention benefits. *The Futurist* (1988) outlined the merits of the home computer security system of the next century, employing 'biometric devices' to verify visitors' identities and keep out burglars. The security computer of the 'intelligent house' 'could even keep track of who has trips or errands scheduled, when the dog needs to come back in, or who is taking too long in the shower'. This is a vision of the 'electronic filofax society', in which positivism and utilitarianism mix in search of effective crime prevention and efficient time management, and even the shower is haunted by Bentham's ghost.

The issues of social concern regarding surveillance, from the panopticon to the Police National Computer, were reflective of the concerns of industrial society, bureaucratization and modernity (Dandeker, 1990). In the overlapping shift to late modernity we become even more clearly an *information* society and the potential for surveillance, as well as new crimes and injurious offences, for example via computer networks (Hollinger, 1996), has opened up entire new horizons – but also poses new problems of rights and accountability.

ON LEGITIMACY, HUMAN RIGHTS AND CRIMES AGAINST THE ENVIRONMENT

It was discussed earlier how traditional notions of the 'legitimacy' of policing and the criminal justice system had been challenged by the commercializing forces of privatization. That the legitimacy of policing and the criminal justice system is still in place despite considerable challenge and tarnishing in recent years suggests either that 'legitimacy' is not as important to the business of government as we might conventionally assume, or that it is an increasingly plastic and malleable concept. The notion of 'legitimacy' implied by Cohen in the quote referred to earlier in this chapter was one born of 'classical' sociological assumptions about how states or governments survive. It is clearly arguable that – as Mrs Thatcher intended – the 1980s drove a very large BMW through a number of classical sociological, liberal and socialist beliefs and principles.

This does not mean however that the insights of classical sociology are no longer of use. Rather, there is a need for a reacquaintance with how they apply in a changed world. As Bryan Turner (1993) has illustrated, classical Weberian sociology copes rather well with a system that ever increasingly moves away from democratic accountability to executive control, bureaucratic obfuscation and downright duplicity.[10] As Turner (1993: 495) notes, 'those [legal–rational] powers which happen to be in control of the legal apparatus and the bureaucratic machine *will have* legitimacy. In Weber's sociology of domination, this legitimacy *does not* come *from below* in terms of *referenda or elections*' (emphasis added; this is perhaps unsurprising as elections are not, after all, strictly 'fair').

Hence, governments which speak and act for free-market interests are, quite simply, untroubled by the idea of 'franchising' responsibilities of the state and elements of legitimacy to market actors. Legitimacy becomes a commodity in the same sense as the franchising of a 'brand name' bestows consumer identification and confidence – sign this contract and buy this licence to run private prisons and you have 'legitimacy'.[11] This 'commodification' of legitimacy raises other issues. In Britain, the United States of America and elsewhere, the state is *de facto* (and in some cases *de jure* (South, 1984; Moyle, 1995)) giving way to the private sector and extending legitimacy to the use of force by the latter (for example, by private prison guards, by private prison escort services, or by private security agents confronting anti-motorway protesters). It is thereby diminishing its own monopoly of power. In these circumstances it may be that the citizen will need to turn for protection and redress, where illegalities are committed by private agents, not to the nation state and its politically compromised laws *but to supra-societal human rights*, as 'guaranteed' (albeit with obvious limitations), for example, by the European Convention on Human Rights (Turner, 1993: 502).

This may seem a far step to take, but already in Europe, the European Court of Human Rights is a superior court over the higher courts of member nations of the European Union. In fact, to place a human rights perspective on the agenda for challenges to, and reforms of, the public and private justice systems is long overdue. A model of justice that prioritizes and highlights human rights can be seen as superior and preferable to the 'due process' model of criminal justice. As Greer (1994: 60) observes:

> The 'human rights' perspective is a subtle variant on [the due process] approach. Although both may be said to share the same moral foundations, the due process model can unfortunately degenerate into a species of legal formalism acquiring a largely technical and mechanical application, while the human rights model always stresses the importance of minimum *ethical* standards [cf. Maher, 1984]. (emphasis added)

'Rights' are produced and understood within the *formal* sphere of law, given, for example, by bodies of constitutional or case law. As Hirst (1980: 95–6) has argued, '"rights" . . . are generally presented as derivations of ontological doctrines in which institutions and laws are conceived as the expression or recognition of certain prior or privileged attributes of subjects'.[12] Private agents and agencies have no need to recognize or privilege the rights of subjects unless formal state law compels them – if formal state law is itself compromised by its legitimation of private agents acting in control capacities, then supra-national guarantors may be essential as the courts of last resort.

The Internationalization and Marketing of Policing?

The need for supra- or international guarantors of rights may be given further urgency by the possible creation of an international market in policing, with services sold across borders. Developments relating to *public* policing, such as established forums like TREVI – and the implications of the Schengen Agreement – despite its recent falterings (McLaughlin, 1992: 481; Johnston, 1992a: 200), plus the establishment of a European police agency, 'Europol', (McLaughlin, 1992: 482–3) suggest moves toward the Europeanization and coordination of policing (albeit not without anticipated and already realized difficulties (Fijnaut, 1991; Sheptycki, 1995[13])). Even though post-Maastricht deliberations have slowed progress towards closer political and economic union, provisions of the established Treaty of Rome provide the basis for cooperative development of collaboration and exchange (potentially a *market*) in relation to state-provided services such as policing (Dorn, 1993).

At the same time, *private* policing, already operating across borders, will be provided by more and more bodies *not* recognizing accountability to coordinating or centralized European authorities (unless pan-European or other international legislation or regulation is introduced). In such a future scenario, the citizen will need protection from the lawlessness of the market. As Nils Christie (1993) has observed, those who are consistently critical of public police organizations might well consider the proposition that with a social practice as important and fundamental to democracy as 'policing' is, then the alternative of privatized, market-led control agencies would hardly be a desirable alternative![14]

In moving towards concluding this chapter, there is a need to expand a little further on the theme of human rights and to note two further issues for the 'end of the century' criminology agenda. Both relate to the violence of humanity as a species. One reflects what Stan Cohen (1993) has most recently drawn attention to, the neglect within criminology of the study of the suffering and atrocities committed in cases of human rights violations. The other refers to the human rights of current and future generations of humanity to inhabit a liveable and sustainable planet.

On Human Rights and Human Atrocities

Cohen (1993, reprinted 1996) has argued that criminology has not necessarily ignored state crimes and human rights issues but has certainly not followed these issues through to illuminate their devastating and awful consequences: 'the subject has often been raised and then its implications conveniently repressed' (1996: 489). Cohen argues that there are several reasons why human rights issues and discourses should be placed more centrally on the criminological agenda. First, the rhetoric of human rights is actually a major source of justifications for new laws and hence more criminalization. As Cohen (1996: 492) puts it: 'Significant waves of moral enterprise and criminalization over the last decade are derived not from the old middle-class morality, the Protestant ethic nor the interests of corporate capitalism, but from the feminist, ecological and human rights movements.' Second, the American-oriented ethnocentrism of some recent human rights research is unhelpful and shapes perceptions of crimes against humanity in limited and partial ways (for example, dwelling on exposés of intelligence agencies involved in 'nasty doings'). This partial view needs to be challenged and corrected. And third, while criminology has embraced victimology and discovered the hidden victims of crime through local surveys, on the global stage the subject has paid no attention to the victims of mass crimes against whole populations. As Cohen observes, 'I am aware that phrases such as "crimes of the twentieth century" sound bombastic – but for vast populations of the world, this is a fair characterization of those "gross violations of human rights": genocide, mass political killings, disappearances, torture, rape by agents of the state' (1996: 492).

On the Rights of Future Generations and the Preservation of the Environment

Arguably, in addition to such 'crimes of the century', consideration should be given to the crimes that humanity is currently committing against the environment and hence the living conditions of present and future generations. As Ferris (1991: 26) eloquently argues:

Post-enlightenment liberalism and socialism which shaped the parameters of contemporary thinking about social policy [and much criminology] were both premised on the conquest of nature. It is becoming very difficult to evade awareness of the costs of this 'victory'. Rather than liberation from the historic bonds of scarcity we have to recognize at least the possibility of the destruction of the planet. Such considerations form the core of the ecological critique of industrialism. Ecological movements world-wide have drawn attention to the problems and placed the idea of limits on the policy agenda. It is no longer a question of saving 'socialism' or 'capitalism' but humanity itself on a threatened planet.

It is recognized by many commentators in other social and natural science disciplines, and yet rarely in criminology, that the earth and its resources are being wasted. Twentieth-century industrial society has overexploited the planet and its resources through processes in which human beings become commodities in chains of production and distribution, and profit is put before sense or sensibility. In these processes, multiple and numerous crimes, violations, deviations and irregularities are perpetrated yet go largely unchecked. As Snyder (1991: 226 and *passim*) observes:

> The paucity of action taken thus far on environmental issues portrays vividly the power of the corporate sector. This is an area . . . which *challenges* the lifestyle and philosophy which is the basis of all capitalist systems – the idea that humans have a right to make use of all the resources of the planet, that other life forms such as animals and birds are there to serve our needs, and that we have no long-term obligations to future generations or to the natural world. (emphasis in original)

Criminology has barely begun to consider the questions and challenges raised here.

CONCLUSION

This chapter has presented a picture of fragmentations, pluralist systems of control, the historical continuity of old and the emergence of new forms of crime. It is, of course, impossible to accurately predict what the 'future' really holds. However, the picture being presented is one which connects with themes that some writers have characterized as reflecting the late or post-modern condition of society in which law and social control exhibit tensions between the concentration of power at the 'centre' versus tendencies toward decentralization (Turner, 1990; on policing and 'the post-modern turn' see Shearing, 1992; Reiner, 1992; South, 1994a). In such a situation, *traditional* expectations about the criminal justice system and the administration of sanctions may no longer apply.

At the end of the century, causes for pessimism about social control systems may be that they so often deliver problems rather than solve them, and that they are ever-extending (Cohen, 1985). On the global stage, sources of violation against humanity and the planet proliferate, and have evidently not diminished as a result of the 'progress', enlightenment or civilization of twentieth-century modernity. Some causes for optimism may lie in the late modern politics (Giddens, 1990) of new social movements, a developing popular intolerance of things that 'have always gone on' but are too frequently ignored (for example, child abuse, domestic violence, pollution, animal cruelty, and so on);

and perhaps in support for human rights and environmental issues generally.

I may be wrong about how strong these latter causes for optimism are. However, in the headlong rush towards the millenium, it may be preferable to participate as at least a partial optimist rather than a fully paid-up pessimist.

Notes

1. A recent editorial in *Professional Security* magazine (March, 1996: 5) stated: 'is it really possible that some people are unaware that all over the country security officers are carrying out a number of "policing" duties in a highly efficient and cost-effective manner?'
2. I am grateful to Patrick Flynn for ideas drawn on here.
3. The Aviation and Maritime Security Act 1990 creates powers to enforce security procedures at airports and ports.
4. An interesting historical comparison might be made here by reference to various studies of the powers and duties of gamekeepers, informers and prosecutors under the Black Acts (Thompson, 1975, *Whigs and Hunters*), although of course, the modern commercial significance of the private security sector is somewhat different.
5. Not pursued here are questions around how 'policing' both 'reverts to' (Pasquino, 1978) and 'develops into' a practice about governance and governmentality (Stenson, 1993).
6. Though it is instructive to note that the necessity of intervention and regulation in markets was illustrated even in the experience of the radical free-market policies of Margaret Thatcher when British Prime Minister. As Jessop and Stones (1992: 177) show:

   In promoting its neo-liberal programme the Thatcherite regime has been obliged to adopt complex and even contradictory strategies. In promoting liberalisation and internationalisation in the City, for example, it further weakened the already crumbling patterns of informal self-regulation; in turn this prompted new forms of state-sponsored, formally organised, corporatist regulation. Likewise, in privatising natural or *de facto* monopolies, it has been obliged to establish regulatory bodies.

7. Bottoms and Wiles (1996: 23–4) note, for example,

   One of the most obvious aspects of social control in the contemporary city, which clearly distinguishes it from earlier eras, is the use of technical control devices ... Although there are many examples of specific types of crime being prevented by technical devices, the development of increasingly sophisticated technical controls against crime *has gone together with a constant rise in the overall crime rate.* (emphasis added)

8. CCTV has been greeted by some as a great success, the way forward for intervention in city and town 'street crime', and reported as receiving a

high degree of public support (Honess and Charman, 1992), especially in the context of it helping to resolve crimes in high-profile cases such as the Jamie Bulger murder. Nonetheless, other commentators have drawn attention to a variety of problems. These include civil liberties concerns and the general implications of becoming a more surveillance-oriented society (Fyfe and Bannister, 1995); as well as the possibility that 'popular belief' in the 'success' of CCTV may lead to bystander indifference, non-reporting of crime and complacency about safety on the streets (Groombridge and Murji, 1994). As Hough (1996: 68) observes:

> Considerable claims have been made about the crime prevention impact of CCTV, but there is little properly conducted work assessing the impact in the target area, the extent of displacement and the extent of 'habituation effects' (as the novelty of the technology wears off). As ever with technology, it is more likely to yield a return the more it is conceived of as a *support* for human activity rather than a *substitute* for it. (emphasis in original)

9. This section of the chapter draws on a short piece entited 'So what's new: some trends in security and surveillance', published in *Criminal Justice Matters*, vol. 20. Summer 1995: 17

10. The fate and impact of the Scott Report (1996) into the illegal sale of arms is an excellent example. The earlier 'Spycatcher' case bequeathed to English phraseology an admission from the most senior civil servant in England that he was being 'economical with the truth', thereby confirming suspicions that the scripts for *Yes Minister* were highly accurate portrayals of Whitehall. I should also add here that it is not my intention to idealize the accountability of earlier administrations.

11. Although, it must be reasonable to ask how much further can the privatization of the prison system be pushed. We are seeing the rapid growth of a 'private archipelago of punishment', accountable through contract not duty, through profits and share performance not principle and vocation (see Beyens and Snacken, 1996). This is an unacceptable basis for the exercise of criminal justice.

12. Note that Hunt (1993: 106) takes issue with Hirst's formulation.

13. Sheptycki (1995: 613, abstract) argues that European 'transnationalization of the police enterprise is ongoing, emergent and, to a great extent, opaque . . . What appears to be emerging is a patchwork quilt of agencies, stitched together by the efforts of transnational liaison officers. It is common or garden folk-devilry that establishes a pattern for that patchwork quilt.' In other words, heralding the birth of the 'Europolice' may be premature, despite Europol and other initiatives.

14. For an exhaustive discussion of models of police accountability, including reference to public and private policing, and democracy, see Jones *et al.*, 1994.

References

Adam Smith Institute (1984) *The 'Omega' Report: Justice Policy* (London: Adam Smith Institute).

Baumgartner, M. (1988) *The Moral Order of a Suburb* (New York: Oxford University Press).

Beyens, K. and Snacken, S. (1996) 'Prison privatization: An international perspective', in R. Matthews and P. Francis (eds), *Prisons 2000: An International Perspective on the Current State and Future of Imprisonment* (London: Macmillan).

Black, D. and Baumgartner, M. (1980) 'On self-help in modern society', in D. Black (ed.), *The Manners and Customs of the Police* (New York: Academic Press).

Bottoms, A. and Wiles, P. (1996) 'Crime and policing in a changing social context', in W. Saulsbury, J. Mott and T. Newburn (eds), *Themes in Contemporary Policing* (London: Policy Studies Institute).

Christie, N. (1993) *Crime Control as Industry: Towards Gulags Western Style?* (London: Sage).

Cohen, S. (1985) *Visions of Social Control* (Oxford: Polity Press).

Cohen, S. (1993/1996) 'Human rights and crimes of the state', reprinted in J. Muncie, E. McLaughlin and M. Langan (eds) (1996) *Criminological Perspectives: A Reader* (London: Sage).

Dandeker, C. (1990) *Surveillance, Power and Modernity* (Cambridge: Polity Press).

Davis, M. (1992) *Beyond Blade Runner: Urban Control, The Ecology of Fear*, (New Jersey: Open Magazine)

Dorn, N. (1993) 'A single-market in European policing?', unpublished paper presented at the British Sociological Association Annual Conference, University of Essex.

Ellickson, R. (1991) *Order Without Law: How Neighbours Settle Disputes* (Cambridge, Mass.: Harvard University Press).

Ferris, J. (1991) 'Green politics and the future of welfare', in N. Manning (ed.), *Social Policy Review* (London: Longman).

Fijnault, C. (1991) 'Police cooperation within western Europe', in F. Heidensohn and M. Farrell (eds), *Crime in Europe* (London: Routledge).

Flynn, P. (in preparation) PhD thesis on 'The Private Security Industry', Department of Sociology, University of Essex.

The Futurist (1988) March.

Fyfe, N. and Bannister, J. (1995) 'City watching: closed circuit television surveillance in public spaces', unpublished paper presented to the 1995 British Criminology Conference, University of Loughborough.

Giddens, A. (1990) *The Consequences of Modernity* (Cambridge: Polity Press).

Goodwin, G. and Humphreys, L. (1982) 'Freeze-dried stigma: cybernetics and social control', *Humanity and Society*, 6 November, pp. 391–408.

Greenberg, S., Rohe, W. and Williams, J. (1985) *Informal Citizen Action and Crime Prevention at the Neighbourhood Level* (Washington, DC: National Institute of Justice, US Department of Justice).

Greer, S. (1994) 'Miscarriages of criminal justice reconsidered', *Modern Law Review*, vol. 57, no. 1, pp. 58–74.

Greer, S. and South, N. (1997) 'The criminal informant: police management, supervision and control', in S. Field *et al.* (eds), *Invading the Private? State Accountability and the New Policing of Europe* (Aldershot: Dartmouth).

Groombridge, N. and Murji, K. (1994) 'As easy as A B and CCTV', *Policing*, vol. 10, no. 4, pp. 282–90.

Hirst, P. (1980) 'Law, socialism and rights', in P. Carlen and M. Collison (eds), *Radical Issues in Criminology* (Oxford: Martin Robertson).

Hollinger, R. (ed.) (1996) *Crime, Deviance and the Computer* (Aldershot: Dartmouth).

Honess, T. and Charman, E. (1992) *Closed Circuit Television in Public Places* (London: Home Office).

Hough, M. (1996) 'The police patrol function: what research can tell us', in W. Saulsbury, J. Mott and T. Newburn (eds), *Themes in Contemporary Policing* (London: Policy Studies Institute).

Hunt, A. (1993) *Explorations in Law and Society: Toward a Constitutive Theory of Law* (London: Routledge).

Jameson, F. (1984) 'Postmodernism or the cultural logic of late capitalism', *New Left Review*, p. 146.

Jessop, B. and Stones, R. (1992) 'Old city and new times: economic and political aspects of deregulation', in L. Budd and S. Whimster (eds), *Global Finance and Urban Living: A Study of Metropolitan Change* (London: Routledge).

Johnston, L. (1992a) *The Rebirth of Private Policing* (London: Routledge).

Johnston, L. (1992b) 'British policing in the nineties: free market and strong state?', *International Criminal Justice Review*, vol. 2, pp. 1–18.

Jones, T., Newburn, T. and Smith, D. (1994) *Democracy and Policing* (London: Policy Studies Institute).

Lyon, D. (1994) *The Electronic Eye: The Rise of Surveillance Society* (Cambridge: Polity Press).

Lyotard, J. (1984) *The Postmodern Condition* (Manchester: Manchester University Press).

Maher, G. (1984) 'Balancing rights and interests in the criminal process', in R. Duff and N. Simmonds (eds), *Philosophy and the Criminal Law* (Stuttgart: Franz Steiner).

Mann, M. (1970) 'The social cohesion of liberal democracy', *American Sociological Review*, vol. 35, no. 3, pp. 423–39.

Marx, G. and Reichman, N. (1984) 'Routinizing the discovery of secrets: computers as informants', *American Behavioural Scientist*, vol. 27, no. 4, p. 430.

Matthews, R. (1995) 'Privatisation, social control and the state', in F. Sack *et al.* (eds), *Privatisierung Staatlicher Kontrolle: Befunde, Konzepte, Tendenzen* (Baden-Baden: Nomos Verlagsgesellschaft).

McLaughlin, E. (1992) 'The democratic deficit: European Union and the accountability of the British police', *British Journal of Criminology*, vol. 32, no. 4, pp. 473–87.

Moyle, P. (1995) *Private Prisons and Police: Recent Australian Trends* (Annandale: Pluto Press Australia).

Narr, W-D. (1992) 'The security market, the state monopoly on violence and civil rights', *Burgerrechte und Polizei*, vol. 43, no. 3, pp. 6–13.

Pasquino, P. (1978) 'Theatrum politicum. The genealogy of capital – police and the state of prosperity', *Ideology and Consciousness*, vol. 4 (Autumn) pp. 41–54.

Reiner, R. (1992) 'Policing a postmodern society', *Modern Law Review*, vol. 55, no. 6, pp. 761–81.

Ritzer, G. (1993) *The McDonaldization of Society* (Newbury Park: Pine Forge Press).

Ryan, M. and Ward, T. (1989) *Privatization and the Penal System* (Milton Keynes: Open University Press).

Sarre, R. (1994) 'The legal basis for the authority of private police and an examination of their relationship with the "public" police', in D. Biles and J. Vernon (eds), *Private Sector and Community Involvement in the Criminal Justice System* (Canberra: Australian Institute of Criminology.

Saulsbury, W., Mott, J. and Newburn, T. (eds) (1996) *Themes in Contemporary Policing* (London: Policy Studies Institute.)

Schultz, E. (1994) 'Employee beware: the boss may be listening', *Wall Street Journal*, 29 July, C1 and C13.

Scott, T. and McPherson, M. (1971) 'The development of the private sector of the criminal justice system', *Law and Society Review*, vol. 6. no. 2.

Shapland, J. and Vagg, J. (1988) *Policing by the Public* (London: Routledge).

Shearing, C. (1992) 'The relation between public and private policing', in M. Tonry and N. Morris (eds), *Modern Policing* (Chicago, Ill.: University of Chicago Press) pp. 399–434.

Shearing, C. and Stenning, P. (1981) 'Modern private security: its growth and implications', in M. Tonry and N. Morris (eds), *Crime and Justice: An Annual Review of Research* (Chicago, Ill.: University of Chicago Press) pp. 193–245.

Shearing, C. and Stenning, P. (1983) 'Private security: implications for social control', *Social Problems*, vol. 30, no. 5, pp. 493–506.

Shearing, C. and Stenning, P. (eds) (1987) *Private Policing* (Beverly Hills, California: Sage).

Sheptycki, J. (1995) 'Transnational policing and the makings of a postmodern state', *British Journal of Criminology*, vol. 35, no. 4.

Snyder, L. (1991) 'The regulatory dance: understanding reform processes in corporate crime', *International Journal of the Sociology of Law*, vol. 19, pp. 209–36.

South, N. (1984) 'Private security, the division of policing labour and the commercial compromise of the state', in S. Spitzer and A. Scull (eds), *Research in Law, Deviance and Social Control 6* (Greenwich, Conn.: JAI Press).

South, N. (1987a) 'The security and surveillance of the environment', in J. Lowman, R. Menzies and T. Palys (eds), *Transcarceration: Essays in the Sociology of Social Control* (Aldershot: Gower).

South, N. (1987b) 'Law, profit and "private persons": private and public policing in English history', in C. Shearing and P. Stenning (eds), *Private Policing* (Beverly Hills, California: Sage).

South, N. (1988) *Policing for Profit: The Private Security Sector* (London: Sage).

South, N. (1989) 'Reconstructing policing: differentiation and contradiction in post-war private and public policing', in R. Matthews (ed.), *Privatizing Criminal Justice* (London: Sage).

South, N. (1994a) 'Privatizing policing in the European market: some issues for theory, policy and research', *European Sociological Review*, vol. 10, no. 3, pp. 219–33.

South, N. (1994b) 'Who does "policing"? privatization to vigilantism', in C. Martin (ed.), *Changing Policing: Business or Service?* (London: Institute for the Study and Treatment of Delinquency).

Specter, M. (1994) 'Guns for hire: policing goes private in Russia', *New York Times* (International section), 9 August.

Spitzer S. (1987) 'Security and control in capitalist societies: the fetishism of security and the secret thereof', in J. Lowman, R. Menzies and T. Palys (eds), *Transcarceration* (Aldershot: Gower).

Spitzer, S. and Scull, A. (1977) 'Privatization and capitalist development: the case of the private police', *Social Problems*, vol. 25, no. 1, pp. 18–29.

Statewatch (1995) 'Legally permitted surveillance', *Statewatch*, vol. 5, no. 2, p. 1.

Stenning, P. and Shearing, C. (1980) 'The quiet revolution: the nature, development and general legal implications of private policing in Canada, *Criminal Law Quarterly*, vol. 22, pp. 220–48.

Stenson, K. (1993) 'Community policing as a governmental technology', *Economy and Society*, vol. 22, no. 3.

Thompson, E. (1967) 'Time, work discipline and industrial capitalism', *Past and Present*, vol. 38, pp. 56–97.

Thompson, E. (1975) *Whigs and Hunters* (London: Allen Lane).

Turner, B. (ed.) (1990) *Theories of Modernity and Postmodernity* (London: Sage).

Turner, B. (1993) 'Outline of a theory of human rights', *Sociology*, vol. 27, no. 3, pp. 489–512.

Weber, M. (1978) *Economy and Society* (2 vols) (Berkeley: University of California Press).

6 Crime, Policing and the Provision of Service

Barry Loveday

INTRODUCTION

Every public service has been subject to the reforming zeal of a Conservative government committed to marketing the public sector in the name of improved efficiency. Yet it was not until the 1990s that the police were subjected to a similar experience. The police service was deemed to be an essential public order force and tool for the government as it embarked on a programme which would inevitably lead to confrontation with public sector unions in the 1980s. As Howard Davies was to argue succinctly in his Social Market Foundation pamphlet on the police:

> Until the end of the miners' strike in 1985, there was perhaps a sound political reason for leaving the police undisturbed ... The industrial relations confrontations of the early 1980s certainly placed a high premium on the maintenance of an unquestionably loyal, disciplined and strike free police service. Subsequently the logic of non-intervention became less clear. (Davies, 1992: 28)

The dependence of the Thatcher government on the police did thereafter rapidly decline. It was probably the end of such government dependence that enabled the Major administration to embark upon a radical reform programme of the police in the early 1990s. A succession of Reviews and White Papers followed. The White Paper on Police Reform (Home Office, 1993a) was to be succeeded by the Sheehy Inquiry (Home Office, Northern Ireland Office and the Scottish Office, 1993), the Police and Magistrates' Courts Act (Home Office, 1994) and the Posen Review into core and ancillary duties (Home Office, 1995a). A succession of Criminal Justice Acts also substantially widened police public order powers. If to this were to be added the recent Cassels Report on the role and responsibilities of the police, and recent police reports from the Audit Commission (particularly *Helping with Enquiries* (1993) and *Streetwise* (1996a)), it would be difficult to identify a time when the police had been subject to such close analysis and detailed external prescription.

124

Alongside this prescription, of course, is the implementation of new public management which places heavy reliance on performance measurement in the public service. Between them, the Home Office, the Association of Chief Police Officers (ACPO) and the Audit Commission are responsible for a range of performance indicators which, it is claimed, now enable government and the police service to evaluate (and presumably improve) the latter's efficiency and effectiveness. Most recently, for example, the Audit Commission has requested police forces to provide not just a costed policing plan but costed outputs (Audit Commission, 1991).

Yet behind all of the management rhetoric, jargon and multiple performance measures, it is also clear that there is a continued uncertainty both as to what the police function is, and what it should be. Within the police service, some of the old shibboleths have, it should be stressed, been effectively buried by this process. One fruitful outcome of the Posen Review into core and ancillary duties has been, for example, the recognition by the police service of the valuable social service role it has always exercised but usually disdained. The likely emasculation of police budgets which would have resulted from a decision to fund police on its crime control activities alone appeared to concentrate minds remarkably. As will be argued, police recognition of the significant part played by service calls could be of great importance for future policing strategies. This is because the social dislocation and collapse experienced in many marginalized communities (which now exist in every police force area), occasioned largely by government policy during the 1980s and 1990s, could provide the biggest challenge to contemporary policing for the next decade.

In this chapter it will be argued that factors influencing criminality may involve high unemployment rates among young males and that this was accepted officially by the previous Conservative government, as recent changes to police grant determination clearly demonstrates. It will be argued that now, as in the past, low-income groups continue to experience the highest rates of victimization and this is, significantly enough, reflected in the higher levels of victimization (such as domestic burglary) experienced by ethnic minority groups, particularly those of Afro-Caribbean origin. This intra-racial victimization is supported by evidence from the earlier American victimization studies of the 1970s. The ability of the police to respond to demand for their service, is, however, influenced by a number of factors which are both internal and external to that organization.

Fear of reprisals and further harassment of the victim can be expected to significantly reduce the likelihood of victims calling the police and this inhibition is likely to be experienced most frequently in areas of greatest need. Additionally the ability of police to respond has been reduced by the growth, over time, of specialist and internal bureaucracies. This has curtailed the ability of the police to provide an effective patrol presence in areas of greatest need. It is also argued that the larger the unit of policing then the lower the level of uniform patrol provision that can be expected. The chapter concludes by assessing the provision of private security patrols and the continuing decline in status of uniform patrol activity in the police service.

POLICE–CRIME CONNECTIONS

It is useful initially to identify what role the police can be expected to play in the continuing 'fight against crime'. This 'fight' has, of course, become a central strategic purpose for the police during recent years. Indeed, it was the perceived failure of the police to successfully fight crime and deal with the crime problem which initiated the avalanche of reforms beginning with the White Paper on Police Reform in 1993 (Baker, 1993). Crime control has, of course, always constituted an important element of police activity. Yet the government's determination to ensure that only this activity would be rewarded financially only served to demonstrate the relative naivety of those who propounded this course of action. The ability of the police to make a major impact on crime remains, of course, a matter of continuing debate. Some commentators (such as Reiner, 1992) have suggested that the police ability to control crime may significantly exaggerate the influence of that service. On the other hand, it is also argued, particularly by the Audit Commission, that the police can be expected to effect real reductions in crime if they are suitably organized, managed and targeted towards known offenders. As the Audit Commission has argued recently:

> By adopting the recommendations in this report, the police can help to prevent crime and raise clear-up rates significantly, which itself will help deter would-be criminals. The ultimate price for the police is the development of a strategy in which the crime rate could be brought under control. (Audit Commission, 1993, Summary: 2)

The argument presented by the Audit Commission was particularly well-received by the Conservative government. It would, of course, be helpful to a government embarrassed by a crime rate which had doubled since 1979 when it took office if the explanation was provided by police inefficiency. By identifying this inefficiency, it also let the government off a very nasty hook. The same argument could also be used by the government to confound a view, espoused since the demise of Mrs Thatcher as Conservative Leader, that environmental factors influenced by government policies might explain the high crime rates which confronted it.

The Audit Commission remained committed to the view that crime can be reduced and the crime rate controlled (Audit Commission, 1993). This is probably best summarized by the often repeated statement that around 7 per cent of offenders are responsible for 65 per cent of known offences in England and Wales (Audit Commission, 1993). While it is recognized that repeat offenders have traditionally been responsible for a significant proportion of crime, it would be unfortunate if this sustained a view that proactive targeting of known offenders could alone be expected to control the crime rate. It is, however, on just such a perception that the Audit Commission appeared to base its recommendations. This approach is, however, likely to be contested, particularly in the light of research evidence generated by Farrington (1994) and others. Farrington's research, conducted by way of a cohort analysis, reveals that more than a third of males will, by the age of 30, have been convicted of a criminal offence (excluding motoring offences). Moreover, it is, for instance, of interest to note that at a time when the government introduced key objectives and targets for police forces to achieve in relation to reductions in violent crime or domestic burglary, Home Office research raised serious doubts about the overall utility of the criminal justice system in 'fighting crime'. In the 1992 British Crime Survey, Home Office researchers were to argue that the national clear-up rates for crimes recorded by the police stood at 29 per cent. However, they added that if crimes cleared up were expressed as a percentage not of recorded crime but of offences estimated by the British Crime Survey, then the clear-up figure would fall to well under 10 per cent. Moreover the proportion of crimes resulting in a conviction was much lower, standing at 3 per cent. Given this, Home Office researchers were to conclude that: 'these figures underline the limitations of the formal criminal justice system as a mechanism for controlling crime and emphasise the need to look beyond it to other approaches' (Mayhew, Aye-Maung and Mirrlees-Black, 1992: 103).

This conclusion, most recently supported by the Audit Commission's study into young people and crime (Audit Commission, 1996b) suggests that greater emphasis would need to be placed on both the spatial location of victimization and on the profile of offenders in terms of age, education training and job prospects. The marginalized residents of declining public housing estates identified by the British Crime Survey as high-risk areas experience poor housing and also very high levels of male unemployment. Although in these areas the recorded crime rate will be only a fraction of the real victimization rate, it is almost certainly the case that a high arrest rate cannot be expected to control or necessarily deter criminal activity. Nor is it altogether clear whether successful prosecutions and punitive measures taken against known offenders can be expected, of themselves, to significantly influence levels of criminal activity either.

Following successive British Crime Surveys conducted by the Home Office, there is now more awareness of the nature and extent of crime in England and Wales. It is the number of offences estimated to have been committed, rather than recorded offences, that questions the strategy to control crime recommended by the Audit Commission. If the recorded burglary rate only represents approximately 40 per cent of the total estimated, then this, when added to other crime data, suggests that criminal behaviour now in fact permeates contemporary life and is much more extensive than may have previously been assumed. Moreover, evidence continues to suggest that crime is much less susceptible to 'control' by the police or the criminal justice system than the government claims. If this is the case, then setting key national performance targets for the police to reduce either recorded violent crime, or domestic burglary, could be at best an irrelevance. Moreover, even if police forces managed to achieve the dubious distinction of reaching targets set by the Home Secretary this might only raise future questions about police recording practices.

The complexities surrounding crime and policing only serve to highlight the simplistic nature of policies that passed for a crime strategy under the previous Conservative government. A strategy of fighting crime which does nothing to confront the underlying factors, both social and economic, cannot be expected to achieve any real success. This represents an obvious challenge to the assumptions made by the Audit Commission on the nature of the crime problem and how the police should respond to it.

THE SOCIAL CONTEXT OF CRIME

Crime and Unemployment

One factor consistently denied by the Conservatives was the link between crime and unemployment. It must certainly be recognized that immediate and direct causal links between unemployment and crime would have to be rejected as being overly deterministic (Box, 1987). Yet the combined impact of relative deprivation and the absence of gainful employment (or indeed any prospects of gainful employment) may, in many urban communities, enhance a disposition which encourages criminal behaviour particularly among the young. Cultural factors may also play a significant role. Overwhelmingly crime is identified as an activity of the young male. While the maximum age of offending has increased, the absence of gainful employment (particularly when linked to drug use) may generate high levels of opportunistic property crime in specific spatial locations (Home Office, 1995b). The remarkable trajectory of property crime in the 1980s and 1990s and the close correlation between property offences and unemployment rates have already been identified, most notably by David Dickinson (1994).

Dickinson's (1994) research, of course, only serves to underline the huge significance of unemployment when this occurs among young males under the age of 25 (see Figure 6.1). Moreover Dickinson's research has only highlighted the close correlation which exists between largely opportunistic crime (domestic burglary) and the absence of gainful employment among young males. There are now some 700,000 young males between the ages of 16 and 25 who do not have gainful employment and may never have had experience of it. Interestingly it is in poorer, striving areas, those which have been most affected by industrial and manufacturing decline in the 1980s and 1990s, that the incidence of opportunistic crime (and drug abuse) has risen fastest. Dickinson's thesis appears to be supported by Wells who also identified close links between unemployment and the incidence of property crime (Wells, 1995).

A detailed analysis of the debate over unemployment and any causal relationship with property crime cannot be undertaken here. It is sufficient to note that an increasing number of commentators have been forced to recognize that much closer links exist between crime rates and the economy than was previously thought (Pyle and Deadman, 1994). More interesting, perhaps, has been the official recognition (and acceptance) that a link between unemployment and crime does exist.

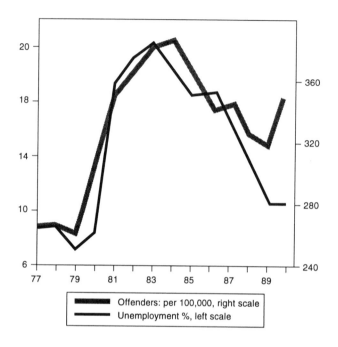

Figure 6.1   Unemployment and burglaries (males under 25 years)

Source: Dickinson (1994).

While Conservative government ministers, in public, rejected any connection between crime and unemployment, changes to the funding formula for the police grant provide indications of a different viewpoint.
Thus it is interesting to note that in the determination of police grant,
a new indicator of need has joined those of 'long-term' and 'short-
term' unemployment (Loveday, 1996: 84; Colpa, 1996/7). The new
indicator is the percentage of unemployed males under the age of 25
in each police force area. The weighting given to this indicator is also
instructive. In comparative terms, this indicator of need is significantly
higher (excluding police establishments) than any other (see Table 6.1).

The Nature of Victimization

The interesting change in grant determination may, of course, reflect
the reality of crime. This reality continues to be the inverse relationship between income levels and victimization. Low-income households

Table 6.1   Indicators of police grant allocation*

Police establishment	
Police establishment	£19,231.70
Daytime population	
Vehicle crime	£ 2.16
Personal crime	£−0.29
Call management	£16.81
Public order	£−0.71
Indicator total	£17.97
Police index I	
Call management	£0.41
Population density	
Personal crime	£0.17
Other crime	£0.11
Indicator total	£0.28
Households renting	
Personal crime	£7.01
Residents in overcrowded households	
Personal crime	£23.22
Striving population	
Vehicle crime	£3.25
Young male unemployment	
Public order	£40.45

* Indicators and their weights in the Police SSA 1996/7 components and subcomponents in which they are used.

Source: Home Office briefing document, December 1995; Association of County Councils, 15 December 1995.

continue to experience crime victimization more frequently than high-income households. This is, of course, best demonstrated by official data on victimization between types of area (Home Office, 1995b) (see Table 6.2).

Further evidence, if it were needed, of the correlation between low income and victimization, is provided by data on victimization by ethnic group. Here again, evidence suggests that certain ethnic groups can expect to experience higher rates of victimization than others. In this case, the fact that black families experience nearly twice as much victimization as white families over a range of offences only serves to emphasize their position on the economic ladder (see Table 6.3).

High victimization rates amongst this group are not a matter of surprise,

Table 6.2   Victims of burglary and car crime by type of area, England and Wales, 1993 Indices

	Burglary	Car crime*
Thriving	58	52
Expanding	60	63
Rising	177	148
Settling	82	82
Aspiring	90	106
Striving	162	190
All areas	100	100

* Thefts and attempted thefts of/from cars taking place in private and semi-private parking areas by the home or in nearby streets. Risks are based on car owners.

Source: Home Office (1995b).

Table 6.3   Victims of crime[1] by ethnic group, England and Wales, 1993 (%)

	White	Afro-Caribbean	Asian	All ethnic groups
Household offences				
Home vandalism	4.3	3.9	4.8	4.3
Burglary	6.3	12.9	8.0	6.5
Vehicle crime (owners)				
Vandalism	8.1	12.1	9.8	8.2
All thefts	19.6	25.7	23.0	19.7
Other	10.2	9.5	8.9	10.1
All household offences	32.6	36.2	34.3	32.6
Personal offences				
Assaults	3.8	6.6	3.1	3.8
Threats	3.5	4.0	3.2	3.4
Robbery/theft from person	1.7	2.7	3.4	1.8
Other personal theft	3.7	5.2	3.2	3.7
All personal offences[2]	8.5	13.2	9.3	8.6

[1] Percentage in each ethnic group who had been a victim once or more.
[2] Excludes sexual offences.

Source: *Social Trends*, Home Office 1995: para. 9, 10.

if only because in contemporary Britain, members of the black community can expect to experience longer periods of unemployment in greater numbers than any other ethnic group. From this constituency are drawn the offenders who were identified in 1995 by the Commissioner of the Metropolitan Police as 'street offenders'. It would probably have been helpful therefore if the Commissioner had also added that the incidence of victimization was also highest amongst members of the black community.

Data from early American crime surveys serve further to reinforce the substantial difference in victimization rates experienced in particular black ethnic families. These data suggest that while official emphasis may have focused on black offenders and white victims the real issue which demanded attention was the high rate of victimization of blacks by blacks. In analysing, for example, the 1973 National Crime Survey, Bowland (1976) discovered that blacks were consistently experiencing higher rates of victimization than whites and that this was related to specific neighbourhoods and spatial locations: 'Persons who live in the same areas or frequent the same places as offenders, are more likely to be victimized than persons who are able to avoid contact with high offender populations' (Bowland, 1976: 33). As Bowland also observed: 'Murder and assault exhibited a high degree of localisation in the poverty slum areas of each city . . . most robberies took place in the same poverty slum areas as assaultive crime although a number occurred in areas contiguous to the residential areas of offenders' (Bowland, 1976: 35).

Of equal interest here is the discovery by the United States of America Crime Survey (1973) that 'robberies in poverty slum areas typically involved a black offender and a black victim'. As a further analysis of the American crime data was to suggest, most violent offences were intra-racial and that 'contrary to certain popular beliefs', victims of violent crimes, as a whole, were most apt to have identified their assailants as members of their own race. For single-offender crimes, four out of five victimizations of whites, and nine out of ten victimizations of blacks, were intra-racial (Dodge, Lentzner and Shenk, 1976: 19). As Tables 6.4 and 6.5 demonstrate, black victimization is overwhelmingly a consequence of black offenders. Yet because victimization was a black rather than a white phenomenon in the poor areas, these offences remained very largely 'invisible'.

These data generated in the 1970s highlighted the spatial location of crime and the socioeconomic position of most victims in a more emphatic way than perhaps any other information had provided to date.

Table 6.4   Robbery victimization rates by race of offender(s) and race of victim(s)* (rates per 1000 population)

Race of offender	Race of victim			Race of offender	Race of victim		
	W	NW	T		W	NW	T
Atlanta				Milwaukee			
W	4.6	10.5	15.0	W	4.6	9.9	14.6
NW	0.3	13.7	14.0	NW	0.2	22.5	22.7
Baltimore				Minneapolis			
W	4.1	17.1	21.2	W	7.5	8.4	15.9
NW	0.6	29.0	29.6	NW	4.7	9.5	14.2
Boston				New Orleans			
W	8.4	19.7	28.1	W	2.3	15.0	17.3
NW	4.2	22.8	27.0	NW	0.7	14.7	15.4
Buffalo				New York			
W	3.9	8.8	12.7	W	3.5	14.3	19.7
NW	1.4	19.6	21.0	NW	2.2	26.1	28.2
Chicago				Newark			
W	5.0	11.3	16.6	W	2.3	15.3	17.6
NW	0.0	37.0	38.0	NW	1.0	31.3	32.5
Cincinnati				Oakland			
W	5.3	7.2	12.5	W	4.5	19.5	24.0
NW	2.0	14.4	16.6	NW	1.3	11.3	12.6
Cleveland				Philadelphia			
W	5.6	9.4	15.0	W	2.7	16.3	19.0
NW	2.2	30.2	32.4	NW	0.5	38.1	38.7
Dallas				Pittsburgh			
W	3.6	5.5	9.1	W	3.6	9.4	13.0
NW	0.2	9.6	9.8	NW	1.8	16.7	18.5
Denver				Portland			
W	7.3	7.7	15.0	W	6.5	7.7	14.2
NW	2.4	10.0	12.7	NW	1.2	13.0	14.2
Detroit				San Diego			
W	3.1	21.3	24.3	W	4.4	5.2	9.6
NW	1.1	37.4	38.5	NW	1.3	7.3	8.6
Houston				San Francisco			
W	5.6	8.3	13.8	W	7.8	20.2	28.0
NW	0.9	21.5	22.4	NW	1.8	12.8	19.6
Los Angeles				St Louis			
W	4.6	7.0	11.6	W	4.2	9.4	13.6
NW	1.6	25.6	27.0	NW	0.2	16.0	16.3

* Figures in this table, derived from unpublished census tabulations, refer to individual robberies only, i.e. commercial robberies have been excluded. Also excluded are a number of individual robberies, usually less than 3 per cent, where the action was not able to identify the characteristics of the offenders.

Note: W = whites, NW = non-whites, T = total.

Source: Skogan (1976) *Sample Surveys of the Victims of Crime.*

Table 6.5   Percentage distribution of crimes of violence by race of victim and offender, 1973

	Race of offender					
	Single			*Multiple*		
Race of victim	*White*	*Black*	*Total*	*All white*	*All black*	*Total*
White	79	21	100	61	39	100
Black	8	92	100	7	93	100

Source: Unpublished data from the Bureau of the Census in Skogan (1976) *Sample Surveys of the Victims of Crime.*

More recent crime surveys have served to further emphasize these characteristics.

The same 1973 American crime survey also discovered that certain household characteristics were associated with victimization. Thus black respondents were more likely to indicate that they or another household member had been the victim of criminal activity in their neighbourhood than were white respondents (Parks, 1976: 91). This could have been explained by income levels, as Parks argued: 'As the wealth of the neighbourhood increased, respondents and members of their households were less likely to have been victimised' (1976: 91).

One conclusion might have been that while black victimization was the most frequent type of victimization in these areas, this did not result in any salience being attached to the problem of black victims of black offenders. While white victims of black offenders did count, black victims did not.

The relationship between victims and offenders is, in geographical terms, also a very close one. Contrary to some claims which are made in relation to the 'itinerant' and, increasingly, highly mobile criminal, most offenders do not travel very far from their homes to commit offences. In fact, the very short distances travelled by offenders to commit offences, means that, in spatial terms, the impact of crime will be greatest in the poorest areas. Evidence of the relative non-mobility of the criminal has in fact already been provided by several police forces. In London, for example, Operation Bumblebee (1993) provided a useful insight into the distances travelled by offenders (see Table 6.6 which shows the results of a sample of 1145 offenders charged between 1 June 1991 and 11 January 1992).

As with a similar analysis of crime patterns conducted by South Yorkshire Police, the most striking phenomenon proved to be the very

Table 6.6   Metropolitan Police Operation Bumblebee: distance travelled
from home address by offenders

		%
Under 1 mile	604	52.8
1–3 miles	261	22.8
3–5 miles	125	10.9
5–10 miles	97	8.5
Over 10 miles	58	5.1

Source: *Police Review* (1992).

proximity of the offender to the victim. These offenders do not need
motorways. They walk to work. Moreover, in analysing types of offence, it was discovered that the more serious the offence, the more
likely it was to be committed closer to the residence of the offender.
Violent crime, sex crime and robbery are offences which are usually
committed close to the offender's home. Lesser offences are likely to
be committed further away. Yet as the South Yorkshire study demonstrated, the travelling criminal could easily encompass weekend shoplifters who travelled to Sheffield where 'the informal redistribution of
income' would be a primary activity (South Yorkshire Police Crime
Survey, 1992).

High Victimization Areas, Crime Rates and Calls for Police Assistance

It is now generally recognized that marginal public housing estates
and inner city areas experience a much greater incidence of crime than
most other residential locations. Foster and Hope (1993) identified factors which can be expected to exacerbate this trend. Yet if
victimization is highest in these areas, then it is also possible that
non-reporting of offences may also be higher. To an extent the level
of non-reporting will be linked to the amount of crime experienced in
an area. It would appear to be the case that significant inhibitory factors may exist which can in certain locations make non-reporting far
more likely than the reporting of crime. In such estates, the inhibiting
factors are likely to encompass fear of further victimization, harassment and fear of reprisals. It is sufficient to note that fear of either
harassment or further reprisal does appear to be significant. This may
be the case even when residents in these estates do not identify such
fears as an issue.

Roger Graef has vividly relayed the potential (and real) dangers which may be experienced by victims who call for police assistance following criminal victimization (Graef, 1996). Calling for police assistance can immediately isolate the victim within these communities, while the police are unable or unlikely to provide the protection which a call for service may itself generate. As Graef notes, the police know that:

> On these huge housing estates, teenagers may have an area of acres and acres and thousands of people. Because the groups are so large, they become very confident and violent and that means the people within that area become more and more insecure. They will not make statements or talk to the police because they are frightened of what might happen to them. And the poor people who live there are really frightened. They cannot shout. They are alone. (Graef, 1989: 160)

Retribution for calling for police assistance can be of such an order that it acts as an overwhelming deterrent for those who are victimized. As Graef again highlights in a case which occurred in the north of England, the consequences of calling for police assistance can prove to be life-threatening for those who do. When a family called the police following the savage beating of a father who had objected to local youths throwing stones at his windows, they had to move from the area (Graef, 1996). Following their move, threats and further harassment followed them. As the wife and mother of two children, explained:

> We thought that once we moved-peace! We went to Moor Park Estate – not far away but we thought far enough. Kids wanted to still go to their school – that is just when real trouble started. Jamie was stabbed inside the head, the chest, the thigh on his way from school. They got hold of me daughter. They put her against a wall. They threw all sorts in her eye. She had to go to hospital. They kicked her so hard between the legs she was taken to hospital and . . . that was just a few incidents. (Graef, 1996)

Another vivid example of local harassment was demonstrated by the murder of a nineteen-year-old boy on the Clopton public housing estate in Stratford-upon-Avon, in 1995. In trying to protect his father from threatening verbal abuse from a group of youths, Anthony Erskine was kicked to death in broad daylight by the same youths who had tyrannized the estate over a number of years. Ironically, it had been the young man's family who had been instrumental in demanding the introduction of a beat patrol in the area and it was for this reason (amongst others) that the son was to pay the 'ultimate price' (McComb, 1996).

The Stratford-upon-Avon case serves to highlight a number of issues which need to be explored in relation to the delivery of a police 'service'. Even though police resources are of course finite, it might be asked why a relatively poor estate with evidently high levels of victimization and harassment of residents had to petition the police to provide a uniform patrol presence. Moreover, it must be asked why, once established, did the police patrol prove to be so ineffectual not just in terms of failing to protect life but also in failing to deal with the persistent harassment of residents which had initiated their petition. If the local police commander was to conclude that the Erskine murder only demonstrated how serious crime had become nationally, this was probably the wrong lesson to draw from the case. Indeed the most notable feature of the case was its consistency. The Erskine murder occurred on a low-income public housing estate where young males experienced low-paid work or unemployment and where the need for police service could be expected to be highest. It was also an area where police patrol activity had earlier been either low or non-existent.

The Erskine case, along with those cases explored by Graef, raise fundamental questions concerning the provision of police service in high-crime areas. First the demand for police presence remains highest in high-victimization areas, where it is perceived there is limited patrol presence. Second, some form of response to this problem may now be necessary if only because of the increase in the proportion of incidents going unreported because of 'police-related factors', factors which encompass a perception that either the police could do nothing or that they would not be interested. As the authors of the British crime survey argue: 'The increase in police related reasons for not reporting does not suggest any improvement in attitudes among victims as to the ability or commitment of the police to deal with the relatively less serious incidents which typically go unreported' (Mayhew, Aye Maung and Mirrlees-Black, 1992: 26).

To conclude this section, it appears that where demand for police service is highest, police provision of service can be expected to be lowest and also least effective. As the Operational Policing Review (1990) demonstrated (see Table 6.7), demand for uniform presence is high across all types of residential areas. However, as the same review found, in the poorest areas demand cuts across age groups and may also reflect a deeper reality that fear of crime in these areas approximates to actual levels of victimization (Kinsey, Lea and Young, 1986).

Table 6.7   Police numbers by age and type of area (%)

	Total	Age				Type of area				
						Small town	Large town	Sub-urbs	Inner city	Rural
		16–24	*25–44*	*45–59*	*60+*					
Base	*(1085)*	*(158)*	*(383)*	*(283)*	*(300)*	*(361)*	*(165)*	*(187)*	*(245)*	*(127)*
Too many	2	6	2	1	1	2	2	2	2	1
Too few	70	56	65	76	78	66	73	62	81	67
Right number	25	36	29	19	17	27	22	30	16	28
Don't know	4	2	4	4	4	5	2	6	2	5

Source: Operational Policing Review, 1990.

Given this, one question which needs to be addressed concerns why residents of usually high-density urban inner city areas consistently claim that too few police officers are available on uniform patrol. A further question concerns why the police service has found it increasingly difficult to fulfil its most basic task of patrol even when police establishments are increased. Some explanation may be provided by reference to bureaucratic growth in the police organization and the rise of specialization, both of which may have reduced the ability of police forces to provide patrol activity. Additionally the continuing low status accorded to patrol makes provision of this service difficult to sustain. It is to a discussion of these factors that this chapter now turns.

THE POLICE RESPONSE

The Provision of and Demand for Service

It is relatively common to stress that increasing demands on the police means that in practice the service will find it difficult to respond effectively to them all. Demand for police service now regularly exceeds available resources. In addition, changes in legislation may increase demand on existing manpower, while new technology (most notably mobile telephones) can substantially increase the number of calls for police service. The Audit Commission, in developing a strategy to make more effective use of limited resources, has encouraged the introduction of a range of new initiatives for police forces. These extend from proactive, intelligence-led targeting of known criminals through to the introduction of directed street patrol (Audit Commission, 1995, 1996a, 1996b). Yet the Audit Commission's recommendations on patrol have

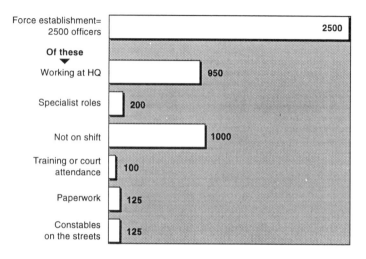

Figure 6.2   Police officers deployed in a typical local population
of one million

Source: Audit Commission (1996).

been confronted by its belated discovery that at most 5 per cent of
police strength is likely to be out on patrol at any one time (Audit
Commission, 1996a) (see Figure 6.2). This replicates an earlier analysis of this phenomenon, notably Richard Kinsey's (1985) celebrated
study of Merseyside police officers.

A number of studies have demonstrated that the ability of the police
force to provide adequate uniformed street presence can be significantly affected by a number of factors which are internal to the force.
These include the size and number of specialist departments, the abstraction rate, the management overhead and shift patterns adopted to provide a 24-hour cover for an area. As the Audit Commission report
Streetwise concludes, in an average-sized police force of 2500 officers,
around 1150 of them will be swallowed up by provision of headquarters staff and specialist units, each of which reduces the availability of
uniform patrol officers (Audit Commission, 1996a).

Additionally abstractions occasioned by sickness, training and leave
also make substantial inroads into the availability of police officers for
patrol duty. To date no opportunity-cost analysis has been attempted
on what appears to be a public service overly committed to training.
The size of the problem is such that the abstraction problem alone
could easily swallow the additional 5000 officers planned by the government

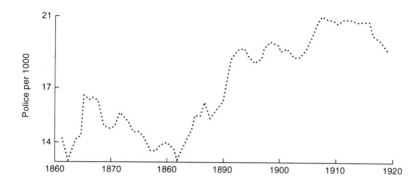

Figure 6.3   The rise of police departments in America, 1860–1920 (total police personnel per 1,000 city population: three-year moving averages plotted; slope of regression line = .012; significance = .00001)

Source: Monkkonen (1981).

by the year 2000. Nor have amalgamations of police forces served to provide any kind of a solution to the continued problem of the non-availability of uniformed officers for patrol. Larger units of policing appear to reduce rather than increase the number of uniform officers available at any one time for these kinds of outside duty (Loveday, 1990). This is probably because bigger units of policing have, in the past, felt it necessary to sustain a much larger range of specialist departments and units, each of which operated at the expense of uniform provision. Whether there was a need for such a range of police specialist departments (and manpower demands generated by them) has not been convincingly answered. The issue of specialization and the apparent inability of police forces to deal effectively with the huge 'on-cost' which the abstraction rate represents, remain crucial in relation to service delivery to the public, particularly those whose need for police service is greatest.

Nor are these issues of any recent provenance. Indeed, the problem of bureaucracy in police forces has a much longer history. This problem has been perhaps best identified in the research conducted by Monkkonen (1981) on American police forces between the years 1860 and 1920. Monkkonen demonstrated that as police forces began to grow in terms of police numbers per 1000 city population, so the actual percentage of police officers on patrol began to steadily decline. The decline was probably most marked in the 1890s which in the literature is often identified as a period of highest visible police patrol (Monkkonen, 1981) (see Figure 6.3).

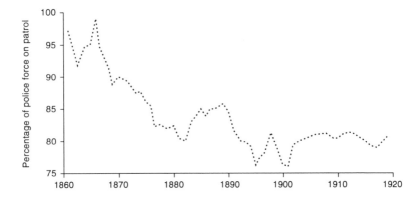

Figure 6.4   The decline of police patrol in America, 1860–1920
(percentage of police force on patrol (three-year moving averages plotted)

Source: Monkkonen (1981).

We should not perhaps draw too many parallels from an analysis of American police forces in the nineteenth century and no comparative data for England and Wales are available. Nevertheless the data available may reflect a more general organizational phenomenon which emphasizes the bureaucratic nature of the police service. This shows that 'the changing proportion of non-patrol to patrol officers demonstrates the bureaucratic growth of police departments' (Monkkonen, 1981) (see Figure 6.4).

The very growth of police bureaucracies made possible even larger and stronger police departments. This, Monkkonen concludes, was because the rise of police strength itself resulted from the increased proportion of police bureaucrats who had the time, position and power to press for more officers per capita of population (Monkkonen, 1981: 145). As Monkkonen argues: 'we can conclude that it was no accident or natural phenomenon causing the increasing in police strength but growing internal specialization and bureaucratization' (Monkkonen, 1981: 146).

Interestingly, the trajectory into self-sustained growth evidenced by Monkkonen's analysis did not translate into increased availability of patrol officers. Neither did it increase police efficiency in terms of criminal arrests despite increased specialization within the organization. As Monkkonen notes, on the basis of analysis of arrest rates and the size of police forces:

We can either speculate that the new police bureaucrats more successfully increased the strength of the institution, that they produced more arrests (cleared more crimes by arrest) or alternatively that the new bureaucrats successfully repressed crime with victims, each incremental increase producing fewer arrests, presumably because of fewer crimes. (Monkkonen, 1981: 146)

Monkkonen argued that the decline in arrests which characterized the rise of the police bureaucracy may be explained by the changing focus of police activity itself. He argues that through the nineteenth century, police attention increasingly shifted from control of the 'dangerous classes' to attempts in the early twentieth century to 'control criminal behaviour' (Monkkonen, 1981: 147). As the century progressed and with it technological innovation, police forces began to specialize. To an increasing degree each specialization eroded the uniform branch which was viewed more frequently as a resource pool from which police managers might draw personnel to support new specialisms. In England, Martin and Wilson (1969) were to identify in the late 1960s the arrival of the manpower crisis in the police and associate it with the rise of specialization during the postwar period. As they argued, however, if there *was* a manpower crisis in relation to uniform patrol duties, there was never a shortage of recruits for CID, traffic or a range of other specialist activities which began to take off during this period (Martin and Wilson, 1969).

Police Patrol

Whilst the rise of specialist functions proved to be at the expense of uniform patrol, this rise was to be sustained by a number of factors which, collectively, served to lower the status of patrol work. In a predominantly male culture which emphasized the value and attraction of 'action-orientated policing' the mundane reality of beat patrol often appeared to be less than attractive. Purpose, action and status accrued to specialist activities which also attracted high and increasing levels of media interest. Indeed the image of policing, generated by the media, may have actually sustained these specializations within the police culture and organization. To this, of course, can be added the personal benefits of more office-based work, office hours, and the opportunity to exercise greater individual initiative in the work situation. Moreover, to work for the CID was also seen as one important way to substantially improve promotion opportunities. As Reiner (1991) has argued, chief officers have themselves risen by way of the CID, and this route has often become an established pathway to ACPO rank within many police forces. It was perhaps not surprising that the organizational culture tended to question the value of uniform patrol which was left increasingly to probationers, 'career failures' or those who evidently did not aspire to higher status in the police service. This was made more emphatic by the threat of being returned to uniform as a 'disciplinary measure' for those specialist officers who broke the disciplinary code. This disciplinary measure was invoked by Robert Mark in his battle to clear up the Metropolitan Police CID during the 1970s. He introduced 'the provincial system hitherto unknown in the Met, of returning to uniform, any detective involved in disciplinary inquiries who was thought no longer fit to work unsupervised'. This, he argued, 'was perhaps the most formidable corrective of all' (Mark, 1978: 96–7).

The decline in status of the uniform patrol function in the 1960s was a relatively recent development. Until then the centrality of the patrol function was to be regularly emphasized in Anglo-American literature on policing. Thus, for example, the 1954 edition of the American Municipal Police Administration series argued that 'the patrol force' remained the 'backbone of the police department'. Police administrators depended heavily on the information gathered and reported by the uniform force, which was in contact 'every hour of the day of the year' with citizens whose life and property it was formed to protect (Municipal Police, 1954: 255).

The relationship between uniform patrol duty and specialist activities was also identified very clearly in the same study. As was argued:

> The work of the patrol force really includes all police functions. Therefore, the more effective the patrol division, the less need there is for the other more specialized operating divisions. Other operating divisions are necessary, only to the extent that the patrol function falls short of being 100 [per cent] effective. Efforts made to improve or strengthen the other divisions at the expense of the patrol division will result in a vicious circle, for weakening of patrol only heightens the burden on the special units. (Municipal Police, 1954: 225)

Commenting on the fact that patrol officers usually arrived first at the scene of the crime it was concluded that the work of patrol officers was of far-reaching importance whilst the quality of service rendered by the police department as a whole was largely dependent on their competence (Municipal Police, 1954: 255).

As was argued in the 1950s in relation to overall police effectiveness, familiarity with the beat would enable the officer to 'know the habits of the people living in the beat area, whilst allowing him/her to become familiar with those districts which were most frequent scenes of crime'. Moreover the close proximity of the officer to the area would enable the officer to 'size up the social environment and influences which must be controlled if crime is to be prevented' (Municipal Police, 1954: 256). Along with a preventative and deterrence function, it was accepted that the patrol officer also had other highly significant functions to perform which went beyond the 'symbolic'. Patrol officers were also available to citizens for consultation, advice, information and professional assistance in emergencies and were frequently used for these purposes by the public.

Yet by the 1950s, the problem confronting many police departments and forces was the apparent inadequacy of manpower to sustain this central police patrol function. In Britain two highly publicized experiments in patrol activity were monitored both by domestic and American police forces. In Aberdeen and Salford, experiments in 'team policing' were designed to improve police response to calls for assistance but also to increase interest 'in patrol among the rank and file' (Municipal Police, 1954: 267). In the Aberdeen experiment fixed beats were ended and were replaced by a larger patrol area worked by a team of constables under a sergeant. Supported by a police vehicle which enabled police to be moved from one area to another, the main feature of the Aberdeen system was its mobility 'and the fact that constables acted as a team rather than as individuals' (Municipal Police, 1954: 267).

One consequence of the Aberdeen experiment was that 'a substantial saving in manpower had been effected' (Municipal Police, 1954: 267). In Salford a similar experiment in 'team policing' provided 'greater flexibility'. This was because patrol areas in each of the districts chosen for team policing were interchangeable while boundaries of beats were changed, sometimes three times each day, to accommodate changing needs. The determination of duties for team policing was also decided on a daily basis. Local commanders, it was noted, 'considered recent incidents and location of crimes and street accidents, complaints from the public of general nuisances, and any property requiring special protection and similar matters' (Municipal Police, 1954: 267).

As with the traditional beat system, the constable remained individually responsible for a definite area while on duty. The biggest difference in the sort of team policing approach was that the beat could be changed immediately to fit any situation. The Salford team policing experiment had a number of advantages. It increased the interest of patrol officers and broke up the 'monotony of patrol in the same area, week after week, waiting for something to turn up'. Moreover the flexibility of the team approach led to an increase of nearly 50 per cent in incidents reported to the police (Municipal Police, 1954: 267).

The interest in the Aberdeen patrol experiment was translated into operational policing in London during this time. This was in large part a response to the growing manpower crisis experienced there. As Sir Harold Scott argued:

> The [manpower] shortage shows itself most on beats. So often one hears the remark 'we never see a policeman on the beat in our part of London' and up to a point this is certainly true. When the various duties which are unavoidable have been provided for and allowance made for men absent on leave, sick or receiving time off in compensation for overtime, the number left at a station is often so small that it is impossible to man beats fully. (Scott, 1957: 51)

As Scott argued, there was no real substitute for the officer on the beat or patrol. Moreover if beats could be fully served he believed crime could be expected to go down (Scott, 1957: 26). It also demonstrated that the manpower crisis for patrol activity predated the 1950s. Scott also noted that: 'with the steady increase in specialised duty and the shortage of men, the situation has worsened in a way that can only be described as disastrous. In 1932 of the men required for beat and patrol duty, 88 per cent were available. In 1952 the figure had fallen to 44 per cent' (Scott, 1957: 51).

Scott was to enthusiastically embrace the 'Aberdeen experiment' with its team policing approach because it appeared to allow the police, with fewer police officers, to provide an area with the same level of service. Prior to his departure, Scott planned a major expansion of team policing throughout the Metropolitan Police area (Scott, 1957: 57). Had this occurred, it would only have reinforced the steady movement towards specialization and bureaucratization which was already a major charter of the Metropolitan Police.

Organization of Beat Patrols

The debate in the 1950s over the patrol function suggested that the fixed beat and inflexible shift system had to be amended if patrol was to adequately respond to changing demand. A range of approaches in helping to respond to periods of high demand on police resources were to be identified. For example, tabulation for service calls on an hourly basis was recommended so that comparative data on peak and trough periods of demand for police service could be identified (Municipal Police, 1954: 273). Geographical fluctuations in demand needed to be accommodated, as did the likely need for overlapping shifts when demand was highest. Additionally the introduction of a fourth shift working during hours of peak demand was also contemplated (Municipal Police, 1954: 273).

One further issue was the determination of police beats in relation to local government district boundaries. In America one major aim continued to be the creation of police boundaries which were coterminous with those of other local government services. This was because the 'generation of data' could be shared with other local services and could be expected to form the basis of an effective crime prevention strategy. As was argued, because past police beats and districts did not conform to boundaries adapted by other local city departments 'there was no comparison possible between police statistics and data on fire, health and social welfare'. Coterminous boundaries were valuable. One consequence was that: 'not only would comparable police statistics be of value to other social agencies but the police would benefit by being able to use other social statistics in crime prevention work' (Municipal Police, 1954: 274).

The Centrality of the Police Patrol Function

The continuing significance of the police patrol function was most immediately identified by the American President's Commission on Law Enforcement and Administration which reported in 1967. While it noted that police 'did not create and could not resolve' the social conditions which stimulated crime, it argued that it was the police officer to whom the public looked for 'personal safety and for the ability to walk their streets and be secure in their homes' (President's Commission, 1967: 92).

Moreover the need for a patrol function was also emphasized in relation to the number and nature of offences experienced by victims of crime. As the Commission's report noted in relation to operational problems of law enforcement, its own analysis showed that 61.5 per cent of over 9000 major crimes against the person – including rapes, robberies and assaults – in Chicago over a six-month period 'occurred on the streets or in other public premises (President's Commission, 1967: 95). In terms of effectiveness of patrol and its deterrent function, however, there did appear to be a clear problem. Public surveys in the early 1960s had already shown that a major reason for the non-reporting of offences by the public was a belief that the police 'could not do anything'. As the President's Commission noted: 'If this impression of the ineffectiveness of the police is widely held by the public, there is every reason to believe that it is shared by criminals and would-be criminals. Under such circumstances "deterrence" is, to say the least, not operating as well as it might' (President's Commission, 1967: 96).

This phenomenon was, however, more than balanced by the discovery of the central importance of police patrol for crime clearance. While many crimes remained unsolvable, in the great majority of cases, personal identification by a victim or witness was found to provide the greatest opportunity for the possible identification of an offender. The President's Commission was to analyze 1905 reported offences over a specific period in Los Angeles. In the minority of cases where police were given a suspect's name, the majority were effectively resolved by way of arrest or some other way' (President's Commission, 1967: 97). With the majority of crimes, however, where no suspect was named (1375 of the total 1905 cases analyzed) only 181 cases were cleared by the police. The Commission concluded that no amount of 'scientific' crime detection or increases in detective manpower could expect to significantly reverse this central feature of reported crime. Clearance, it argued, remained almost entirely dependent on information provided to police officers at the scene of the crime. In the absence of such information, clearance became very unlikely. Nevertheless, the 'crime solution' was found to be highly dependent on good patrol work. In the same Los Angeles study, it was found that 36 per cent of all arrests were made within half an hour of the commission of a crime and 48 per cent were made within two hours (President's Commission, 1967: 97). Moreover nine-tenths of all arrests were made by patrol officers rather than by detectives (although 25 per cent of these arrests were made on the basis of leads provided by detectives).

The central feature of primary detection and clearance of crime was the patrol officer, and the ability of those officers to find witnesses or victims who were able to identify the offender. The salience of victims and witnesses was to be identified most emphatically by Murphy when he was Commissioner of the New York Police Department (NYPD). Murphy was to initiate a detailed analysis of crime clearance by the NYPD Detective Bureau. The Bureau was asked to identify the percentage of crime referred to the Detective Bureau which was cleared by them. As Murphy and Plate state of the 1967 study: 'The results were devastating. The clearance rate for robberies was 5.38 per cent. The clearance rate for burglaries was 1.85 per cent. The clearance rate for grand larcenies was 2.7 per cent. These were the clearance rates.

Who knew how low the conviction rates would be?' (Murphy and Plate, 1977: 185). As Murphy and Plate argued, the truth about detectives was that, taken as a whole, they were not likely to be 'effective police officers'. While there were always exceptions, as a general rule crimes were solved not by detectives but by ordinary patrol officers, he argued:

> Precinct police officers were usually the ones to identify the witnesses and the victims. Most criminal cases never progressed beyond this state of knowledge. Cases that could not be cleared on the basis of the original set of facts were likely not to be cleared at all. In reality the vast majority of a department's detective work was being performed by patrol officers in the course of their duty. (Murphy and Plate, 1977: 187)

This conclusion was graphically reinforced in 1992 by American Police Foundation evidence which demonstrated that the larger the detective bureau in a police department, the lower the arrest rate for certain offences appeared to be. Although in England the very low primary arrest rate among the CID was to be identified by Martin and Wilson in the late 1960s, the Police Foundation's statistical analysis conducted in the 1990s demonstrates that the inverse relationship between arrest rates and detective strength remains a crucial element in explaining the continued underperformance of police forces (see Figure 6.5).

Moreover the role of the uniform patrol officer was seen by the President's Commission as being one which involved a far wider remit than that of arrest and crime control. The President's Commission was to consider whether the role of the police might not be extended to cover additional duties. One issue identified early on as a future police function involved the police as protectors of the community 'against social injustices'. This, it argued, while not at the time considered to be police business, 'should become so'. As police were uniquely situated to observe what was happening in the community and were also in constant contact with the conditions associated with crime, they could and should act as important facilitators to improve those social conditions which generated criminality. The Commission argued that the police, acting as facilitators, could represent the community in securing those public services to which it was fully entitled (President's Commission, 1967: 98).

Public Expectations of Police

As successive surveys demonstrate, it would appear that the public expect more than merely a 'fire brigade' style of policing or a quick

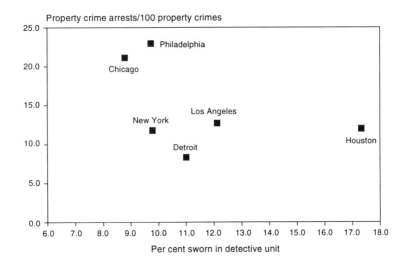

Figure 6.5   Detection and property crime arrests

Note: There appears to be a slight negative relationship between the percentage of a department's sworn personnel assigned to detective units and the number of property crime arrests made per 100 property crimes.

Source: Police Foundation, Washington, DC (1992).

response to calls for service. Aligning police service provision more closely to public demand is of course a feature of the quality of service initiatives to which police forces have become increasingly committed. The primary objective would seem to be that police provision should be heavily influenced by external demand rather than by internal, self-generated professional priorities. That said, recent evidence as shown in Table 6.8 suggests that the public believe that in the long term, the real requirement of the police is for them to tackle the underlying causes of crime.

Interestingly the public also appear to prefer 'community style' as opposed to 'crime-fighting modes' of policing. Indeed, as the Operational Policing Review was to discover, the public showed clear preferences about policing styles (see Table 6.9).

The difference between community-style policing and crime fighting is, of course, crucial as it serves to demonstrate the difference in perception between the public and police professionals as to what constitutes effective policing. In the main, professional perceptions of effective-

Table 6.8   Perception of effective crime control strategies

	Social class				
	All	AB	C1	C2	DE
Tackling causes of crime	40	45	46	38	34
More community service	8	10	7	8	9
Adventure courses in UK	2	0	2	1	3
Harsher prison conditions	23	19	20	27	23
Prison for 12-year-olds	21	17	18	19	26
Removing right to silence	4	4	4	5	2
Don't know	3	4	3	2	3

Source: *The Guardian*, May 1993.

Table 6.9   Public preferences and policing styles: overall preference
between PC Smith and PC Jones, by age (%)

	Total	Age			
	Base (1085)	16–24 (158)	25–44 (383)	45–59 (238)	60+ (300)
Overall preference:					
PC Smith – detects and					
arrests offenders	24	27	17	22	32
PC Jones – works with local					
people to solve crime					
problems	74	70	81	75	66
Don't know	2	3	2	3	2

Source: Operational Policing Review (1990).

ness have traditionally been closely linked to the expansion of a range
of specialist activities and the application of enhanced technology aids.

POLICING, CRIME AND COMMUNITY

Giving the Public What It Wants

Returning the police to its most basic yet highly significant patrol function
cannot easily be achieved. Police organizations as bureaucracies will
inevitably seek to defend established routines and specialist interests

where they are able to do so. However, the overall measure of effectiveness of the police is probably linked to the extent to which that service is able to integrate with communities. In terms of effective crime control this will depend on the extent to which they can encourage the public to provide information to enable them to arrest offenders. It is clear that a range of initiatives will be needed to respond to the now traditional problem of 'inadequate personnel'. Police 'overheads', particularly 'on-costs', are in the process of being more closely scrutinized, particularly where on-cost is a means of sustaining and expanding internal specialist bureaucracies. This challenge may be met more effectively by smaller rather than larger units of policing, where the opportunity cost of diversion of police resources away from patrol activity becomes more immediately observable to both police managers and the public. Team policing and directed patrol based on effective crime analysis might be seen as merely further application of the Aberdeen and Salford experiments of the late 1940s. Precisely how the uniform patrol is structured should be, of course, a professional decision. Yet, as has been succinctly argued by Lea and Young (1984) in relation to patrol:

> Effective policing depends on receiving a high amount of information from the community. This usually involves the public informing the police about a crime (either as victims or bystanders) and the police acting upon this. The public are needed as alarm systems, as providers of information, and as witnesses in court. (Lea and Young, 1984: 62)

The crucial role of police patrol, however is not universally acknowledged. As the Cassels Report argues, the consequence of financial constraints on the police, together with increasing demand, may mean that the 'ability of the police to meet public expectations by way of visible patrol will continue to be tightly constrained'. The same report concludes that in the long term the patrol function can be expected to diminish (Cassels, 1996, para. 4.7: 27). As the report goes on to argue, evidence that the police find it increasingly difficult to provide a level of visible patrol which inspires public confidence may lead local communities to seek other alternatives (Cassels, 1996, para. 4.7: 28).

Yet the availability of uniform officers for patrol duties may remain the most significant indicator of police force efficiency and overall effectiveness. How to provide maximum uniform presence at times of highest demand will, of course, offer a continuing challenge to police managers. More flexible shift arrangements, enhanced pay for patrol officers, inverting the pyramid of promotion and pay to reward those officers who remain in uniform, are all areas which need to be explored. It is clear, however, that the apparent inability of the police to sustain effective patrol cover must be a matter of grave concern. The patrol function remains central to public perceptions of police legitimacy and may need to be enhanced in relation to the continuing growth of the private security industry.

Private Provision of Patrols

If the abstraction rate continues to account for around 50 per cent of officers via training, sickness, leave, sporting activities, management and specialist duties, one consequence could be that in areas of high victimization residents may turn to alternative suppliers of patrol activity. As yet, the provision of private patrol has been relatively limited in England and Wales. This activity remains an area which the New Right, particularly the Institute of Economic Affairs and the Adam Smith Institute, regard as entirely appropriate for an expanded private sector provision. Recently David Pyle (1995) has argued in favour of private patrols in terms of their cost and availability and also because of the benefits of 'exit accountability' which accrue to private consumers of service who may wish to seek alternative suppliers.

The Association of Chief Police Officers and the Home Affairs Committee have recently recommended the regulation of the industry (Home Affairs Committee, 1995). It is clear, however, that consumers of the private sector services are not overly concerned with the lineage of either the companies or the personnel employed by them. Rather, evidence (albeit limited) appears to suggest that consumers of private patrol services are primarily concerned about direct protection of property and are prepared to accept high levels of intrusiveness into personal space to achieve this (see, for example, McManus, 1995).

In an important study of a limited number of mobile private security patrols, McManus has highlighted the real dilemma which the private sector poses both for public police forces and for residents in areas surrounding those patrolled. The evidence suggests that the inequalities of private provision will be exacerbated by the displacement of crime from areas which are patrolled to areas which are not. Yet, overwhelmingly, McManus found the primary explanation for residents' choice of private security patrols was a deep concern about the lack of public police patrol in these areas (McManus, 1995: 85). It was this, rather than a preference for private policing, which encouraged residents to purchase the service. Nevertheless, analysis of resident responses to private patrols highlighted the sense of a 'psychological advantage' that residents appeared to obtain from knowing that someone was 'watching out' in their neighbourhood. As McManus notes: 'The fundamental message which I was receiving from respondents was that people needed to feel safe and secure. Foot patrol gives this assurance of security' (McManus, 1995: 85). Moreover, this had a much stronger effect than any number of alarms, locks or other preventative devices.

The research showed that if this assurance was available it did not appear to matter whether it was provided by private security or a public police force. Furthermore, while the primary aim was protection of property, resident responses indicated that the feeling of enhanced personal safety served to confirm their 'legitimation of the patrols' public disorder–deterrence function if only in a symbolic sense' (McManus, 1995: 84). Where private patrol was limited and demands placed on the police appeared high, McManus found that 'service calls' to police were low and often directed to the local council. Tenants felt in one area that the council would be better able to resolve their problems than the police (McManus, 1995: 92). Overall the research conducted by McManus appears to confirm the value of proactive, preventative functions of albeit private security patrol. It also provided further evidence of traditional preventative public policing being eroded by the incursion of the private sector as security companies moved into areas of what was formerly 'public police work'. This, McManus concluded, would continue to blur the boundaries between the public and the private sector (McManus, 1995: 97). Indeed, the impact of the private patrol function was personally experienced by McManus when he joined private guards on patrol in the research sites. As he noted:

Local knowledge is an obvious asset and comes naturally through regular street patrol. This local knowledge is the essence of community policing and has always been seen by the public police as the main attribute of the constable. As I observed the patrol personnel at Moston and Bridton, I became aware of this part of their role as being analogous of the traditional constable. (McManus, 1995: 98)

As the above discussion highlights, it would appear that underestimating the importance of preventative patrol in the community can ultimately begin to undermine the legitimacy of the police.

Targeting Need

The above discussion suggests that the future orientation of policing must be community-based. This will necessarily increase demands on the visible presence of police by way of uniform patrol. Normally the immediate visibility of police in areas of high demand may not necessarily provide greater reassurance or satisfaction amongst members of the community. This has most recently been discovered by the Audit Commission in its evaluation of patrol activity (Audit Commission, 1996a). Yet if crime in these areas is to be successfully addressed, then, as Alpert and Moore (1993) have argued, a new 'paradigm of policing' will need to be developed. This may place less emphasis on a rapid response to incidents, retrospective investigation and the solution of crimes as 'indicators of police efficiency'. Responding to specific incidents would be replaced by 'a problem-orientated approach' which recognizes that a large proportion of incidents emerge from a small number of situations and locations (Alpert and Moore, 1993: 116).

Re-engaging the Community

In this chapter it has been argued that the current crisis confronting police forces is the disengagement of the police from communities which may legitimately demand most of them. A corresponding problem, and one which represents the biggest potential challenge to the police, is the disengagement of residents in high-crime areas from the police. Increasingly residents are using local authorities, particularly housing departments, as alternatives to the police when reporting a matter which traditionally would have involved the police. To the extent that the police pursue high-profile crime-fighting activities, it is likely that local authority departments will be used more frequently by residents in high crime areas when lodging a complaint. Moreover the threat of reprisal against a complainant who involves the police is also a major deterrent. Involving the police and criminal justice system may only exacerbate a victim's problems in high-crime areas. Thus for most victims who reside in high-crime areas, much policing activity (if not all), like that of the highly expensive criminal justice system, remains utterly irrelevant to their needs.

Re-engaging the police service may take many forms. Already police associations are recognizing the acute nature of the problem which is reflected in the decline of uniform police patrol. In 1996 a Police Federation report argued forcefully for the resurrection of the patrol function. The Federation report was to find that while patrol was a core task of policing, it was not highly regarded by force managements, while patrol staff continued to feel that they were the 'least esteemed' section of the service. This feeling, it added, was compounded when around one-third of notional patrol strength was not available due to extractions of all kinds, as the report went on to note:

> The working conditions of patrol officers are the most onerous, involving the greatest pro rata personal risks, exposure to the elements, round the clock shifts, disruption of family life; frequent changes of duty and constant abstractions from allotted roles in order to be a source of instant manpower for other tasks. (Police Federation, 1996: para. 21)

If this was not enough, managerial indifference to the status of the patrol officer was manifested in the quality of provision for their needs inside police stations. Inadequate locker and changing accommodation and poor facilities for briefing and report writing were found to be common. As the same report noted, all this was in sharp contrast to the management style generally experienced by officers of similar rank and service who were in specialist roles.

Indeed, it was probably because of this that an initial Federation survey of police patrol officers was to find that 'approaching half of patrol officers hoped to be performing a specialist role within the next two years' (Police Federation, 1996), while one-third stated that they wanted to stay as patrol officers. Probationers made up the bulk of officers on foot patrols and it was these officers who were most anxious to move from patrol. As the report went on to state: 'It is regrettable that the present condition of patrol is such that a high proportion of officers, at the outset of their careers, wish to transfer from what is supposed to be the most important of all police functions' (Police Federation, 1996: para. 22).

Interestingly, given the remarkably low status accorded to patrol work, the same Federation survey was to discover that approximately two out of every five patrol officers (who responded to the survey) had made an arrest during their most recent tour of patrol duty. Despite this interesting confirmation of relatively high primary detections and arrest rates achieved by way of uniform patrol, the most widespread feeling among patrol officers was found to be that they were undervalued and the 'recipients of the worst aspects of human resource management' (Police Federation, 1996: para. 35). The Police Federation concluded that a new approach was needed by which patrolling was seen as the basis of all police operations to which specialists might contribute. Otherwise, in the absence of developing such initiatives the provision of private security patrols can be expected to grow, filling the vacuum created by the disengagement from this activity in many high-crime areas by public police forces.

If the police service is to respond to the problem of high victimization and the prolonged period of social dislocation which has helped generate this, it could be argued that the police service needs to develop some kind of 'strategy for poverty'. This would encompass inter-agency initiatives but would have as a primary objective a palpable reorientation of policing to encourage policing *for* communities rather than against offenders. This orientation would undoubtedly present a formidable challenge to the police service. It might nevertheless resurrect the original aims set for the police in the early nineteenth century which emphasized prevention over detection of crime as a primary police function (Reiner, 1992).

The preventative function of the uniform police remains a primary function even if crime rates are unlikely to be significantly affected by police activity (even if that takes the form of targeting known offenders). As has been argued, the history of policing has really been one of steady decline in the availability of uniform patrol officers and in the number of primary arrests effected. Ironically this may itself have been a function of the increase in police strength. To the extent that specialist duties have replaced uniform patrol in terms of police activity, the decline in primary detections will have reflected this. As an American Police Foundation Study (1992) demonstrated, there is a negative relationship between the size of the police department's detective unit and the number of property crime arrests achieved. A similar negative relationship was the size of the detective unit and arrest rates for violent crimes (American Police Foundation, 1992). In an interesting reversal of expected outcome, it found that police departments with the highest percentage of police officers in detective units had the lowest rates of violent crime arrests per 100 violent crimes (American Police Foundation 1992: 234–5). Effectively removing police officers from uniform patrol to specialist duties will have a significant impact on primary detections achieved by the police. These primary detections can be expected in the main to involve offences which immediately involve members of the public. It is they who will provide information which may enable the police to resolve the incident.

CONCLUSION

The police response to public service calls may be held back by organizational inertia. The highly bureaucratic nature of the police organization provides the biggest obstacle to improving police service to areas of greatest need. There is currently no real incentive to change existing structures or practices. In retrospect, it is interesting to note that the *Inquiry into Police Responsibilities and Rewards* did at least attempt to change (among much else) the police promotion system by inverting the promotion pyramid. It intended to achieve this by paying more to those who worked closest to the public. It was never really likely, however, that such a radical system of rewards would be implemented when it so clearly challenged both the existing status hierarchy and specialist units which sustain it within the police organization. Having survived Sheehy and the internal reorganizations encouraged by the Audit Commission, the 'on-cost' of police 'management' continues to remain high. Inbuilt resistance to anything which challenges the status quo remains strong and can be expected to provide a continuing brake on real change.

The nature of internal bureaucratic constraints in the police service raises other important questions concerning the police function. If police patrol is difficult to sustain, to what extent can the police service be expected to achieve the Audit Commission's objectives of controlling crime and reducing the crime rate? There is in fact little evidence to suggest that the police service would ever be likely to either control or reduce the crime rates. Ultimately the police service can be expected to influence recorded crime by changing crime recording methods. Most recently this activity has drawn comment from the authors of the British Crime Survey (Mayhew, Aye Maung and Mirrlees-Black, 1992) who discovered significant variations in the incidence of reporting and recording burglaries by the police. It is against this background that the key national objectives for the police under the Police and Magistrates' Court Act must be viewed. Setting key objectives and targets for police forces in the fight against crime only emphasizes a continuing commitment to a performance culture. Yet this will fail to provide any effective measure of police activity. This is because there will always be a bureaucratic pressure to manipulate crime statistics to enable the police to achieve unrealistic targets set for them by government (Loveday, 1996).

The continuing crisis of uniform patrol provision and the protection of existing bureaucracies raise questions concerning the managerial purposes and competence of police managers. It is, after all, the failure to provide public reassurance and support to those in greatest need which has relegated policing to the level of irrelevance in many high-victimization estates. Yet the evidence suggests that the expansion of police organizations has been unrelated to any increase in the level of public service provision. This expansion has, as with any bureaucracy, been more closely linked to specialization and the achievement of internal bureaucratic goals (Lane, 1994). These goals have helped sustain a status hierarchy which has been almost entirely unrelated to the delivery of service to the public. It has, however, significantly improved the working lives and incomes within the police bureaucracy. Moreover, as research suggests, police expansion can be expected to benefit the organization rather more than the public. This is because there appears to be an inverse relationship between police numbers (and the size of police departments/police forces) and the inability to sustain an effective level of uniform patrol activity. These and related issues must be of continuing concern to those whose primary aim is the improved efficiency and overall effectiveness of the police service.

Preliminary evidence suggests that larger police forces are unable to translate higher levels of manpower into greater levels of patrol activity. Indeed the opposite appears to pertain. Smaller police forces may sustain greater levels of patrol activity than the largest police forces. The interesting existence of an inverse relationship existing between police force size and levels of patrol activity needs further exploration but may be closely linked to higher levels of bureaucracy status achievement and police specialization. Similarly there appears to be sufficient evidence to suggest that an inverse relationship may exist between the size of the detective branch within police forces and the arrest rate. The bigger the detective branch then the lower the arrest rate will be, particularly for certain types of offences. Moreover primary detections along with overall detections can be expected to fall as the specialist detective function expands.

Indeed where specialization of bureaucratic growth reduces uniform patrol, primary crime clearances can be expected to fall. This will reflect a corresponding fall in police public contacts and a further decline in the rate of reported crime. Additionally, where uniform patrol provision falls, a corresponding increase in the incidence of 'police-related' reasons for not reporting offences can be expected. Any further decline in the rate of reported crime can only be expected to further question the value of police statistics on reported crime, an issue which is already the subject of a more general debate (Jenkins, 1995).

For policing futures, the problem of patrol activity, its value within the police organization and the response of police forces to perceived public need will each need to be assessed. These issues, along with that of the professional policing model which has removed the police from effective crime control and the protection of the most vulnerable in an increasingly unequal and divided society, will limit police managers. Yet staffing problems which appear to traditionally confront the police service would appear to be largely self-inflicted. These may be the result of a mixture of bureaucratic growth and increas-ing specialization. These problems may be beyond the ability of the police to effectively reform if, as the evidence suggests, the growth of police forces has been predicated upon the continued expansion of the police bureaucracy. Indeed bureaucratic growth, despite civilianization and 'de-tiering' of police forces, has been a noticeable feature of most 'western' police forces and departments. This trend is probably irreversible and not susceptible to internal police reform.

The problem of effective policing is also increasingly linked to the costs of policing. It has already been suggested by some chief constables that beyond the year 2000, police pension costs alone could account for around three-quarters of current police expenditure in police force areas. Pension costs, along with high salary costs, now make policing a highly expensive public service. Arguably, public police forces are now perhaps too expensive to sustain any further expansion. This may be particularly the case when such expansion does not provide the service which the public increasingly demands and expects.

References

Alpert, G. and Moore, M. (1993) 'Measuring police performance in the new paradigm of policing', *Performance Measures for the Criminal Justice System*, October (Washington, DC: United States Department of Justice).
American Police Foundation (1992) *The Big Six: Policing America's Biggest Cities* (Washington, DC: Police Foundation).
Audit Commission (1991) *Pounds and Coppers: Financial Delegation in Provisional Police Forces* (London: HMSO).
Audit Commission (1993) *Helping with Enquiries* (London: HMSO).
Audit Commission (1994) *Cheques and Balances* (London: HMSO).
Audit Commission (1996a) *Streetwise: Effective Police Patrol* (London: HMSO).
Audit Commission (1996b) *Misspent Youth: Young People and Crime* (London: HMSO).

Baker, K. (1993) *The Turbulent Years: My Life in Politics* (London: Faber & Faber).

Bayley, D. (1995) *Police for the Future* (Oxford: Oxford University Press).

Bowland, B. (1976) 'Patterns of urban crime', in W. Skogan (ed.) *Sample Surveys of the Victims of Crime* (Chicago, Ill.: Ballinger Publications).

Box, S. (1987) *Recession, Crime and Punishment* (London: Macmillan).

Cassels, J. (1996) *Independent Report on the Role and Responsibilities of the Police* (London: Police Foundation/Policy Studies Institute).

Colpa Police Funding Formula (1996/7) (London: Home Office).

Davies, H. (1992) *Fighting Leviathan* (London: Social Market Institute).

Dickinson, D. (1994) *Crime and Employment* (Cambridge: Department of Applied Economics, University of Cambridge).

Dodge, R., Lentzner, H. and Shenk, F. (1976) 'Crime in the United States of America: a report on the National Crime Survey', in W. Skogan (ed.), *Sample Surveys of the Victims of Crime* (Chicago, Ill.: Ballinger Publications).

Farrington, D. (1994) 'Human development and criminal careers', in M. Maguire, R. Morgan and R. Reiner (eds), *The Oxford Handbook of Criminology* (Oxford: Oxford University Press).

Foster, J. and Hope, J. (1993) *Housing, Community and Crime: The Impact of the Priority Estates Project* (London: HMSO).

Graef, R. (1989) *Talking Blues: The Police in Their Own Words* (London: Collins Harvill).

Graef, R. (1996) *Law and Order Policing*, text (London: Channel 4).

Home Affairs Committee (1995) *First Report on the Private Security Industry* (London: Home Affairs Committee).

Home Office (1993a) *Police Reform: A Police Service for the Twenty First Century*, Cmnd 2281 (London: HMSO).

Home Office (1993b) *Royal Commission on Criminal Justice*, Cmnd 2262 (London: HMSO).

Home Office (1994) *Police and Magistrates' Courts Act* (London: HMSO).

Home Office (1995a) *Review of the Core and Ancillary Tasks*, Final Report (London: HMSO).

Home Office (1995b) *Social Trends* Central Statistical Office (London: HMSO).

Home Office, Northern Ireland Office and the Scottish Office (1993) *Inquiry into Police Responsibilities and Rewards*, Cmnd 2280 (London: HMSO).

Jenkins, L. (1995) *Accountable to None* (London: Hamish Hamilton).

Joint Standing Committee (1990) *Operational Policing Review* (Surbiton: Police Federation).

Kinsey, R. (1985) *The Merseyside Crime and Police Surveys*, Final Report (Liverpool: Merseyside Police Authority).

Kinsey, R., Lea, J. and Young, J. (1986) *Losing the Fight Against Crime* (London: Basil Blackwell).

Lane, J. (1994) *The Public Sector Concept: Models and Approaches*, 2nd edn (London: Sage).

Lea, J. and Young, J. (1984) *What Is to Be Done About Law and Order?* (London: Penguin).

Loveday, B. (1990) 'The road to regionalisation', *Policing*.

Loveday, B. (1996) 'Crime at the core?', in F. Leishman, B. Loveday and S. Savage (eds), *Core Issues in Policing* (London: Longman).

Mark, R. Sir (1978) *In the Office of Constable* (London: Collins).

Martin, J. and Wilson, G. (1969) *The Police: A Study in Manpower. The Evolution of the Service in England and Wales 1829–1965* (London: Heinemann).

Mayhew, P., Aye-Maung, A. and Mirrlees-Black, K. (1992) *The British Crime Survey of England and Wales* (London: Home Office).

McComb, R. (1996) 'Grieving for a family that cared', *Birmingham Post*, 5 January.

McManus, M. (1995) *From Fate to Choice: Private Bobbies, Public Beats* (Altershot: Avebury).

Monkkonon, E. (1981) *Police in Urban America 1860–1920* (Cambridge: Cambridge University Press).

Municipal Police Administration (1954) Fourth Edition (Chicago, Illinois: International City Managers Association).

Murphy, P. and Plate, T. (1977) *A View from the Top of American Law Enforcement* (New York: Simon & Schuster).

Operational Policing Review (1990) Joint Standing Committee (Surbiton: Police Federation).

Parks, R. B. (1976) 'Police response to victimization: effects on citizen attitudes and perceptions', in W. Skogan (ed.), *Sample Surveys of the Victims of Crime* (Chicago, Ill.: Ballinger Publications).

Police Federation (1996) *Patrolling* (Surbiton: Police Federation).

President's Commission on Law Enforcement (1967) *The Challenge of Crime in a Free Society* (Washington, DC: United States Government).

Pyle, D. (1995) *The Cost of Crime* (London: Institute for Economic Affairs).

Pyle, D. J. and Deadman, D. F. (1994) 'Crime and the business cycle in post-war Britain', *British Journal of Criminology*, vol. 34, no. 3.: 339–357.

Reiner, R. (1991) *Chief Constables* (Oxford: Oxford University Press).

Reiner, R. (1992) *The Politics of the Police*, 2nd edn (London: Harvester Wheatsheaf).

Scott, Sir Harold (1957) *Scotland Yard* (London: Penguin).

Skogan, W. (1976) *Sample Surveys of the Victims of Crime* (Chicago, Ill.: Ballinger Publications).

Wells, J. (1995) *Crime and Unemployment: Economic Report*, vol. 9, no. 1 (London: Employment Policy Institute).

7 Policing Divided Societies: Trends and Prospects in Northern Ireland and Britain
Paddy Hillyard[1]

INTRODUCTION

Northern Ireland is a society which has long been divided in terms of politics, religion and national aspirations. This chapter explores the forms of policing which have been developed to deal with the problems of social disorder stemming from these divisions and considers future prospects. As the strategies of social control have long historical roots, the first section of the chapter sketches a brief history of some of the key features of policing under colonial rule in Ireland. The purpose of this is twofold. First, it will provide a deeper structural understanding of the development of security strategies; and second, it will also provide a corrective to the dominant Anglo-centric view of the development of policing in Britain, which typically overlooks the fact that modern police history on these islands began in Ireland. After examining current developments in Northern Ireland, the chapter considers trends in policing England and Wales and draws out a number of similarities in the development of policing in the two jurisdictions. The central idea which is explored in this section is that forms of policing are a product of conflict, social divisions and the distribution of power in any particular society, and that these forms impact upon and radically affect both the economic and social structures of that society. The final section considers the future, not only for Northern Ireland, but for Britain more generally, of policing divided societies.

Before any analysis can proceed, two further introductory comments are necessary. First a comment on the notion of a 'divided society'. There can be no doubt that Northern Ireland is a divided society in the traditional use of the term, which privileges divisions based on ethnic, religious or national divisions. It was born out of a colonial conflict which was exacerbated when in the seventeenth and eighteenth centuries the colonialists attempted to restore order through a system of plantation, creating a lasting conflict between the planter and the Gael, with the former wanting to maintain their loyalty to Britain and the latter to reassert their independence. These different national aspirations, which were broadly mapped on to different religious affiliations, still run as fault lines through the social order, expressed in high levels of social segregation in housing, education and cultural activities. An analysis of the 1991 Census, for example, suggests that about one-half of the population live in areas more than 90 per cent Catholic or 90 per cent Protestant (Murray, 1995). The school system, despite the development of a number of integrated schools, is also highly segregated along Catholic and Protestant lines. There are also sharp cultural differences within the two main groups; they read different newspapers, play different games and belong to different social and sports clubs.

This stark view, however, must be qualified because the extent of these divisions varies considerably with respect to social class, geographical location and increasingly age. Moreover, in terms of everyday activities such as working, shopping and drinking, there is considerable interaction and people in the North of Ireland are as addicted to television soap operas as everyone else in the world! This then raises the important sociological question as to why 'divided societies' are primarily defined along religious, ethnic and national dimensions. In Britain, although there is considerable residential, educational and cultural segregation along class lines, few people would apply the label 'divided society'. It is a label for 'the other'. This is an important point because one of the themes pursued in this chapter is that although policing a divided society such as Northern Ireland may be unique, it will be argued that similar features are emerging in the policing of an increasingly polarized Britain.

The second introductory comment concerns the role of British academics and the British/Irish problem. It is remarkable that most sociologists of law, critical legal theorists and criminologists in Britain, with only a few exceptions – for example Brogden (1987) in the field of policing – have totally ignored Northern Ireland despite the fact that it represents one of the most important constitutional issues facing the government and provides numerous insights into policing, law, order and disorder.[2] This collective silence appears to stem from a shared culture in which the British/Irish problem is seen at best as irrelevant or at worst a petty squabble between two warring factions within Northern Ireland. The silence has produced a form of censorship which must rank in importance alongside the direct forms of censorship under the repressive legislation and the broadcasting ban (see in particular Curtis and Jempson, 1993). Crucially, this Anglo-centric focus has meant that sociological and criminological research and theory have been deprived of the comparative insights which even a cursory glance at some of the literature would have produced. Moreover, it has produced a distorted view of the development of policing in Britain.

THE HISTORICAL ROOTS OF POLICING IN IRELAND

The form of policing in Northern Ireland predates the setting up of the state in 1921. In the eighteenth and nineteenth century, when the whole of the island of Ireland was under British rule, there were widespread protests of various kinds, not least against British rule, which posed major threats to the social order (Broeker, 1979; Clark and Donnelly, 1983; Townshend, 1983). There was a crisis of legitimacy and the forms of policing which were developed were a direct expression of the social, political and economic circumstances of the time. Provision for a police force was made in 1786, some 43 years before similar developments in England. Following the Gordon riots in London in 1780, the government put forward a Bill in 1785 for a police force for the London metropolitan area, but this was roundly defeated to cries of 'French despotism' (Palmer, 1988: 30). A year later, however, a similar Bill was passed, setting out provision for a police force for the Dublin metropolitan area, under a central command within a single jurisdiction.

At the same time, Dublin Castle was secretly considering a whole range of ideas for a 'universal system' of policing in Ireland. One plan was to have each county governed by three Police Commissioners who would appoint a High Constable for each police district and a Chief Constable with 'a little body of petty constables' for each barony. The force would be entirely Protestant (Palmer, 1988: 111). A much less ambitious plan was accepted which rejected the idea of a national police force and made temporary provision for a police force in districts where there were disturbances.

In 1814, 'the idea of a force of men active in disturbed districts' (Palmer, 1988: 112) was consolidated when the then Irish Secretary, Robert Peel, established the Irish Peace Preservation Force. It had ready access to guns and men could be dispatched to areas with disorders. By 1818, the 'Peelers', as they became known, could be found in ten counties. They were housed in fortified 'barracks' – a term which is still used to describe police stations in many parts of Ireland today. This highly militarized and coercive form of policing not only determined the form of its eventual successor, the Irish Constabulary, but was also important in serving as a model for policing the empire (see Jeffries, 1952; Tobias, 1972).

The first regular rural police force was established in Ireland with the passage of the Irish Constabulary Act 1822, which abolished policing under the existing local constables and peace officers of the county and set up forces in each area under central control. Contrary to much academic and popular discourse, it was devised by Goulburn and not Peel. It was strongly opposed in Parliament particularly on the grounds that it would destroy local government in Ireland and centralize state power. The former Irish Chief Secretary, Charles Grant, argued that it would 'place the whole of Ireland under an armed police force'. Grant went on to argue that long-term peace in Ireland would come about only with the establishment of viable local institutions and the righting of social and economic wrongs. He asked whether the government really believed that the people of Ireland would accept 'unconstitutional measures . . . to which [the government] dare not resort for the administration of England'. He ended, prophetically, by arguing that unconstitutional laws in Ireland might, by the passage of time, habit, and precedent, be more easily 'put in force in England' (all quoted in Palmer 1988: 242).

By this time the Peelers had some 2300 men in sixteen counties but the new Act saw their numbers quickly decline as the Irish Constabulary was developed. Within two years, there were nearly 6000 in the new force compared with approximately 100 Peelers. Further centralization of the police in Ireland occurred in 1836, when the various local forces were brought together under the control of a supra-provincial inspector-general, except for the police in Dublin, Belfast and Derry. These police developments were later to have a profound impact on the development of policing in Britain and the Empire. Many of the ideas expressed in the secret plans for a 'unified system of policing' formulated in Dublin Castle in 1787, together with the practical experiences of the Irish Constabulary, were drawn upon in the development of the new police systems in England and Wales.

By 1840 there were therefore two highly centralized and militarized police forces in Ireland whose personnel and resources were increasing rapidly. In 1840, for example, in total there were over 8000 police or 106 per 100,000 of the population, while by the middle of the century, there were 13,500 police officers or 208 per 100,000. At the same time the number of troops based in Ireland was at least 25,000 (Boyle, Hadden and Hillyard, 1975: 172–3). By the time of the Great Famine in 1846 there were nearly 30,000 security personnel in place to police a population of some 8 million people, roughly the same size of force which has been in place in the north of Ireland since 1969 to police a population of around 1.5 million people.[3]

Throughout this period the army and the police were provided with an impressive battery of coercive legislation to deal with the perceived disorder. For example, the government introduced an Irish version of the English Riot Act – the Irish Riot Act 1787 – in an attempt to deal with the situation in rural areas where there was widespread organized protest. It contained a number of harsh clauses to deal with the special character of the protest.[4] The Irish Riot Act was initially renewed every three years, but was then made permanent in 1800 – a pattern which was to become common for all subsequent emergency legislation in these islands.[5] In the nineteenth century there were further repressive laws. In 1829, Peel remarked that 'for scarcely a year during the period that has elapsed since the Union has Ireland been governed by the ordinary law' (quoted in Palmer, 1988: 117). But this pattern was to continue to the end of the union in 1921, a period in which no fewer than 105 separate Acts of coercion were enacted (Farrell, 1986: 5; see also Broeker, 1979; Townshend, 1983). Most of the current legislation to deal with political violence was portended by these Acts (Hogan and Walker, 1989).

Moreover, these formal methods of policing operated alongside a complex informal system of justice. In 1868, for example, an official observed in a quote which summarizes so much about the unhappy relationship between England and Ireland and between colonial law and the law of the people:

> We are under two different and repugnant systems of law. One enacted in Parliament and enforced by the Courts – the other is concocted in the whiskey-shop and executed by the assassin. And the law of the people is far better enforced than that of the Government. More who break it are generally sure to be detected, for their offences are generally public, the punishment is as severe as any man can inflict or suffer, and the chances of escaping it are few. The popular law, therefore, is obeyed; the Government law is disregarded. (Senior, 1868)

Lewis (1977), in the first sociological analysis of crime in Ireland, was more objective in his observations. Instead of focusing on the legal definition of crime and differences between crimes against the person and crimes against property, he concentrated on motives and argued that most crime in Ireland had an 'exemplary' or 'preventive' purpose. Acts of violence and murder were carried out on behalf of a class of people – the Irish peasantry. Far from being self-serving and individualistic, as with most crime in England at the time, it was social and collective (Lewis, 1977).[6]

What this brief historical analysis shows is that policing in Ireland in the period prior to the setting-up of the Northern Ireland state was characterized by a centralized, armed police force backed up by a large army and a battery of extraordinary legislation.[7] The notion of the 'rule of law' had little meaning in the absence of authority and legitimacy and the presence of an informal system of justice. Coercion was the dominant characteristic in much of the period and, as Strauss put it, 'The excessive use of force by the authorities was an indication of the popular opposition to "common and statute law" and the other activities of Dublin Castle' (Strauss, 1951).

THE PARTITION OF IRELAND

The Government of Ireland Act 1920 created two home-rule parliaments in Ireland, one in the Northern six counties and the other in the remaining 26.[8] After a period of armed conflict, the British Army and the Ulster Special Constabulary were able to impose some sort of order on a reluctant Roman Catholic minority. Partition, far from being the only possible democratic solution, simply served to reproduce and exacerbate the divisions between Protestant and Catholic in a smaller territory and it was inevitable that the forms of social control which had dominated the whole of Ireland for hundreds of years should be reproduced in Northern Ireland.[9] As Joe Lee (1989) in his comprehensive and insightful history of twentieth-century Ireland argues:

> The border was not devised to keep two warring groups apart. The Catholic minority in the Northern Ireland was proportionately larger than the Protestant minority in Ireland as a whole. This brought the warring groups together more than it separated them . . . [Its objective] was . . . to ensure Protestant supremacy over Catholics even in predominantly Catholic areas. The British government of 1920 bore

no immediate responsibilities for the racial and religious antagonism in Ulster. It does bear responsibility for imposing a 'solution' to the Ulster question that contained within it the seeds of fresh struggle . . . A border justifiable only on the basis of racial supremacy was bound to do so. (1989: 45–6)

Following the establishment of the first parliament in Belfast in 1921, which was dominated by the Unionist Party, a new police force – the Royal Ulster Constabulary (RUC) – was established to replace the Royal Irish Constabulary (RIC)[10] and measures were taken to safeguard its position from rebellion. The new force, one-third of which were to be Catholics, was recruited partly from the ex-RIC but more importantly from what was known as the A Specials – the full-time section of the Ulster Special Constabulary. This had been formed prior to the setting up of the state after the British government became concerned about the lack of troops in the Northern counties. Most of its recruits came from the Ulster Volunteer Force, which had been set up illegally in 1912 in response to the British government's decision to grant a limited measure of self-government or 'Home Rule' to the island of Ireland and from the Imperial Guard which had been formed after the truce in the War of Independence in July 1921 (Farrell, 1983). As a result of recruiting predominantly from this latter source, the composition of the RUC became overwhelmingly Protestant with only 21 per cent drawn from the Catholic community. By the 1930s this had dropped to 17 per cent, and by the start of the troubles in 1969 to 11 per cent. The Catholic composition of the RUC now stands in the 1990s at some 8 per cent.

The RUC was supported in its policing role by the B Specials – a part-time section of the Ulster Special Constabulary. At the same time the police were given considerable powers under the Civil Authorities (Special Powers) Act Northern Ireland 1922 – in popular parlance the Special Powers Act – which effectively annulled the fundamental legal rights of citizens against arbitrary arrest and imprisonment, and it gave almost unrestricted powers to the Minister of Home Affairs to make whatever regulations he considered necessary to maintain order.

It is not the purpose of this chapter to describe in detail the next fifty years of policing. Suffice it to say that the characteristics of social control differed little from those in the whole of Ireland in the previous century with similar concerns about coercion, centralization and the religious composition of the force. The Civil Rights Movement took up these issues in their demands for reforms in the late 1960s.

The main point to emphasize is that the form of social control in Northern Ireland was a product of the divisions which were entrenched and exacerbated by partition. Like 'the dreary steeples of Fermanagh and Tyrone' to borrow from Winston Churchill's famous passage in 1922 in which he attempted to imply that Britain was a benign government acting to deal with an insoluble problem, the same policing form has a nasty habit of 'emerging once again'.

DEVELOPMENTS IN POLICING NORTHERN IRELAND:
1969–95

Following the outbreak of the troubles, the introduction of the British Army in 1969, and the rise of the Irish Republican Army (IRA) as a military force in late 1970, a number of key developments in policing took place over the next ten years. Three of the most important trends have now acquired descriptive labels – militarization, Ulsterization and professionalization – and have been extensively described already (see for example, Boyle, Hadden and Hillyard, 1975; O'Dowd, Rolston and Tomlinson, 1980; Weitzer, 1990; Hillyard, 1994). But a fourth trend – the increased use of undercover and clandestine surveillance, and the heavy reliance on the use of informers to supply information on those involved in political violence, which began in earnest in the late 1970s, has still to acquire a label. As similar trends are now clearly identifiable in Britain, there is need for a descriptive label to capture this development. In this chapter 'covertization' will be used to describe this important trend.

The trend towards further militarization of the police following the breakdown of law and order in 1969 was inevitable. While in 1970 the Hunt Committee recommended an unarmed, civilianized service answerable to the public it served, this was not to come to fruition (Hunt Report, 1969). Although the government moved quickly on setting up a police authority, disbanded the B Specials and established a new force, the Ulster Defence Regiment (UDR), under the control of the British Army, the plans to disarm the RUC were dropped in the face of attacks by the IRA. The subsequent years saw an increased militarization of the police as the level of political violence increased. The Special Powers Act was repealed and in 1973 the Northern Ireland (Emergency Provisions) Act was introduced which provided the police and army with extensive new powers and made provision for radical changes in the criminal justice system, including the abolition of trial by jury. Further exceptional powers were introduced in the Prevention of Terrorism Act 1974 which applied to the whole of the United Kingdom (Hillyard, 1993). Both pieces of legislation have been further amended and extended in recent years, a process which Ni Aolain (1996) has called 'the fortification of an emergency regime'.

During these early years of the conflict the army took the primary role, although by the mid-1970s the government switched strategy, a move which was to have a profound consequence for the police's counter-insurgency role and an equally important consequence on the social composition of the security forces. In 1976, Merlyn Rees, the then Labour Secretary of State for Northern Ireland, announced a new policy known as 'the primacy of the police' or Ulsterization. This meant that the police were given primary responsibility for the security situation and this was followed by an expansion in both the RUC and the UDR. This shift meant that instead of the political violence being policed principally by the army, and therefore made up of people from outside Northern Ireland, it was now policed by people from within Northern Ireland. As both the RUC and the UDR were predominantly Protestant, this shift further polarized society in Northern Ireland and increased the Protestant character of the security forces. At the outbreak of the troubles the total person power of the RUC, B specials and the British Army was almost 11,600. Following the reforms three years later this number had tripled to 33,000. By the end of the decade the number of full-time and part-time members of the security forces dropped to around 30,000 – roughly the same number of security personnel policing the whole of Ireland in the middle of the nineteenth century. It represented some 206 per 100,000 of the population.

The third trend, professionalization, has taken place without the same level of public attention. The RUC now uses a range of modern management and training techniques and has adopted a clear set of force objectives. The Chief Constable's annual reports are replete with statements noting the new professionalism. This professionalization will be taken further if recommendations of a recent White Paper are adopted. It argues for the adoption in Northern Ireland of the police reforms introduced in England and Wales under the Police and Magistrates' Courts Act 1994. In essence these reforms impose a much stricter managerial structure of accountability on the police. In return for control of the budget, the Chief Constable will be required to produce a clear statement of objectives, which in the first instance will be produced by the Secretary of State for Northern Ireland and then extended by the Police Authority for Northern Ireland. These objectives will then be monitored by means of performance indicators (Northern Ireland Office, 1996).

A study by Weitzer (1990) of the RUC has suggested that it is now one of the most professional police forces in the world, having shown outstanding professionalism, as well as bravery, in the face of twenty-five years of continuing hostility from a determined and ruthless terrorist organization resulting in the death of 189 of its members. He argues:

> Under British rule the RUC's mission changed from that of defending a social order based on Protestant supremacy to enforcing the law impartially in a society undergoing transition away from Protestant domination . . . [It] clearly pays greater attention than in the past to Catholic sensitivities and shows less favouritism toward Protestants. (1990: 68)

In his view, then, significant reforms have taken place, but he also acknowledges that the demands of the counter-insurgency role places very real restrictions on police liberalization. He then suggests a number of ways in which counter-insurgency policing can itself be partially liberalized.

There are, however, problems with Weitzer's analysis. To begin with it overlooks the numerous lapses of the impartial and professional application of the rule of law: the harassment of members of the Catholic community on the streets; the beating of suspects in custody; the shoot-to-kill incidents; collusion between the security forces and Protestant paramilitaries; and the intimidation of lawyers. Second, it implies that once the political violence stops and the RUC can move away from a counter-insurgency role, then liberal imperatives will dominate. Weitzer also seems to suggest that the fundamental problem of the alienation of large sections of the nationalist population will disappear. This all assumes that ideology alone is sufficient to change the form of policing and neglects the structural problems and the historical legacy which are responsible for the divide in the first place.

The fourth trend, the greater use of covert methods (covertization) was given added impetus in August 1979 following the assassination of Lord Mountbatten and the killing of 18 soldiers at Warrenpoint. The then British Prime Minister, Margaret Thatcher, visited Northern Ireland and was told that the strategy of Ulsterization had failed and that the army should once again take the dominant role. Thatcher's response was to appoint Sir Maurice Oldfield, who had recently retired from MI6, to the post of Security Co-ordinator. His remit was to sort out the differences in approach between the two forces, although he went much further and put in place a new security strategy which relied heavily on covert operations. This has been summed up in a security report at the end of 1981:

> Current policy emphasizes 'low profile' and covert intelligence operations – plain-clothes surveillance, camouflaged observation posts, covert photography, fewer foot patrols and more [patrols] in unmarked vehicles. The SAS has been in the vanguard of the change to covert action, but SAS-trained soldiers from conventional units are now carrying out an increasing share of the undercover operations. (Charters, Graham and Tugwell, 1981)

Developments in the technology of surveillance have facilitated the shift towards more covert policing. Northern Ireland became an attractive market as well as a site for the testing of equipment by some of the biggest manufacturers in internal security or IS, as the manuals euphemistically describe the purpose of their wares. The security services have used a variety of different covert technologies including: helicopter monitoring equipment with surveillance and night vision cameras; telephone taps; advanced communications and automatic vehicle tracking systems; computerized data and intelligence banks with remote access to terminals in police vehicles and at border check-points; and surveillance equipment which can monitor houses and other areas.

The increase in surveillance has been accompanied by a greater use of informers. Historically, of course, informers have been used in Ireland over many centuries in an attempt to combat political violence. But from the late 1970s the importance of the informer to the army, the police and MI5 expanded greatly. Typically they were recruited after being arrested, and from all accounts the techniques used to persuade people to become informers were often unscrupulous. John Stalker (1988) expressed considerable concern about the way informers were used:

> I suspected that government guidelines were regularly being breached, and almost certainly in the three cases I was investigating. The absolute rule laid down by the Home Office in a document they describe as *Guidelines for the Police in the Use of Informants* is that an informant must never initiate crimes that would otherwise not take place. An informant must never be used as an agent provocateur, and he must not be allowed by the police freely to commit crime himself in return for giving information. The reality in Northern

Ireland is worlds away from those perfectly proper rules. In order to establish his terrorist credentials in the Province an informant may have to commit serious crime, possibly even murder. (1988: 71)

Another glimpse into this underground and unaccountable world emerged during and following the trial of Brian Nelson. Nelson was the intelligence officer for the paramilitary Protestant Ulster Defence Association and at the same time he worked for the Field Research Unit (FRU), an army unit set up in 1980 to gather its own intelligence. While on remand he wrote a 90,000-word account of his experiences on which a BBC *Panorama* programme was based. Nelson alleged that the FRU had knowledge about who was being targeted and in some cases it assisted with photographs of intended targets and premises. He also alleged that it helped him organize and collate his intelligence files. One target, who was subsequently killed, worked as an informer for the RUC and was part of the IRA's counter-informer unit. It is also alleged that the FRU knew that Pat Finucane, a solicitor, was a target. Finucane was subsequently murdered in 1989. Nelson's account illustrates well the considerable collusion between the army and the loyalist assassination squads (Amnesty International, 1994; *Statewatch*, 1994a).

Militarization, Ulsterization, professionalization and covertization have taken place against the backdrop of considerable criticisms by the Catholic community of the RUC and security services, the use of the emergency powers and the abolition of juries and the partial abolition of the right to silence. There has been and continues to be very little confidence in the formal system of law and order. As a result informal methods of justice have emerged. Attempts were made, for example, in the early 1970s in nationalist areas to set up people's courts and the IRA have introduced, often with the support of elements of the community, their own forms of policing and punishment to deal with what they consider to be illegalities. What is important about these systems, if the brutal nature of some of the punishments is discarded, is that, like the formal system, they are a product of historical and structural factors (Hillyard, 1985; Munck, 1985, 1988). Partly as a result of the lack of acceptance of the legitimacy of the RUC and partly in an attempt to assert their own legitimacy in certain areas, the paramilitaries developed popular forms of justice. Both systems have used a variety of devices in order to justify their existence including appeals to the 'other'. At a very basic level this has involved the mobilization of political discourses about the legitimacy or illegitimacy of the state itself (Hillyard, 1985).

CONFLICT, ECONOMY AND SOCIAL STRUCTURE

All too often, descriptions of the changing nature of policing stop at this point and there is little attempt to explore the impact of these changes on the broader structures of society. Yet these developments do not take place in a vacuum: they have a profound impact on both the economy and the social structure. The Northern Ireland economy has long been in decline and there are now more people on the unemployment register than in the manufacturing sector. That said, the conflict has itself created new employment opportunities, not only for those who join the security services but also for those who are employed in various other parts of the control industry, from checking the bags of customers as they enter shops to patrolling private spaces. In addition, there are hundreds of people employed in dealing with the consequences of the political violence, such as replacing windows or providing a service to those affected by an explosion. Moreover, thousands of new jobs have been created in Northern Ireland and elsewhere to produce IS equipment. Indeed, it is calculated that as many as one-quarter of the full-time workforce in Northern Ireland is now employed directly or indirectly in some aspect of the conflict (Tomlinson, 1994: 14).

Ulsterization has had a particular impact on employment and has changed the composition of the security personnel radically. Instead of being policed by people from outside Northern Ireland, three-quarters of the security forces personnel are now from within Northern Ireland, and the vast majority are Protestant (Hillyard, 1988). As the manufacturing sector declined, policing, in the widest sense of the word, increasingly provided significant employment opportunities for the Protestant community. The Catholic community, because of their alienation from the state and their lack of confidence in the forces of law and order, had few equivalent opportunities. Thus, it can be suggested that, on one level, policing policy can be seen as playing a part in maintaining the unemployment differential between the two communities which throughout the troubles has shown Catholics as being two times more likely to be unemployed than Protestants (PPRU, 1994).

The economic costs of the conflict have also been considerable. Tomlinson (1994: 32) has estimated that the total cost of the war since 1969 has been at least £23.5 billion. In 1994 the total cost of the British Army, the RUC, the prison and court systems came to around £1 billion, constituting one-seventh of all public expenditure in Northern Ireland. To sustain this level of expenditure, a substantial subvention of around £3 billion per annum (that is, the difference between

the amount raised in taxes in Northern Ireland and the amount of public expenditure) has to be made by British tax-payers.

From this broader perspective, it is possible to suggest that the control of political violence has had a profound and historic effect on the
social divisions and social structure in Northern Ireland. The liveli-
hood and material circumstances of a large segment of the population
is now dependent on the conflict. In addition, the polarization of the
two communities has increased not only because of the direct effects
of violence, but also because of its impact on the labour market. The
problems of moving away from what is now a deeply entrenched social
control economy are considerable. Put crudely, any settlement which
includes agreement over the future form of policing will have direct
consequences for thousands employed in the security services and
throughout the control industry.

The problem of redeployment specifically applies to a number of
British personnel working in Northern Ireland. It is claimed that as
many as 60 per cent of MI5 operatives work in Ireland, and if there
was a comprehensive peace settlement, the services of these operatives
will no longer be required and they will face the prospect of redun-
dancy or redeployment. Indeed, the decision to expand the role of MI5
to conduct intelligence-gathering in criminal cases in Britain may well
be related to MI5's future employment prospects in Ireland.

From the above discussion, it is clear that there are a number of
important sociological observations about policing which can be drawn
together at this point. First, it is clear that the form of policing in
Ireland has always been a product of the configuration of specific power
relations. In eighteenth and nineteenth century Ireland, policing was a
direct expression of British rule. Following partition and the establishment of a state with a built-in Unionist majority and a minority which
was proportionately greater than the Protestant minority in the whole
of Ireland, it was inevitable that the social divisions between the two
communities would be further exacerbated and that the characteristics
of policing and social control would differ little from the system which
preceded it. Policing was a direct expression of Protestant rule in Northern
Ireland. Similarly, any hopes of a less repressive and more representative police service following the demands of the Civil Rights Movement were bound to be short-lived before there was a return in the
face of IRA violence to a militarized form of policing backed up by
the army, a battery of repressive legislation, and radical and far-reaching reforms of the criminal justice process. Second, the development
of different forms of policing have had a profound impact on the economy

and social structure. Social control in the North of Ireland is now very much a part of the market economy and the Protestant community has a very real material interest in policing and social control. Third, notwithstanding the amount of money spent on, and the sophistication of, the repressive apparatus, the intensity of conflict has altered little over the period. From a comparative perspective Northern Ireland has remained one of the most internally politically violent of the recognizably continuous liberal democracies between 1948 and 1977 (O'Leary and McGarry, 1993).

POLICING IN NORTHERN IRELAND AND TRENDS IN BRITAIN

There are clear signs that similar developments are occurring in the face of very different, but nevertheless equally important, social divisions and conflict within British society. The principal social divisions are between the rich and the poor and between ethnic minorities and the majority white population. The share of the disposable household income of the poorest fifth of the population declined between 1979 and 1990–91 from 10 per cent to 6 per cent, while that of the richest 20 per cent increased from 35 per cent to 43 per cent. In cash terms this meant a loss for the poorest of £17 billion and a gain of £35 billion for the rich (Townsend, 1994). These divisions are now greater than at any time since income statistics were introduced.

The principal conflict, although it is rarely put this way, is centred around crime. Every year millions of people suffer some form of loss, damage or injury as a result of crime. Some of this harm is dealt with through informal negotiation in the family, school or workplace, while other harms are dealt with through some form of administrative action or the civil law. But an increasing proportion of the incidents leading to harm are now being criminalized and made subject to criminal law. The dominant characteristic of this criminalization process is that the state takes over the conflict between the two parties (Christie, 1977).[11] Thus on one side in this conflict is the state and its professionals together with an increasing number of people employed by private security firms. On the other are thousands of individuals, mostly young men, many of whom are poor and lacking in education, with a disproportionate number drawn from the ethnic minority community, who are defined as being involved in criminal incidents.

The numbers involved in what is sometimes referred to as 'the war against crime' has been increasing rapidly.[12] The number of police personnel has grown from 108,000 in 1979 to 141,000 in 1994, an increase of nearly 10 per cent. At the same time the police have expanded the number of civilian staff they employ from 36,000 to 48,000 (Home Office, 1995a). There are now 228 police officers for every 100,000 people. The increase in private security personnel has been even more rapid. It is estimated that there are now approximately 162,000 people employed in the private security industry, a 50 per cent increase in ten years. In 1990 the annual turnover was estimated at 1.5 billion per annum and it is an industry which is growing by 20 per cent annually (Jones and Newburn, 1995). Similar expansion has occurred in sections of the penal system. For example, the number of prison officers has more than doubled between 1971 and 1994 to 38,000, which represents 74 per 100,000 of the population.

It is unsurprising therefore that the number of individuals subject to some action by the criminal justice 'army' has also steadily increased. The number of people arrested in England and Wales has grown from 1.2 million in 1981 to 1.75 million in 1994 – a rise of 45 per cent.[13] The number of people imprisoned is now 57,000 – the highest ever recorded (*The Guardian*, 30 September 1996). In 1971 the incarceration rate was 78 per 100,000, while in 1995 it had risen to 98 per 100,000. Figures recently published by the Home Office (1996b: 128–9) show a very strong racial component in the incarceration rates. Excluding foreign nationals and children under 16, the incarceration rate for whites in 1995 was 134 per 100,000 and 1049 per 100,000 for black people (see also FitzGerald and Marshall, 1996).

Moreover, it is clear that the policing of such conflict, as in Northern Ireland, is becoming increasingly militarized and covertized. An important turning point for the militarization of the police was the coal dispute of 1984–85 when the police were forced to adopt military-style tactics to defeat the miners (Fine and Miller, 1985), since which time the battle against drugs and organized crime as well as the continuing struggle to deal with political violence connected with Northern Ireland has played an ever-increasing part in creating a more military style of policing. For example, the number of police officers trained in the use of firearms has increased over recent years and the presence of armed officers at airports and in other public places has become much more commonplace. The recent decision of a number of police forces to provide all their officers with CS spray is another indication of the general direction towards militarization.

At the same time, policing in Britain is becoming more proactive and much more covert. One turning point in the covertization of the police was the publication of a report in 1993, from a most unlikely source – the Audit Commission (1993). It argued that the police were in danger 'of losing the battle against crime', and therefore recommended a shift to a much more proactive strategy based on the collection and analysis of intelligence. To obtain this intelligence it proposed the increased use of surveillance and informers. Indeed, while recognizing the high cost of surveillance, it considered the use of informers to be cost-effective, a view which has been strongly challenged recently by Dunningham and Norris (1995).

Another step in this direction was the government's decision to extend MI5's 'counter-subversion' role to normal policing activities. In 1989, MI5 successfully campaigned to take over the lead role for counter-terrorism inside the United Kingdom from the Special Branch. In 1993, the then Home Secretary, Kenneth Clarke, in a letter to Tony Blair (then Shadow Home Secretary), indicated that MI5 would only become involved in the fight against drugs and organized crime if, 'the level of such criminal activity would have risen to such a point, and would evidently have done so, that it constituted a threat to national security' (*Statewatch*, 1994b). However, even at the time of writing the letter, MI5 was consolidating its position with the development of new links with the police force as a result of its anti-terrorist work. It had considerable experience in covert surveillance, such as telephone tapping, mail-opening and bugging homes and offices, and had a distinct advantage of having few problems with accountability.[14] It therefore came as no surprise that the government introduced a Bill at the end of 1995 to extend the role of MI5 to the prevention and detection of serious crime. The subsequent Security Services Act 1996 will radically extend the use of surveillance, informants and infiltrating agents, technical devices such as hidden bugs, video cameras and tracking devices in the detection of serious crime (*Statewatch*, 1996). A number of MPs expressed concern about the lack of clarity on what was meant by serious crime and the lack of any clear mechanisms of accountability of MI5, but to no avail.

A more visible manifestation of a more covert form of policing is the phenomenal spread in the use of closed-circuit television (CCTV), mainly under the control of local authorities and private security firms, to survey public and private spaces. The spread has been encouraged by the provision of over £22 million of government money in two separate 'Challenge Competitions' and a further £15 million has been promised for a third competition. Successful applicants are expected to contribute a further £7 million towards the cost of the schemes, bringing the total expenditure on CCTV in three years to at least £60 million.

These developments in British policing are creating, as in Northern Ireland, new jobs for thousands of people. There are new opportunities in the public police and in private security firms, in the manufacture of equipment for crime control, and numerous other related areas such as the insurance industry and universities. Crime control in all its manifestations is an expanding area of the economy which has been encouraged by privatization and increasingly by the unification of Europe.[15] As Christie (1993) has pointed out, the crime control industry is uniquely placed to deal with the major problems facing Britain and other modern societies, such as the ever-increasing inequalities in wealth and access to work and the associated possibility of social unrest because, 'It provides profits and work while at the same time producing control of those who might otherwise have disturbed the social process' (Christie, 1993: 11). And, of course, it has unlimited potential for growth. In such a context where thousands of people have a vested interest in the expansion of the industry, crime control in all its dimensions will become even more deeply embedded in the social structure of modern Britain.

THE FUTURE

From this analysis the development of policing does not look particularly hopeful anywhere in Ireland or Britain. In Northern Ireland there is little optimism that there will be a comprehensive settlement which would include the development of new forms of policing. The distribution of power between the two communities is too one-sided and the most powerful player – the British government – partly as a result of its own precarious position, has dragged its feet in the process. In addition, it has been totally unwilling to put pressure on the Protestant community to encourage it to reach a comprehensive settlement, notwithstanding the mounting costs to the British Exchequer of the conflict. At the same time, the Protestant community has not produced any leader who is prepared to lead and say that it is in everyone's interest to talk and negotiate a settlement which would bring a lasting peace. There is thus a very real danger that there will be a return to conflict and the targeting of key economic sites in Britain. In such a context there is likely to be further militarization and covertization of policing in Northern Ireland. In any event, even if there is a settlement, the growing inequalities in both the north and south of Ireland will lead to an intensification of a different war – the 'war against crime'.

In Britain there is little prospect that a change of government will radically reduce the growing social divisions. A new Labour government might improve the employment opportunities for a section of young men who are currently excluded from the labour market, but it is hard to see how it will be able to stem the tide of unemployment resulting from the broad trends in the global economy. Moreover, the Labour Party is as committed as the Conservative Party in making a political issue out of law and order and hence intensifying the conflict around crime.

Gatrell (1990), in his classic piece on the police state, argued that the history of crime is largely a history of social divisions, of how better-off people disciplined their inferiors. It has always been about how bureaucrats, experts and the police have used crime to justify their own expanding functions and influences. As he points out, the history of crime is a grim subject, 'not because it is about crime but because it is about power'. It is a quote which sums up well what the British/Irish crisis is about too.

Notes

1. I would like to thank Peter Francis, Michael Naughton and Margaret Ward for comments on an earlier draft of this chapter.
2. It is invidious to select out any one person, but a relevant example in terms of the arguments developed here is Reiner's (1985) *The Politics of the Police*, which provides an extensive analysis of the 'birth of the blues', yet there is no mention of the extent to which their birth owes much to their parents' experiences in Ireland. As Palmer (1988: 27–8) has commented, 'The reluctance of modern English police historians to cross the Irish sea would have surprised Robert Peel who made the crossing many times'.
3. Apart from Palmer's definitive history of policing in Ireland, see also Boyle (1973, 1987) and Breathnach (1974).
4. Much of the rural protest was organized by secret societies requiring an oath. The Irish Riot Act made administering an illegal oath punishable by transportation for life.
5. For example, the Civil Authorities (Special Powers) Act (Northern Ireland) 1922 was enacted from year to year and then made permanent in 1933. The Prevention of Terrorism (Temporary Provisions) Act has to be renewed annually by Order but it no longer has an expiry date. Currently, Lord Lloyd is conducting an inquiry into counter-terrorism legislation and it is expected that he will recommend a permanent replacement of emergency powers (Ni Aolain, 1996: 1375).

6. It is interesting to note that Lewis anticipated Schafer's analysis of the 'convictional criminal' by well over a hundred years (Schafer, 1971).
7. There were, of course, quiet periods and towards the end of the century the RIC developed a stronger civil policing role. However, in essence it always remained a colonial force imposing order on a disaffected population.
8. The British Cabinet had wanted the nine counties of Ulster included in Northern Ireland, but it agreed under Unionist pressure to include only six counties as this was the size of the territory which they could safely control.
9. The impact of this history in the south of Ireland has also been significant. As Fennell (1993: 12) has pointed out: 'Since the repressive regime of the eighteenth century, a lot has changed in criminal justice but it should not be forgotten that the origins of this structure are bloody: the legacy it left, a commitment to a recognition of the unequal nature of the balance between the citizen and the state.'
10. Queen Victoria bestowed the title Royal on the Irish Constabulary in 1867 after it had 'saved' the country from a Fenian uprising. The prefix was also granted to the new Ulster Constabulary when it was set up in 1922. It is interesting to observe that the prefix has never been granted to any British police force.
11. As Christie (1981: 74) points out: 'Crime is not a "thing". Crime is a concept applicable in certain social situations where it is in the interests of one or several parties to apply it. We can create crime by treating systems that ask for the word. We can extinguish crime by crea ng the opposite type of systems.'
12. Feeley and Simon (1994: 193–6) also conceptualize the response to violence and other forms of illegalities as a 'war' and develop an interesting comparison between the *intifada* and South Central Los Angeles but their emphasis is on notions of actuarial justice and governmentality rather than on the political economy of this form of social order.
13. It is estimated that over a third of those arrested in 1994 were freed without any further action after their details were recorded by the police.
14. Under the Security Services Act 1989 a Commissioner submits an annual and very brief report to Parliament which is never debated. Complaints may be made to a Tribunal but it has never found in favour of a complaint.
15. The unification of Europe is leading to a considerable expansion of the surveillance and intelligence capacities of all European police forces under the Schengen and Europol agreements.

References

Amnesty International (1994) *United Kingdom: Political Killings in Northern Ireland* (London: Amnesty International).

Audit Commission (1993) *Helping with Enquiries: Tackling Crime Effectively* (London: HMSO).

Boyle, K. (1972) 'Police in Ireland before the Union', *The Irish Jurist*, n.s., vol. 7, pp. 115–37.

Boyle, K. (1973) 'Police in Ireland before the Union', *The Irish Jurist*, n.s. vol. 8, pp. 90–116, 323–48.

Boyle, K., Hadden, T. and Hillyard, P. (1975) *Law and State: The Case of Northern Ireland* (London: Martin Robertson).

Breathnach, S. (1974) *The Irish Police from Earliest Times to the Present Day* (Dublin: Anvil Books).

Broeker, G. (1979) *Rural Disorder and Police Reform in Ireland 1812–36* (London: Routledge & Kegan Paul).

Brogden, M. (1987) 'An act to colonize the internal lands of the island: empire and the origins of the professional police', *International Journal of the Sociology of Law*, vol. 15, pp. 179–208.

Charters, D., Graham, D. and Tugwell, M. (1981) *Trends in Low Intensity Conflict* (Ottawa: Operational Research and Analysis Establishment, Department of National Defence).

Christie, N. (1977) 'Conflicts as property', *British Journal of Criminology*, vol. 17, pp. 1–19.

Christie, N. (1981) *Limits to Pain* (Oxford: Oxford University Press).

Christie, N. (1993) *Crime Control as Industry* (London: Routledge).

Clark, S. and Donnelly, J. S. (eds) (1983) *Irish Peasants: Violence and Political Unrest 1780–1914* (Wisconsin: University of Wisconsin Press).

Curtis, L. and Jempson, M. (1993) *Interference on the Airwaves: Ireland, the Media and the Broadcasting Ban* (London: Campaign for Press and Broadcasting Freedom).

Dunningham, C. and Norris, C. (1995) 'The detective, the snout and the Audit Commission: the real costs in using informants', unpublished paper presented to the British Criminology Conference, University of Loughborough, July 1995.

Farrell, M. (1983) *Arming the Protestants: The Formation of the Ulster Special Constabulary and the Royal Irish Constabulary 1920–1927* (Dingle: Brandon).

Farrell, M. (1986) *The Apparatus of Repression* (Derry: Field Day).

Feeley, M. and Simon, J. (1994) 'Actuarial justice: the emerging new criminal law', in D. Nelken (ed.), *The Futures of Criminology* (London: Sage).

Fennell, C. (1993) *Crime and Crisis in Ireland: Justice by Illusion* (Cork: Cork University Press).

Fine, B. and Millar, R. (eds) (1985) *Policing the Miners' Strike* (London: Lawrence & Wishart).

FitzGerald, M. and Marshall, P. (1996) 'Ethnic minorities in British prisons', in R. Matthews and P. Francis (eds), *Prisons 2000: An International Perspective on the Present State and Future of Imprisonment* (London: Macmillan).

Gatrell, V. A. C. (1990) 'Crime, authority and the policeman-state', in F. M. L. Thompson (ed.), *The Cambridge Social History of Britain, 1750–1950, Volume 3, Social Agencies and Institutions* (Cambridge: Cambridge University Press).

Hillyard, P. (1985) 'Popular justice in Northern Ireland: continuities and change', in S. Spitzer (ed.), *Research and Law, Deviance and Social Control*, Vol. 7 (Greenwich Connecticut: Jai Press).

Hillyard, P. (1988) 'Political and social dimensions of Emergency Law in Northern Ireland', in A. Jennings (ed.), *Justice under Fire: The Abuse of Civil Liberties in Northern Ireland* (London: Pluto Press).

Hillyard, P. (1993) *Suspect Community: People's Experience of the Prevention of Terrorism Acts in Britain* (London: Pluto Press).
Hillyard, P. (1994) 'The normalization of special powers', in N. Lacey (ed.), *A Reader on Criminal Justice* (Oxford: Oxford University Press).
Hogan, G. and Walker, C. (1989) *Political Violence and the Law in Ireland* (Manchester: Manchester University Press).
Home Office (1995a) *Digest 3*: Information on the Criminal Justice System in England and Wales (London: HMSO).
Home Office (1996b) 'More winners switch on CCTV to stamp out crime', *News Release*, 186/96, 21 June.
Home Office (1996c), *Prison Statistics England and Wales, 1995*, Cm 3355 (London: HMSO).
Hunt Report (1969) *The Advisory Committee on Police in Northern Ireland*, Cm 535 (London: HMSO).
Jeffries, C. (1952) *The Colonial Police* (London: Max Parrish).
Jones, T. and Newburn, T. (1995) 'How big is the private security sector?', *Policing and Society*, vol. 5, pp. 221–32.
Lee, J. J. (1989) *Ireland 1912–1985: Politics and Society* (Cambridge: Cambridge University Press).
Lewis, G. C. (1977) *Local Disturbances in Ireland* (Cork: Tower Books).
Munck, R. (1985) 'Repression, insurgency and popular justice: the Irish case', *Crime and Social Justice*, vol. 21/22, pp. 81–94.
Munck, R. (1988), 'The lads and the hoods: alternative justice in an Irish context', in M. Tomlinson, T. Varley, and C. McCullagh (eds), *Whose Law and Order?* (Dublin: Sociological Association of Ireland).
Murray, D. (1995) 'Culture, religion and violence', in S. Dunn (ed.), *Facets of the Conflict in Northern Ireland* (London: MacMillan).
Ni Aolain, F. (1996) 'The fortification of an emergency regime', *Albany Law Review*, vol. 59, no. 4, pp. 1353–87.
Northern Ireland Office (1996) *Foundations for Policing: Proposals for Policing Structures in Northern Ireland*, Cm 3249 (London: HMSO).
O'Dowd, L., Rolston, B. and Tomlinson, M. (1980) *Northern Ireland: Between Civil Rights and Civil War* (London: CSE Books).
O'Leary, B. and McGarry, J. (1993) *The Politics of Antagonism: Understanding Northern Ireland* (London: Athlone Press).
Palmer, S. H. (1988) *Police and Protest in England and Ireland 1780–1850* (New York: Cambridge University Press).
PPRU (1994) *1993 Labour Force Survey: Religion Report*, PPRU Monitor 2/94 (Belfast: Department of Finance and Personnel, Stormont).
Reiner, R. (1985) *The Politics of the Police* (Brighton: Wheatsheaf Books).
Schafer, S. (1971) 'The political criminal', *Journal of Criminal Law, Criminology and Police Science*, vol. 62, no. 3, pp. 380–7.
Senior, N. W. (1868) *Journals, Conversations and Essays Relating to Ireland* (London: Corsholle).
Stalker, J. (1988) *Stalker* (London: Penguin Books).
Statewatch (1994a) 'Amnesty Report on Northern Ireland', *Statewatch*, vol. 4, no. 3 (May–June), pp. 18–19.
Statewatch (1994b) 'Turf war: MI5 bids for policing role', *Statewatch*, vol. 4, no. 6 (November–December) pp. 17–19.

Statewatch (1996) 'MI5: A licence to "bug and burgle": MI5 take on a new policing role but many questions remain unanswered', *Statewatch*, vol. 6, no. 1 (January–February) pp. 19–20.

Strauss, E. (1951) *Irish Nationalism and British Democracy* (London: Methuen).

Tobias, J. J. (1972), 'Police and the public in the United Kingdom', *Journal of Contemporary History*, vol. 7, pp. 201–20.

Tomlinson, M. (1994) *25 Years On: The Costs of War and the Dividends of Peace*, the Second Annual Frank Cahill Memorial Lecture, Conway Mill, Belfast, 8 August (Belfast: West Belfast Economic Forum).

Townsend, P. (1994) 'The need of an international welfare state', in A. Jenkinson and K. Livingstone (eds), *The Future of the Welfare State* (London: Campaign for the Defence of the Welfare State).

Townshend, C. (1983) *Political Violence in Ireland, Government and Resistance Since 1848* (Oxford: Clarendon Press).

Weitzer, R. (1990) *Policing Under Fire: Ethnic Conflict and Police Community Relations in Northern Ireland* (London: Routledge).

8 Policing Communities of Risk

Les Johnston

INTRODUCTION

The contention of this chapter is a simple one: that the future lies in community policing. At first sight, this might appear to be a surprising argument. For one thing, debates about community policing are hardly new, having been in circulation for a quarter of a century in both Britain and North America. For another, many versions of community policing, far from being futuristic, are singularly backward-looking, being predicated upon some rural idyll in which social cohesion was the product of collective community sentiments. However, the concept of community policing which will be deployed in this chapter is very different from that dominating conventional debates. The future may well lie in community policing, but the communities being policed will bear little resemblance to those invoked in community police rhetoric. Rather, in this chapter communities are seen not as 'communities of collective sentiment' but as 'communities of risk'.

The chapter is divided into three sections. The first examines the concept of risk, arguing that an analysis of its contemporary forms is fundamental to any understanding of the future of policing. The second explores the concept of community policing, comparing conventional communitarian approaches to the risk-based one proposed here. The final section outlines some of the issues at stake in a future preoccupied with policing 'communities of risk'. Fundamental to any analysis of these issues is an understanding of the connections between policing, security, government and the state. Policing is defined here as a practice whose objective and intent is the promotion of security and the minimization of risk. Security, whether viewed in personal or territorial terms, is a fundamental precondition of government. Therefore, policing may be defined as that governmental practice whose object is security. Neither policing nor government are, however, the exclusive prerogative of the state, a point which becomes more and more significant with the emergence of 'communities of risk'.

RISK: EXPLANATIONS AND IMPLICATIONS

Accounting for Risk

Risk has become a dominant focus of contemporary life and an inherent feature of most forms of human conduct. Eating is risky (pesticides, additives, 'E' numbers, BSE). Breathing is risky (atmospheric pollutants). Work is risky (job-induced stress, fear of unemployment, sexual and racial harassment, repetitive strain injury). Sexual activity is risky (AIDS and other sexually transmitted conditions). Walking the streets is risky (robbers, muggers, stalkers). So is staying at home (burglars, domestic accidents). People's increased awareness of risk has been accompanied by the emergence of specialists whose declared aim is to manage and minimize its effects, including dieticians, ecologists, child protection teams, domestic violence units, counsellors, therapists, crime prevention units, commercial risk managers, vetting agencies, drug-testing services and the like. In addition, state insurance against illness and other personal misfortune has been supplemented – even supplanted – by the services of an expanding private insurance sector willing to offer protection against virtually any insurable hazard. Of course, the paradox of risk is that its very resolution may generate new dangers. The old adage that hospitals are the least healthy places in the world may be an exaggeration, but the tendency of medical intervention to generate new pathologies whilst resolving old ones – what Illich (1975) called iatrogenesis – is well-known. Illich's observation raises two issues: that risk may be constituted in the very technologies which are intended to minimize it; and that the very expertise of those who apply such technologies may be contested. All in all, then, given the apparent ubiquity of risk, the existence of specialized technologies for dealing with it and the fact that disputes about the validity of those technologies are of growing significance, it is hardly surprising that conventional wisdom holds we live in a 'risk society' (Beck, 1992).

There are two dominant explanations for our contemporary preoccupation with matters of risk. The first of these has its roots in the sociology of modernity, with the work of Giddens (1990) and Beck (1992, 1996) being especially relevant. For Giddens the reorganization of risk is an important element in the dynamics of modernity (Waters, 1995). Giddens, like Beck, has a particular interest in the question of 'how trust, risk, security and danger articulate in conditions of modernity' (Giddens, 1990: 54). To that extent, the character of modernity is encapsulated in the tension between two sets of relations: security versus danger and risk versus trust. The second of these is particularly relevant, as the relationship between risk and trust in 'high modernity' (Giddens, 1990) differs significantly from its character during the pre-modern and early modern periods. In the pre-modern period risk was localized, being derived from immediate threats of personal violence and natural disasters. In these circumstances trust was also localized, its basis lying in kinship, religion, place and tradition. During high modernity the situation differs in two respects. First, risk is globalized as, for example, in the case of international warfare or global pollution. Second, risk is personalized, in the form of people's subjective concerns about matters of personal safety or ontological meaning.

Much of Giddens's analysis focuses on the relationship between three elements in modern society: the separation of time and space and its recombination in new forms; the disembedding of social systems; and the deployment of expert knowledge for purposes of reflection on and reconfiguration of social relations. In fact, these three elements overlap one another. Distantiation (or separation) of time and space involves both the 'disembedding' (or extraction) of social relations from their local contexts and the temporal and spatial restructuring of those same relations. One dominant form of disembedding is through symbolic tokens such as money, a medium with the capacity to transfer values across vast expanses of time and space. Another is through the application of expert systems. Each of these mechanisms presupposes an attitude of trust on the part of those who are subject to them. As Giddens puts it, they provide '"guarantees" of expectations across distantiated time–space' (Giddens, 1990: 28). Thus, subjects place trust in the knowledge of those whose expertise, as designers of security systems or new dietary innovations – an expertise which is increasingly commodified – minimizes their risk of falling foul of criminal victimization or obesity. At the same time, however, social life under high modernity is reflexive, with subjects constantly assessing and re-assessing the validity of the (commodified) expertise put before them. The balance between risk, trust and expertise – which itself conditions personal and collective security – is an unstable one.

Beck, like Giddens, also focuses on the sociological characteristics of modernity to analyse risk. For Beck, risk society is a distinct stage of modernity: 'a phase of development of modern society in which the social, political, ecological and individual risks created by the momentum of innovation increasingly elude the control and protective institutions of industrial society' (Beck, 1996: 27). Risk society can only be understood, however, if juxtaposed with class society. The class societies of the industrial era were oriented towards the application of the forces of production to the maximization of economic growth. In those circumstances, populations were obliged to accept the pathological, medical and ecological effects of growth as a mere side-effect of production. Class society also raised questions about equality, since the very production of wealth generated concern about its distribution. Political discourse in class society was, therefore, focused on socialist, social democratic and meritocratic notions of equality and equity.

The innovations which give rise to risk society transform risks from merely localized 'latent side effects' of production to '*supra*-national and *non*-class specific *global* hazards with a new type of social and political dynamism' (Beck, 1992: 13) (emphasis in original). Typical of such global hazards are the dangers posed by nuclear warfare and environmental pollution. Beck argues that global risks of this magnitude homogenize victims and offenders, the instigator of nuclear war or the polluter being destined to share the same fate as those whom they victimize. In that respect, risk society is a society of 'fate', where subjects are no longer concerned with the attainment of 'good' normative ends, but merely preoccupied with 'preventing the worst' (Beck, 1992: 49). The risk society is narrowly obsessed with matters of security and safety to the detriment of any significant engagement with wider social considerations. Even worse, the hazards produced by risk society take it 'beyond its own limits of calculability' (Szerszynski, Lash and Wynne, 1996: 7). For Beck, global risks such as those associated with nuclear, chemical, ecological and genetic technologies cannot be limited by time or space, nor can they be made accountable to established rules of liability and are thus, increasingly, uninsurable. Risk is ubiquitous and its resolution impossible within the confines of modernist thought systems.

From the above discussion it can be seen that Giddens and Beck provide a historical–sociological account of risk and its management, drawing upon the concept of modernity for purposes of explanation and prognosis. An alternative, 'genealogical' account prefers to analyse risk 'as part of *a particular style of thinking* born during the nineteenth century' (Rose, 1996: 341) (emphasis in original). In order to understand this second explanation it is necessary to draw upon Foucault's (1991) distinction between the three dimensions of rule (or governance): sovereignty, discipline and governmentality. Sovereignty consists of strategies exercised by an authority claiming the legitimate monopoly of coercion over a given territory. As such, it is founded upon laws to which subjects are meant to be universally accountable and backed up by the coercive powers of the police and the military. Disputes about sovereignty may occur at many different levels: between competing nation states in the international arena; between nation states and supranational bodies in the transnational arena; or between competing territorial interests within a single nation state. Disciplinary modes of rule are, by contrast, concerned with attempts to control the human body. In pre-modern times disciplinary power was expressed through physical punishment, mutilation, serfdom, the powers of compulsory conscription and other extremes of physical domination. With the development of the modern state and of the formal freedoms associated with citizenship, however, disciplinary power centred on the deprivation of liberty and on the surveillance of subjects in factories, prisons, asylums and schools (Foucault, 1977). Consequently, the expansion of modern disciplinary rule coincided with the development of new professional specialisms in health care, education, psychiatry, welfare and criminal justice.

It is Foucault's third category of rule – governmentality – which is of most direct relevance to the analysis of risk. Governmentality (or 'governmental rationality') emerged during the nineteenth century when 'population comes to appear, above all else, as the ultimate end of government' (Foucault, 1991: 100). The techniques of governmentality are concerned with the management of aggregate populations for the purposes of maximizing welfare and, towards that end, are organized around some statistical mean of health, wealth, security or well-being. Such techniques are closely connected to the development of the human sciences. They are also exemplified in the statistical, actuarial and accounting methodologies which have underpinned state intervention in the social realm for much of the twentieth century. Governmentality is, therefore, concerned with the management of aggregate risks through the application of actuarial, insurential and other technologies (Ewald, 1991; Castel, 1991; Feeley and Simon, 1994).

Contemporary accounts of governmentality raise two issues. O'Malley (1992) points to the impact of political programmes on ruling technologies. On the one hand, neo-liberal ideology has expanded the scope of governmentality beyond mere actuarial technique so that it now includes a wide variety of risk-based technologies: strategies of environmental modification (designing out crime); methods for identifying high-risk individuals and groups (offender profiling, geographical information systems); and policies for reducing criminal opportunity through temporal and spatial manipulation (situational crime prevention). On the other hand, neo-Conservative political programmes have modified and, in some cases, curtailed risk-based interventions, focusing instead on the increased application of punishment and disciplinary-based rule. O'Malley's (1992) analysis confirms that whilst governmentality is a key mode of governance in contemporary society, particular configurations of rule involve determinate combinations of the three technologies, combinations which are conditioned by the effects of political programmes.

This last point raises a further issue. Several commentators (Simon, 1988; Ewald, 1991) maintain not only that governmentality is a dominant mode of rule in the contemporary period, but also that it is a more effective one. Simon suggests that the normalizing objectives of disciplinary rule (the desire to reproduce properly socialized subjects) have given way to actuarial practices 'that are, in turn, more efficient in the use of resources and less dangerous in the political resistances they generate' (Simon, 1988: 773). Others, however (Stenson, 1995, O'Malley, 1992), are, rightly, sceptical of viewing governmentality and the 'New Penology' (Feeley and Simon, 1994) as the pinnacle of some socio-historical project of enhanced social control. After all, such a view is incompatible with O'Malley's (1992) rightful insistence that both the character and the effect of ruling techniques are conditioned by political circumstances.

Both the sociological and genealogical accounts of risk have some merit. The sociological approach points to several important factors: the tension between risk and trust; the commodification of risk management; and the impact of globalization/localization on the state's capacity to manage risk. The main weakness of this approach, however, is its sociological determinism. In Beck's (1992) case the socio-technical determination of risk produces fatalistic consequences. Risk is seen as ubiquitous and socially divisive. Its management is bereft of normative content and, in any case, is doomed to fail. The strength of the sociological approach is its identification of some of the social preconditions of contemporary risk. Its weakness lies in the elevation of those conditions to insurmountable obstacles to political intervention.

The genealogical approach avoids that problem by insisting that risk is constituted within given methodologies, rather than derived from some extra-discursive social source. (The question of whether an exclusively discursive approach is able to give due recognition to the social conditions of risk is a complex matter which need not concern us here). The effect of that insistence is to avoid the extreme political fatalism of Beck (O'Malley, 1992), emphasizing that the application of risk-oriented techniques produces outcomes which are, in part, dependent upon political conditions. Yet, some versions of the genealogical approach continue to retain fatalistic and deterministic elements. Simon's (1988) contention that actuarial justice is the epitome of modern social control – strictly, one should say 'asocial control', since its effectiveness is predicated upon the disaggregation of the social into its individual components – produces a conclusion similar to Beck's: that risk-oriented techniques are unjust, divisive and immune from political intervention.

Police and Risk

For some time it has been apparent that police and criminal justice agencies adopt policies based on assumptions and techniques derived from risk management. Over a decade ago, Cohen (1985) noted that situational crime prevention was concerned not with the causal origins of crime, but with its spatial and temporal manipulation through techniques such as defensible space and target hardening. This movement away from causal speculation about crime towards pragmatic intervention in its control is driven by priorities very similar to those expressed by proponents of commercial risk management. There are, according to Nalla and Newman (1990), five defining principles of risk management: to anticipate risks by proactive means; to appraise the character of a given risk, together with the probability of its being realized; to calculate the anticipated losses or pathologies arising from a given risk; to balance the probability of any risk occurring with the anticipated losses or pathologies arising from it; and to control risks through direct intervention or to displace or transfer them elsewhere (Nalla and Newman, 1990).

In short, risk management is actuarial, proactive and anticipatory, its deployment requiring the collation and analysis of information about and the systematic surveillance of those at risk or likely to cause risk.

The public police's orientation towards information-gathering, proactive intervention, rational calculation and systematic surveillance is, therefore, similar to that of the commercial security sector (Shearing and Stenning, 1981). That public policing is similarly oriented is apparent even in those activities which are, to all intents and purposes, socially and communally oriented. It is no accident that the beat officer under 'Problem Oriented Policing' (PROP) is redesignated a 'beat manager' (Tilley and Brooks, 1996). The reason for this is simple. Though PROP is concerned to analyse the causes of community problems and initiate strategies for dealing with them, its systematic approach for doing so (Scanning, Analysis, Response, Assessment) bears many similarities to risk-oriented practices. Moreover, the application of these principles under conditions of devolved police budgets demands rational calculation of the balance between risks and resources. One response to that calculation may involve the displacement or transfer of problems to other, more appropriate, agencies and locations.

There is, of course, the danger that pragmatic intervention in the management of risk by the police might compromise the principles of public justice. A recent comment from a 'Home Office source' regarding the enhanced role of MI5 in dealing with organized crime suggested that 'Disrupting the activities of organised criminals may be a desirable role if MI5 is not able to bring them to justice' (cited in Gibbons and Hyder, 1996: 5). This is a classic example of the application of 'informal justice' to crime problems, something which is well-documented in the field of commercial security (South, 1988). Doubtless, public police have always engaged in informal practices of one sort or another. The difference is, however, that the principles of commercial risk management are now explicitly adopted as part of the public police mandate.

Ericson and his colleagues (Ericson, 1994; Ericson and Carriere, 1994; Ericson and Haggerty, 1996) suggest that orientation to risk alters the structure and practice of police organization. In particular, that orientation leads to a preoccupation with the collation, collection and dissemination of information for risk management purposes. In effect, the police are, increasingly, part of a network of information-based expert systems, producing knowledge for and collecting knowledge from other security agencies. Two elements of this argument are of particular relevance to the present discussion. First, following the Foucauldian proposition that risk is constituted within determinate methodologies and practices, particular consideration is given to the role of information technology in 'defining' and 'doing' risk-oriented policing: 'information technology has been employed by police organizations to construct the population of police' (Ericson and Haggerty, 1996: 4). This population includes not only those outside the police organization but also those inside. In respect of the latter, various risk-profiling mechanisms are applied to the internal management of risk: employment screening, work activity reports, competence ratings, and health and safety measures. (One is reminded here of Manning's (1979) observation that the main problem for the police organization is not the control of crime but the control of its own personnel.)

Ericson and Haggerty's (1996) point is that information technology defines and manages risks more precisely than hitherto. Though rank and file officers may resist expert systems, in the long term, discretion 'is curtailed, taken away from the individual officer and dispersed into the embedded knowledge systems' (Ericson and Haggerty, 1996: 32). The effect is the creation of working systems where it is difficult to gauge who is in control: systems where hierarchical authority is replaced by transparency and self-regulation; where working cultures and structures are altered; and where definitions of accountability are transformed. Second, intra-organization diversity is accompanied by inter-organizational diversity. Since the police are, increasingly, enmeshed in multi-agency information networks, they are, first and foremost 'information-brokers'. For this reason, Ericson (1994) contends that community policing should, more accurately, be described as 'communications policing'.

TWO VERSIONS OF COMMUNITY POLICING

Policing Communities of Collective Sentiment

It is widely accepted in North America and in many parts of Europe that the future lies in community policing. Yet, in stating that, it is apparent that there is a lack of any coherent definition of the term. Bennett (1994), commenting on this matter, states that in the past there have been various pragmatic attempts to give the term a coherent meaning. These include attempts to identify proactive programmes which benefit the community (police liaison committees, school liaison schemes, community constables); attempts to identify the essential 'core' of community policing programmes (foot patrol, decentralized command, community crime prevention); and the extraction of key concepts from academic analyses of community policing programmes (non-crime problem-solving, police–public partnerships, power-sharing). Though these approaches give some rudimentary shape to community policing, they continue to leave many questions unanswered. For example, should any decentralization of command be seen as evidence of community policing? Is foot patrol an inherent component of any programme?

To argue that community policing has no coherent definition is, however, only partly true. If it is focused on less as a substantive policy than as a rhetorical discourse (Klockars, 1991) one thing becomes immediately apparent. All debates about community policing are predicated upon some conception of community as the embodiment, or potential embodiment, of collective sentiments. This point is well-demonstrated in Mastrofski's (1991) discussion of community policing in the USA. Here, the appeal lies in powerful metaphors which evoke an imagined past in which society was less conflictual and less impersonal. Community policing offers, instead, 'a government that acts to advance the "natural" mechanisms of social control peculiar to a locale' (Mastrofski, 1991: 515–6). The problem is, of course, that such an image of community is both a poor representation of the past and a poor predictor of the future. As Mastrofski (1991) points out, there is a wealth of evidence demonstrating the absence of shared norms about crime and disorder in communities which are, in any case, more often heterogeneous than homogeneous. And even in neighbourhoods where strong informal social control mechanisms are developed, these may be due less to value consensus than to the social or political dominance of particular groups. This is, by no means, a peculiar feature of low-income neighbourhoods. Social conflict, distrust and lack of participation in community initiatives are also a feature of many middle-class communities. The police are, of course, well-aware of this fact. Only the most naive of them would conceive contemporary community as the embodiment of homogeneous structures and common sentiments. Yet, the discursive thrust of community policing is oriented, precisely, towards the reconstitution of collective and consensual communities. Like tourism and heritage, community policing is preoccupied with the reconstruction of nostalgia.

That is not to dismiss the admittedly diverse objectives contained within community policing programmes, many of which are entirely laudable. The problem is that the police are trapped within a paradox of their own making: 'As long as community-as-consensus is perceived as a prerequisite for governance, police will be burdened with the necessity of fabricating one where it does not exist' (Mastrofski, 1991: 527). The effects of this paradox are easy to see. Rosenbaum (1995), a keen but critical advocate of community policing, insists that any effective programme has to recognize that crime control and social order cannot be the exclusive prerogative of the police. Following Jacobs (1961), he concurs with the view that public peace is not kept by the police but by informal networks of voluntary control located within neighbourhoods. The conclusion he draws from this observation is, however, ambivalent. On the one hand, he deems the police to be 'supplemental' to the community when confronting neighbourhood problems. On the other hand, he insists that this supplemental status involves the police taking a 'lead role' in community change: 'The challenge for the police today and into the 21st century is to find creative ways to help communities help themselves' (Rosenbaum, 1995: 43).

This proposal raises two sorts of issues. First, there is the question of whether police-led community policing can be implemented. The wealth of evidence suggests that this is unlikely. Bennett's review of the research evidence draws a number of significant conclusions in this regard: police have not yet assimilated the philosophy of community policing into their routine thinking; decentralization has been hard to implement and may be sabotaged by lower-rank officers; community constables spend relatively little time on community-oriented tasks; public involvement through consultation schemes is limited; public involvement in crime prevention is low and important elements in programmes are often not sustained (Bennett, 1994, 1995). The second issue is more relevant to the present discussion. For Rosenbaum (1995), one of the key components of the police's lead role is 'community building'. First and foremost this involves making efforts to 'facilitate the creation of self-regulating and self-defended neighbourhoods' (Rosenbaum, 1995: 45). This is, of course, a commendable objective. However, it raises a major problem for advocates of community policing. Are self-regulated communities compatible with police leadership? Or, to put it another way, does the concept of self-regulated community demand a fundamental rethink about the governance of policing? It is precisely this issue which is posed by Brogden and Shearing's (1993) model of 'dual policing' in South Africa. Like community policing, that model assumes partnerships between the police and the public. Unlike community policing it is predicated neither upon consensual communities nor upon the state police's continued monopoly of leadership.

Policing Communities of Risk

The paradox of community policing is that despite its communitarian rhetoric, it remains, to use Reiner's (1992) term, 'police property'. Community policing is, first and foremost, state-oriented. In the 1980s radical critics, such as Gordon (1984), observed that the object of community policing was to establish a multi-agency framework connecting the central state with the local state in a coordinated network of social control. In fact, that was a more or less accurate description of the official model (Home Office, 1984). The dispute between advocates and critics was not about the mechanisms to be put into place but about their implications: whether community policing, once imple-mented, would be liberating or oppressive. Subsequent evidence sug-gests that it is neither. Proponents and critics alike misread the constraints imposed by police culture and organization and overestimated the state's capacity for integrated, cohesive action. A decade later the discourse of community policing has altered. As O'Malley and Palmer (1996) observe, the focus on integrating the central and local state has been replaced by one emphasizing the promotion of voluntary, private and cooperative partnerships. Yet, as we have seen, proponents of com-munity policing still continue to see it as a project under police leader-ship. So, can state rule over community policing be reimposed under contemporary conditions? In order to address that issue we need to recap on what was suggested earlier.

In the first section two accounts of contemporary social change were identified, one sociological, the other genealogical. Each of these has major relevance to the issue of state rule. In respect of the first, it is now recognized that the complexities of privatization, commodification, globalization and localization undermine traditional assumptions about the state, various writers having referred to its 'hollowing out', 'stretching' or 'unravelling' (Rhodes, 1994; Bottoms and Wiles, 1996; Crook, Pakulski and Waters, 1993). Much of this discussion has focused on the rela-tively narrow question of whether the (British) nation state possesses more or less sovereignty than hitherto. Yet, the issue is more compli-cated than that, the question of the state's position as a specific and irreducible domain of public rule becoming increasingly questionable. Recognition of the state's increased involvement in 'decentralised societal guidance strategies rather than centralised imperative co-ordination' (Jessop, 1994: 3) has also generated a debate about distantiated rule ('state rule at a distance'), though whether that term adequately cap-tures the state's changing character or merely reinvokes state rule by the back door (Curtis, 1995) remains open to question. Whichever of these various positions one adopts, however, it is clear that the state is experiencing more than a mere 'blurring' of its boundaries. The mor-phology of government is constantly shifting under the impact of sectoral, spatial and temporal changes and, in those circumstances, traditional notions of state rule are problematic. Diverse conditions imply diverse modes of rule.

Diversity of rule is also implicit in the triangular model of govern-ment contained in the genealogical account. The concept of govern-mentality relates specifically to those diverse modes of rule which are oriented towards risk and located in late modern communities. What, then, is the character of these communities? In order to answer this question it is necessary to differentiate between 'government through society' and 'government through community'.

Rose (1996) points out that various contemporary governmental discourses – associationalism, civic republicanism, communitarianism, consumer sovereignty – have dispensed with the aim of governing through society. In effect, he argues, the social is no longer regarded as an objective of strategies of government. In those circumstances, the state – hitherto the political embodiment of the social – is also undermined as a locus of government. The state's capacity to govern in the interests of social justice, social solidarity, social rights and social protection is less and less salient as a ruling strategy. Instead, state rule gives way to community-oriented rule:

> the 'social' may be giving way to 'the community' as a new territory for the administration of individual and collective existence, a new plane or surface upon which micro-moral relations among persons are conceptualized and administered . . . [this] is indicative of a mutation . . . in the ways of thinking and acting that used to be conducted in a 'social' language. (Rose, 1996: 331)

This reconfiguration of government involves, simultaneously, the redefinition of the concept of community. In the past, community, like society, was perceived as a homogenizing force. It is no accident that sociology, as a discipline, was preoccupied with 'community studies' from the nineteenth century to the middle of the twentieth. Much of that research was predicated on a distinction between the homogeneity of community (*gemeinschaft*, rural society, folk society) and the heterogeneity of association (*gesellschaft*, urban society, mass society). One of the projects implicit in community studies was the establishment of conditions conducive to the achievement of the first of these, a project often captured in the drive to inject localities with collective community sentiments – 'community spirit'.

As Rose (1996) suggests, however, community has undergone two significant transformations. The first is one of diversification, the singularity of 'community' giving way to a plurality of 'communities': moral communities (religious, ecological, gendered), lifestyle communities (of taste or consumption), communities of commitment (to personal or nonpersonal issues mobilized locally or globally) and so on. A second change has occurred in the ethical dimension of communities. In the past, individual responsibility for conduct was always partly mitigated by social factors such as family background, social class or education.

Nowadays personal obligations and responsibilities are assembled differently, conduct being 'retrieved from a social order of determination into a new ethical perception of the individualized and autonomized actor' (Rose, 1996: 334).

Rose (1996) illustrates the effects of this reconfiguration by considering the issue of security. In the past social rationalities of government sought to maintain collective security through state intervention on behalf of citizens. Such intervention involved a variety of measures ranging from social insurance to the enforcement of criminal law by a state-funded police force. Under contemporary conditions subjects become active and responsible agents in their own governance, policing and security. Subjects' engagement may take a variety of forms: active participation in official security initiatives, such as neighbourhood watch; direct involvement in unofficial modes of community-based 'self-policing'; and the purchase of physical and manual security products from commercial companies.

As for the last of these, the availability of security commodities is inseparable from the commodification of risk: 'As risk is simultaneously proliferated and rendered potentially manageable, the private market for "security" extends' (Rose, 1996: 342). Social insurance against insecurity gives way to 'private prudentialism' (O'Malley, 1992), individuals gaining access to the benefits of education, health or security by participation in competitive markets and by the management of their own lifestyles. In that environment the conduct of government operates, increasingly, on the basis of 'identity, choice, consumption and lifestyle' (Rose, 1996: 344). Communities, far from being homogenous – or even having homogenizing potential – are diverse, overlapping, pragmatic, temporary and, frequently, divided from one another. That is not all, however. In the past, the sectoral, spatial and temporal dimensions of community were taken for granted. Community might have been difficult to define with precision, but everyone knew it to be the public–collective domain, located within a specific (usually small) geographical territory at a particular period of time. Communities of late modernity are different. The 'virtual communities' of cyberspace exceed the spatial limits of geography. 'Contractual communities' (Shearing, 1995) of subscribing consumers breach the (public) sectoral limits of the past. The processes of globalization – notably 'time–space distantiation' (Giddens, 1990) – place communities in new and complex temporal configurations. Together, these changes eradicate the conventional view of community, emphasizing its growing diversity.

COMMUNITY POLICING, GOVERNMENT AND JUSTICE

Community policing – that form of government through community which is concerned with the provision of security – is likely to be dominant in the future. This has various implications for policing, government and justice. For one thing, the traditional assumption that community policing is specific to narrowly defined geographical areas – localities or neighbourhoods – is no longer tenable. Diversification of community, like 'stretching' of the state, has exceeded the established boundaries of sector, space and time. The diverse communities identified by Rose (1996) as indicative of the 'death of the social' are visible not just in the locality but also at the global level. For some writers on globalization this suggests that 'we must now embark on the project of understanding social life without the comforting term "society"' (Featherstone and Lash, 1995: 2). Their reasons for drawing that conclusion are apparent if one considers the character of global government. For what one observes is not the primacy of society and the nation state, but a moving complex of organizational modes similar to that which might be observed in any regional or local community:

> What globalization means in structural terms . . . is the *increase in the available modes of organization*: transnational, macro-regional, national, micro-regional, municipal, local . . . crisscrossed by *functional networks* of corporations, international organizations, as well as professionals and computer users . . . two interactive worlds with overlapping memberships: a state-centric world, in which the primary actors are national, and a multi-centric world of diverse actors such as corporations, international organizations, ethnic groups, churches. (Nederveen Pierterse, 1995: 50; emphasis in original)

The spatial ubiquity of government through community confirms it to be more than a localized phenomenon. In that respect, it is significant that both Shearing (1992) and Elkins (1995) identify commercial corporations as key sites of governance, raising the question of whether they might come to embody 'corporate governments' composed of 'corporate communities of citizens'. If that situation comes about, of course, the territorial scope of community policing will far exceed anything envisaged by its traditional proponents.

That raises the issue of how the communities policed by distantiated means are characterized. Throughout this chapter, reference has been made to the term 'communities *of* risk'. At first sight, this term might seem a clumsy construction. Would it not have been preferable to use the more conventional idea of communities *at* risk? In fact, the use of the term has been a deliberate one, the point being that communities are not merely 'at risk' from some external threat, but are increasingly defined, oriented, organized and governed around matters of risk. There are several reasons for making this claim. Risk, far from being given in external social conditions, is constituted and reconstituted in daily experience. That experience is, in turn, mediated by the commodification of security, a process which leads to increased demand for policing. That demand is likely to be disparate and varied, rather than consistent and uniform. It cannot be assumed that members of communities will share common perceptions of, and interests in, risk. Indeed, some communities are, themselves, deemed to constitute risks. It is for these reasons that the term 'communities of risk' is the preferred one, the alternative endowing communities with a coherence and risk with an externality which is unwarranted.

If the future is one in which diverse communities are policed diversely, there are a number of implications for policing and justice. One concerns the divisive potential of policing. That is not a new problem, of course. The police have always had to reconcile their practices with the demands of different social constituencies. Sometimes that has proved difficult to achieve. Yet, as long as the state could claim – rightly or wrongly – to enjoy a monopoly over security, policing could always be presented as an indivisible public good. Once government through state and society is undermined, however, that vision can no longer be sustained and the possibility of one person's security being guaranteed at the expense of another's becomes all too transparent. The problem for the police is that their claims to exert leadership over community policing become less and less convincing, the more distantiated community-based modes of government are invoked.

Diversity also poses problems of justice. Government through community is forged, at least in part, through the identity and lifestyle of autonomous consumers exercising choice. Government, in this context, is not merely the product of diversity; it also diversifies:

> These new logics of risk management are thus capable of being deployed within a wide range of strategies. They not only multiply the points at which normative calculation and intervention are required, but fragment the social space of welfare into a multitude of diverse pockets. (Rose, 1996: 343)

The inclusive strategies which define communities also lead to exclusion from them. Those who are either unwilling or unable to participate in commercial or voluntary schemes for protecting themselves from risk are excluded from 'contractual' communities or from communities of 'responsible citizens'. As Rose (1996) suggests, once citizenship is affiliated to consumption and lifestyle, governmental strategies identify non-affiliates – so-called marginal populations – as problematic. Inevitably, this produces injustice. It also raises questions about the equity of policing. Many commentators have suggested that policing faces a 'two-tier' future: 'affiliates' freely subscribing to the 'services' of commercial security; 'marginals' enjoying the attention of a residual public police 'force'. Probably this picture is simplistic. The management of 'anti-communities' (Rose, 1996), hitherto undertaken by the welfare state, is already in the hands of a complex of quasi-autonomous agencies, some voluntary, some private, some state-funded. To that extent, the bifurcation between 'affiliates' and 'marginals' is unlikely to be reflected by any simple sectoral bifurcation in policing.

There is also the impact of risk-oriented techniques on justice. As Castel (1991) suggests, risk-managing techniques are concerned with the accumulation of aggregate data about risk probabilities. As such, they are unconcerned with matters relating to individual subjects, focusing instead on subjects as factorial components of aggregate populations. Though there is nothing inherently unjust about that focus, injustice may arise where it is applied to marginal populations. As Hudson (1996) suggests, this is precisely the difficulty with the application of actuarial technologies, the danger being that 'the new techniques will continue to be directed against the same population, the disadvantaged, who will lose even such limited protection as is offered by the commitment to justice' (Hudson, 1996: 155). More seriously, Hudson suggests that under a regime of risk management extra penalization of those who, according to actuarial methodologies, possess factors associated with risk – race, unemployment, homelessness, single parentage and the like – may also be deemed justifiable.

Another issue concerns the distribution of risk. Socialized modes of protection from risk, such as state insurance and public policing, operate with a clear conception of justice, people sharing a collective burden and having their individual contributions fixed by agreed rules. According to this model, risk and its management are social categories: everyone faces risks and society insures against them. 'Prudentialism' (O'Malley, 1992), by contrast, has an individualistic theory of justice in which people have the responsibility to protect themselves, receiving the security they deserve. This model, like the socialized one, also has a conception of shared risk, though in this case, sharing is restricted to a community of subscribers, rather than extended to the wider society. Consequently, prudentialism denies that risk distribution should accord with any principle of social equity. This position might seem problematical since, as Ewald (1991) rightly insists, risk is collective: 'Strictly speaking there is no such thing as an individual risk . . . Risk only becomes calculable when it is spread over a population' (Ewald, 1996: 202–3). Prudentialism resolves this difficulty, however, by insisting that the collective resolution of risk can be achieved by communal, rather than social, means: a community of risk-takers insuring itself against the pathologies of risk.

All of these issues raise basic governmental problems which cannot be resolved by the old certainties of state rule. If the pessimism implicit in much of the writing on risk society is to be avoided, a politics of community policing has to be developed which, though mindful of the sociological context of risk, avoids the fatalism implicit in sociological determinism. O'Malley's insistence that the impact of policing technologies is 'largely determined by the nature and fortunes of political programs with which they are aligned' (O'Malley, 1992: 252) suggests that such a project is possible. Such a politics would have to recognize the positive potential contained in autonomy, citizenship and choice, whilst remaining aware of the dangers posed by exclusion, marginalization and inequity. Behind such politics lies a basic governmental question: can community reconcile collective objectives with individual ones?

Though some attempt has been made to address these issues at a general level (for example, Etzioni, 1993; Hirst, 1994), they have barely been considered in the context of policing. An exception may be found in Brogden and Shearing's model of dual policing in South Africa and Northern Ireland (respectively Brogden and Shearing, 1993; Brogden, 1995). Here, it is argued, policing within local communities should be understood as a network of interrelated institutions operating at different levels and with different knowledges and resources. Civil society, albeit fractured and fragmented, should be recognized as the primary location of policing – something which, as we have suggested, government through community has already initiated – the state police being defined as a specific, problem-solving agency organized around their capacity to exercise legitimate force. At the heart of this argument is the suggestion that local self-policing be coordinated with local state policing to constitute a dual system. In turn, this would involve the 'resurrection of civil society', ensuring that it 'plays a central role, not only in monitoring and contributing to what the police do, but in taking

direct responsibility for policing as part of a radical process of democratization' (Brogden and Shearing, 1993: 181). The radical democratization is seen as a basic precondition of dual policing since, otherwise,
it would merely invite the inequality and inequity associated with those
'two-tier' systems of policing which are based upon the consumers'
capacity to pay. The dual model is predicated upon a genuine partner-
ship between state and civil policing in the locality. State police would
be responsible for enforcement. Community policing would be provided by commercial, municipal and voluntary elements within civil
society. Overall responsibility for the coordination and integration of
local policing networks would lie with local democratic government,
though authoritative force would remain with the state police and, crucially, national criteria would be established to determine the legitimate limits of local civil autonomy.

Since diverse policing is now with us, it is vital that further work is
undertaken into the political arrangements necessary for its just, effective and democratic functioning. The dual policing model, however,
leaves one final question. Will the future be one in which there is a
simple division of policing functions, with state police becoming 'ban-
dit-catchers' (Brogden and Shearing, 1993), while the community bears
responsibility for community policing? Or does the earlier observation
that public and private security organizations share a common orientation to risk management indicate a more variegated functional future?

References

Beck, U. (1992) *Risk Society: Towards a New Modernity* (London: Sage).
Beck, U. (1996) 'Risk society and the provident state', in S. Lash, B. Szerszynski
    and B. Wynne (eds), *Risk, Environment and Modernity* (London: Sage).
Bennett, T. (1994) 'Recent developments in community policing', in M. Stephens
    and S. Becker (eds), *Police Force, Police Service* (London: Macmillan) pp.
    107–30.
Bennett, T. (1995) 'Evaluating police and public performance in the delivery
    of community policing', in *Workshop on Evaluating Police Service Deliv-
    ery: Report of the Ministry of the Solicitor General of Canada/International
    Centre for Comparative Criminology, University of Montreal*, pp. 316–47.
Bottoms, A. and Wiles, P. (1996) 'Understanding crime prevention in late
    modern societies', in T. Bennett (ed.), *Preventing Crime and Disorder:
    Targeting Strategies and Responsibilities* (University of Cambridge, Insti-
    tute of Criminology: Cambridge Cropwood Series).
Brogden, M. (1995) 'An agenda for post-troubles policing in Northern Ireland
    – the South African precedent', *The Liverpool Law Review*, vol. XVII,
    no. 1, pp. 3–27.

Brogden, M. and Shearing, C. (1993) *Policing for a New South Africa* (London: Routledge).

Castel, R. (1991) 'From dangerousness to risk', in G. Burchall, C. Gordon and P. Miller (eds), *The Foucault Effect* (London: Harvester Wheatsheaf) pp. 251–80.

Cohen, S. (1985) *Visions of Social Control* (London: Polity).

Crook, S., Pakulski, J. and Waters, M. (1993) *Postmodernization: Change in Advanced Society* (London: Sage).

Curtis, B. (1995) 'Taking the state back out', *British Journal of Sociology*, vol. 46, no. 4, pp. 575–89.

Elkins, D. J. (1995) *Beyond Sovereignty: Territory and Political Economy in the Twenty-First Century* (Toronto: University of Toronto Press).

Ericson, R. (1994) 'The division of expert knowledge in policing and security', *British Journal of Sociology*, vol. 45, no. 2, pp. 149–75.

Ericson, R. and Carriere, K. (1994) 'The fragmentation of criminology', in D. Nelken, (ed.), *The Futures of Criminology* (London: Sage) pp. 89–109.

Ericson, R. and Haggarty, K. (1996) 'The population of police', unpublished paper to the Joint Meetings of the American Law and Society Association and the Research Committee on the Sociology of Law of the International Sociological Association, Glasgow, 10–13 July.

Etzioni, A. (1993) *The Spirit of Community* (New York: Touchstone).

Ewald, F. (1991) 'Insurance and risk', in G. Burchall, C. Gordon and P. Miller (eds), *The Foucault Effect* (London: Harvester Wheatsheaf) pp. 197–210.

Featherstone, M. and Lash, S. (1995) 'Globalization, modernity and the spatialization of social theory: an introduction', in M. Featherstone, S. Lash and R. Roberston (eds), *Global Modernities* (London: Sage) pp. 1–24.

Feeley, M. and Simon, J. (1994) 'Actuarial justice: the emerging new criminal law', in D. Nelken (ed.), *The Futures of Criminology* (London: Sage) pp. 173–201.

Foucault, M. (1977) *Discipline and Punish: The Birth of the Prison* (London: Allen Lane).

Foucault, M. (1991) 'Governmentality', in G. Burchell, C. Gordon and P. Miller (eds), *The Foucault Effect* (London: Harvester Wheatsheaf) pp. 87–104.

Gibbons, S and Hyder, K. (1996) 'MI5 crime-fighting role needs tighter control says Sharples', *Police Review*, 19 January, p. 5.

Giddens, A. (1990) *The Consequences of Modernity* (Cambridge: Polity Press).

Gordon, P. (1984) 'Community policing: towards the local police state?', *Critical Social Policy*, vol. 10, pp. 39–58.

Hirst, P. (1994) *Associative Democracy* (Cambridge: Polity Press).

Home Office (1984) Circular 1/1984 *Crime Prevention* (London: Home Office)

Hudson, B. A. (1996) *Understanding Justice: An Introduction to Ideas, Perspectives and Controversies in Modern Penal Theory* (Buckingham: Open University Press).

Illich, I. (1975) *Medical Nemesis: The Expropriation of Health* (London: Marion Boyars).

Jacobs, J. (1961) *The Death and Life of the Great America Cities* (New York: Vintage).

Jessop, B. (1994) 'The changing form and functions of the state in an era of globalization and regionalization', in R. Delorme and K. Dopfer (eds), *The Political Economy of Complexity* (London: Edward Elgar).

Klockars, C. B. (1991) 'The rhetoric of community policing', in C. B. Klockars and S. D. Mastrofski (eds), *Thinking About Policing* (New York: McGraw-Hill) pp. 530–42.

Manning, P. (1979) 'The social control of police work', in S. Holdaway (ed.), *The British Police* (London: Arnold) pp. 41–65.

Mastrofski, S. D. (1991) 'Community policing as reform: a cautionary tale', in C. B. Klockars and S. D. Mastrofski (eds), *Thinking About Policing* (New York: McGraw-Hill) pp. 515–29.

Nalla, M. and Newman, G. (1990) *A Primer in Private Security* (New York: Harrow & Heston).

Nederveen Pierterse, J. (1995) 'Globalization as hybridization', in M. Featherstone, S. Lash and R. Roberston (eds), *Global Modernities* (London: Sage) pp. 45–68.

O'Malley, P (1992) 'Risk, power and crime prevention', *Economy and Society*, vol. 21, no. 3, pp. 252–75.

O'Malley, P. and Palmer, D. (1996) 'Post-Keynesian policing', *Economy and Society*, vol. 25, no. 2, pp. 137–55.

Reiner, R. (1992) *The Politics of the Police* (Hemel Hempstead: Harvester Wheatsheaf).

Rhodes, R. A. W. (1994) 'The hollowing out of the state: the changing nature of the public service in Britain', *Political Quarterly*, vol. 65, no. 2, pp. 138–51.

Rose, N. (1996) 'The death of the social? Re-figuring the territory of government', *Economy and Society*, vol. 25, no. 3, pp. 327–56.

Rosenbaum, D. (1995) 'The changing role of the police in North America: assessing the current transition to community policing', in *Workshop on Evaluating Police Service Delivery: Report of the Ministry of the Solicitor General of Canada/International Centre for Comparative Criminology*, University of Montreal, pp. 29–68.

Shearing, C. (1992) 'The relations between public and private policing', in M. Tonry and N. Morris (eds), *Modern Policing: Policing, Crime and Justice: A Review of Research*, Vol. 15 (Chicago, Ill.: University of Chicago Press).

Shearing, C. (1995) 'Reinventing policing: police as governance', in O. Marenin (ed.), *Policing Change: Changing Police* (New York: Garland Press).

Shearing, C. and Stenning, P. (1981) 'Modern private security: its growth and implications', in M. Tonry and N. Morris (eds), *Crime and Justice: An Annual Review of Research*, Vol. 3 (Chicago, Ill.: University of Chicago Press) pp. 193–245.

Simon, J. (1988) 'The ideological effects of actuarial practices', *Law and Society Review*, vol. 22, p. 772.

South, N. (1988) *Policing for Profit* (London: Sage).

Stenson, K. (1995) 'Communal security as government – the British experience', in W. Hammerschick, I. Karazman-Morawetz and W. Stangl (eds), *Jahrbuch für Rechts und Kriminalsoziologie, 1995*, Die Sichere Stadt-Prävention und Kommunale Sicherheitspolitik (Baden-Baden: Nomos).

Szerszynski, B., Lash, S. and Wynne, B (1996) 'Introduction: ecology, realism and the social sciences', in S. Lash, B. Szerszynski and B. Wynne (eds), *Risk, Environment and Modernity* (London: Sage) pp. 1–26.

Tilley, N. and Brooks, S. (1996) 'Popular coppers', *Police Review*, 2 February, pp. 24–5.

Waters, M. (1995) *Globalization* (London: Routledge).

9 Policing the Virtual Community: The Internet, Cyberspace and Cyber-Crime[1]

David Wall

INTRODUCTION

The 1980s and 1990s has witnessed the development of an exciting new domain which, warts and all, is potentially free of conventional politics, social order and social regulation. Never before has there been so much ready access to such a broad range of human knowledge and experience. However this 'cyberspace', which has been created by the Internet,[2] is not without its contradictions. The optimism arising from its potential to democratize access to hitherto restricted knowledge and thus level out some of the social boundaries that have developed both within and across societies is tempered by the nature of this revolutionary new resource. In addition to the considerable benefits that the Internet creates, there are also many opportunities for new types of offending and new forms of anti-social behaviour. Moreover, cyberspace undermines economic, social and political boundaries, posing a considerable threat to traditional forms of governance and creating a challenge to traditional understandings of order.

Conventional understandings of crime and policing are based upon a collective social experience of traditionally bounded space, not the virtual environment of cyberspace. Since the Internet is clearly here to stay, a number of important questions emerge, such as 'who will regulate "undesirable" behaviour?' and 'how will they police it?' Is, for example, the traditional public policing model, which is based upon principles which have changed little since the early nineteenth century, the most appropriate organization to deal with the new set of demands created by the colonization of cyberspace? Or is it the case that the characteristics of cyberspace are so radical that a completely new approach needs to be taken? Clearly there is a need to look at the implications that cyberspace has for policing and regulation and more generally for the discipline of criminology in the light of the new millennium.

This chapter is divided into five sections. The first part focuses upon the qualities of change that the increasing colonization of cyberspace is giving rise to. The second part explores the phenomena of cyber-crime and contrasts it with our traditional understanding of criminal activity. The third part considers the various responses to cyber-crime and explores the organizations involved in policing it and the strategies that they use. The fourth part looks at the application of the existing public model of policing to cyberspace. The final part of the chapter draws some conclusions about policing the virtual community and the challenges it poses for the discipline of criminology.

TECHNO-SOCIAL CHANGE

Born out of a United States of America Department of Defense military initiative to create a communications system that would survive a thermonuclear attack (Elmer-Dewitt, 1994: 52),[3] the Internet has developed far beyond its original military and academic goals. In the early 1990s, the Internet became more readily available to individuals not affiliated with military, government, research, or academic organizations; at this time it is estimated that there were about one million users (Byassee, 1995: 197). Since then, the Internet's full commercial, political and artistic potential started to be realized and this has led to an exponential growth in the number of users especially after the development of the 'World Wide Web'. During the next four years, the Internet sustained a growth rate of 10 per cent per month, and by 1994 it is estimated that there were more than 20 million Internet users (Evans, 1994: 67). It is predicted that the 'entire global electronic information matrix', which includes the Internet, will probably have more than 500 million users by the end of the century (Mandel, 1993). For example, Digital's AltaVista boasts the following: 'AltaVista gives you access to the largest Web index: 30 million pages found on 275,600 servers, and four million articles from 14,000 Usenet news groups. It is accessed over 21 million times per weekday.'[4]

Such developments have ensured the colonization of areas of human existence that are not physically bounded: 'digital technology is detaching information from the physical plane, where property law of all sorts has always found definition' (Barlow, 1994). This area is now commonly referred to as *cyberspace* (Benedikt, 1991), an often misunderstood term, which has developed from science fiction (Gibson, 1984) into a socially constructed reality. The common understanding of cyberspace is that it is the 'conceptual location of the electronic, interactively available using one's computer, it is a place without physical walls or even physical dimensions in which interaction occurs as if it happened in the real world and in real time, but constitutes only a "virtual reality"' (Byassee, 1995: 199; Tribe, 1991: 15).

If cyberspace is an area in which new forms of social activity are taking place, then we can conceptualize its inhabitants as the *virtual community*. Virtual communities are 'social aggregations that emerge from the Net when enough people carry on public discussions long enough, with sufficient human feeling, to form webs of personal relationships in cyberspace' (Rheingold, 1993: 5). Authors such as Saradar and Ravetz (1996: 1) have gone further than this simple analogy by arguing that the virtual community is in fact the first step towards 'Cyberia', a 'new civilisation that is emerging through our human–computer interface and mediation'. The potentiality of cyberspace is awesome, and some of its possibilities have already been mentioned. The good side is that individuals can now work in three dimensions instead of two: meaning that it is possible, for example, to do office work without office politics and to work where abilities are suited rather than where they are physically placed. Moreover, cyberspace provides an environment where products can be created, manufactured and traded.

Attempts to understand this socially constructed cyberspace are fostering a reformulation of the debate over modernity 'in ways that are not so mediated by literary and epistemological considerations, as was the case during the 1980s' (Escobar, 1996: 113). One of the most visible impacts of the colonization of cyberspace has been the acceleration of some of the qualities which characterize late modernity, particularly the three factors or 'discontinuities' highlighted by Giddens (1990: 6) as separating the modern and traditional social orders. Social orders bind time and space, however they have become disembedded and *distantiated* (Giddens, 1990: 14); 'lifted out' of local contexts of interaction and restructured across indefinite spans of time–space.

It is in the dimensions of time, space and place that the concept of cyberspace cuts across our conventional understanding of social interaction. First, the speed of communications within cyberspace collapses the conventional physical relationship between the overall speed of travel and geographical distance. Indeed, the configuration of hardware systems can mean that distant servers are more quickly accessible than are those in a local vicinity. The relative instantaneity of cyberspace means that meaningful social interaction can be conducted at a distance. Second, cyberspace cuts across geographic, social, political and gendered boundaries and calls into question existing notions of space. Cyberspace has no conventional boundary as it is potentially infinite in size, and the only boundary that it does respect is that through which access is gained. The politics of access to cyberspace is a major issue and is discussed later. Third, the existence of cyberspace questions conventional understanding of the meaning of place. An individual may live in one continent and labour on a distant site. Similarly, the individual is now free to develop social relations that are commensurate with their own interests or lifestyle and are therefore more meaningful than they would otherwise be. Whilst this form of social relationship has the advantage of avoiding the pitfalls of social existence created by destructive *gemeinschaft*, it does have a dark side in that it leads to the social deskilling[5] of the individual. The individual's social life effectively becomes subdivided into specializations. Underpinning the concept of cyber-social relations is the issue of technicality. To gain access to the virtual community, the individual has to fulfil various conditions. They have to have access to the necessary resources which buy them into the services of a web provider. The individual also has to possess specialist knowledge relevant to the operation of the Internet; those who have the knowledge will become the knowledged classes (Kumar, 1978; Blakey, 1996: 19).

What is different about cyberspace, compared to the rapid increases in the pace of life brought about by other technologies such as the telephone, automobile and airplane, is that it is a *hyper-distantiated* world in which there is no longer 'a question of a false representation of reality [ideology] but merely of concealing the fact that the real is no longer real';[6] it is so *hyperreal* that 'truth has been not destroyed; it has been made irrelevant'.[7] Cyberspace has now become an important site for capitalist production and it is also the site where products are now manufactured, purchased and consumed. Cyber-spatial production therefore leads to a transformation of our understanding of property. So instead of the traditional notion of physical property we have now an emphasis upon intellectual properties in the form of images and likenesses, copyrightable, trademarkable and patentable materials. These intellectual properties, like conventional property, have value and are therefore vulnerable to being appropriated.[8] Moreover, even the nature of more familiar forms of property is changing, especially money. It is anticipated that before long the practical development of the concept of electronic cash (cyber-cash or cyberbucks) and 'cyber-shopping' through 'cyber-consumption' networks will supersede conventional money (Lloyd, 1994: 335). There already exists, for example, the First Bank of the Internet (Blakey, 1996: 19). These networks will provide new opportunities for theft and fraud. The transubstantiation of money into cyber-cash will also present a new series of evidential problems in the investigation of theft and fraud.

The problem, states Barlow, is that 'only a very few people are aware of the enormity of this shift, and fewer of them are lawyers or public officials' (Barlow, 1994). Underlying any debate over the governance of cyberspace is the fact that the Internet was designed to resist attack, a characteristic which frustrates attempts at direct governance by removing the possibility of disconnection: the ultimate sanction. At present, the absence of formal structures of governance means that any controls currently exercised over cyberspace are exercised on an informal basis. In theory, control could be exercised from either of two main sites and the locus of power is with those who possess the knowledge to gain access to the Internet and/or with those who provide the hardware which facilitates access to the Internet. In practice, the degree of control to be exercised by either group is limited by the fact that such knowledge is now fairly widely distributed and there are many physical points of access.

In addition to the practical problems of effecting control is the central problem of identifying in which jurisdiction cyberspace lies (Byassee, 1995: 199). One school of thought argues that because cyberspace is a new and quite separate area then it should become a separate legal jurisdiction. But, others have argued that cyberspace cannot exist independently of the real world, which is organized into its geographical jurisdictions. Byassee (1995) contends that the 'interactions between users in cyberspace have effects in real world jurisdictions, and that the inhabitants of cyberspace are also citizens of a physical jurisdiction' (1995: 207). Though unresolved, the few legal cases that have reached the courts have been the subject of 'forum shopping' (Akdeniz, 1996). In other words, prosecutors have sought a site where they felt a conviction would best be secured, for example as in the cases of *United States of America* v. *Robert A. Thomas and Carleen Thomas*[9] and *R.* v. *Fellows and R.* v. *Arnold.*[10]

These characteristics provide a challenge to the principles upon which our conventional understanding of crime and policing are based, and, moreover, raise issues over their regulation and control. It is to these principles which the discussion now turns.

CYBER-CRIMINOLOGY: REDEFINING THE BOUNDARIES OF CRIMINAL ACTIVITY

In order to understand cyber-criminal activity we first need to look at traditional criminal activity. Broadly speaking, traditional criminal activity displays some fairly characteristic and commonly understood features (Gottfredson and Hirsch, 1990; Braithwaite, 1992). First, there is a degree of consensus about what does or does not constitute a crime. Second, criminal activities take place in real time as their time frame is determined by the (physical) circumstances which give rise to them, for example, speed of transport. Third, crimes take place within a defined space: distinct geographical and social boundaries. Fourth, the actions they describe are governed by a body of substantive law created by the legitimate legislature of the area enclosed by the boundary (Johnson and Post, 1996). Fifth, crimes take place within an observable place. The place where the criminal behaviour takes place is usually the same place where the impact of the crime is felt. Sixth, white-collar crimes notwithstanding, the body of knowledge required to undertake traditional crimes is located within working-class subcultures.

In contrast, cyberspace is a virtual environment in which values are largely attached to ideas rather than traditional physical property (Barlow, 1994). These values are constantly being threatened and therefore have to be protected in order to prevent them from being appropriated, damaged or distorted. As a result, cyber-crimes possess qualities which turn existing, traditional, conceptions of crime on their head. They do not respect time, space or place and are instantaneous in so far as they are freed of a physical time frame. Cyber-crimes are also contentious in so far as there does not yet exist a core set of values about them which informs general opinion. Moreover, cyber-crimes require considerable technical knowledge to be enacted.[11]

Classifying Cyber-Crime

There have been a number of attempts to classify cyber-crimes. Some (Young, 1995: 1; Wasik, 1991) have focused upon the individual and have therefore sought to identify types of offender such as hackers, players, updated white-collar criminals, pornographers, perverts, computer spies, computer terrorists. Others have concentrated upon the behaviour. Schlozberg (1983) for example, listed the following six groups of offences (Duff and Gardiner, 1996: 213):

1. Theft, embezzlement and fraud of intangible property.
2. Sabotage and vandalism.
3. Automatic destruction of data.
4. Appropriation of data.
5. Theft of computer services.
6. Alteration and modification of data.

The main problem with these classifications is that they tend to have been established before the commercial exploitation of the Internet and even before the sophisticated development of the graphics user interface which has facilitated the commercialization of the Internet. More recently, in the United States of America, the National Computer Crime Squad[12] of the Federal Bureau of Investigation has identified a number of crime categories which it currently investigates. They are: intrusions of the Public Switched Network (the telephone company); major computer network intrusions; network integrity violations; privacy violations; industrial espionage; pirated computer software; and other crimes where the computer is a major factor in committing the criminal offence. Although the National Computer Crime Squad's charter limits its investigations to violations of the Federal Computer Fraud and Abuse Act 1986,[13] the coverage, according to Fraser (1996), is still rather broad and imprecise, referring to areas rather than activities.

Perhaps the most comprehensive attempt to define cyber-crime was undertaken by the United Nations, whose *Manual on the Prevention and Control of Computer-Related Crime* (United Nations, 1995) was quite candid about the problems of defining cyber-crimes.

> There is no doubt among the authors and experts who have attempted to arrive at definitions of computer crime that the phenomenon exists. However, the definitions that have been produced tend to relate to the study for which they were written ... A global definition of computer crime has not been achieved; rather, functional definitions have been the norm. (United Nations, 1995: para. 21)

The manual concludes that although there is a common acceptance that cyber-crime exists because 'the computer has also created a host of potentially new misuses or abuses that may, or should, be criminal as well' (United Nations, 1995: para. 22), it nevertheless accepts that authors cannot agree as to what cyber-crime actually is. The United Nations were not alone in reaching this conclusion. The European Committee on Crime Problems of the Council of Europe avoided a formal definition of computer crime, discussing instead the functional

characteristics of target activities. The committee left individual countries to adapt the functional classification to their particular legal systems and historical traditions (United Nations, 1995: para. 23). The
United Nations manual did, however, discuss the role of law, arguing
that since criminal law recognizes the concepts of unlawful or fraudulent intent and also of claim of right, then any criminal laws relating
to cyber-crime would need to distinguish between accidental misuse
of a computer system, negligent misuse of a computer system and intended, unauthorized access to or misuse of a computer system, amounting
to computer abuse. It also argued that annoying behaviour must be
distinguished from criminal behaviour in law (United Nations, 1995: para.
24). These points were reflected in the European Commission Select
Committee's recent Green Paper on the protection of minors (1996).

In addition to the problematic classification and definition of cyber-
crime is the difficulty of locating it within an appropriate body of literature. Attempts to liken cyber-crime to white-collar crimes, state Duff
and Gardiner (1996: 213), can be misleading as most forms of hacking
cannot be seen as white collar crime. Much of the problem here is that
the main body of literature on white-collar crime predates the recent
and rapid expansion of the Internet. Rather than attempt to make classifications that will become quickly outdated, it is perhaps better to
explore three generic cyber issues which are raising concerns as we
enter the twenty-first century; cyber-trespass (including cyber-espion-
age and cyber-terrorism), cyber-theft and cyber-obscenity.

Cyber-trespass
Essential to cyber-criminality is a high level of specialized knowledge
associated traditionally with computer hackers, who were, ironically,
crucial to the development of the Internet.[14] Once lionized as the genius
of youth and the pioneering spirit of America (Chandler, 1996: 229)
the original hackers believed in freedom of access to all information.
Those same skills and beliefs are now seen as a potential threat to the
interests both of commerce and the state which are attempting to effect monopoly control over cyberspace. Hackers have now become
demonized as latter-day folk devils (Chandler, 1996; Duff and Gardiner,
1996; Ross, 1990: para. 4; Sterling, 1994). Because of the ideological
baggage that the term 'hacking' has accrued, the term 'cyber-trespasser'
is used here; within this term there is a continuum, with intellectually
motivated trespassers at one end and the politically or criminally motivated (cyber-terrorists) at the other. At best, cyber-trespass is an intellectual challenge resulting in a harmless trespass, at its worst it is

information warfare (Szafranski, 1995: 56).[15] There are four basic types of cyber-trespasser. Young (1995: 10) distinguishes between *utopians* who naively believe that they are helping society by demonstrating its vulnerabilities, and *cyberpunks* who are aggressively anti-establishment and who intentionally cause harm to targets who for one reason or another offend them. In addition, we can also identify two further types of cyber-trespasser: the *cyber-spy* and the *cyber-terrorist*. Both are characterized by their motivation, typically for politics or money, to disrupt the prevailing order. *Utopians* and *cyberpunks* on the other hand tend to create disruption as the result of being at a particular site. Clearly, the practical distinction between the four is hard to delineate because, as stated earlier, cyber-spies and terrorists must by definition be expert hackers to be able to gain access to the sites at which they create disruption.

For the most part, significant acts of cyber-trespass will lie somewhere between these extreme positions. Three types of activity are relevant here. First is the deliberate planting of viruses. These viruses could be designed to disable a particular function or they could be sleeping viruses designed to be neutralized only after a ransom has been paid. Many organizations experienced 'virus planting' in the early 1990s when organizations all over the world received floppy disks through the post which purported to be HIV training packages. They were in fact sleeping viruses which lodged themselves in the recipient's computer system. Victims were instructed to send a sum of money to an address in the United States of America in return for a code that would disable the virus (Chandler, 1996: 241). The second type of activity is the deliberate manipulation of presentational data, such as home pages, so that they misrepresent the organization that they are supposed to represent. The University of York fell victim to this form of attack (*The Herald*, 1996: 6) when an intruder entered the University's Conservative Club home page, defacing minutes of meetings and adding various pornographic images. In addition to the quandary of establishing whether or not this was a prank or a politically motivated act designed to discredit the Conservative Party was the problem of establishing the identity of the perpetrator.[16] It was possible to trace the time and place of the tampering and also the account used to gain access to the computing system, but it was impossible to identify the individual who committed the act. This type of manipulation of presentational data could just as easily be used to manipulate important research findings or publicly viewed policy documents.

The third and fourth types of activity are cyber-spying and cyber terrorism. Cyber-spies enter computer sites to gain access to specific secrets or classified information and entry and exit is usually as discreet as possible in order to avoid detection.[17] Cyber-terrorism, by comparison, results in the deliberate destruction of material and is raising considerable concern within military circles. Various military strategists are preparing to counter 'information warfare', so defined when intruders enter major computer systems and cause damage to their contents, thus causing considerable damage to the target society (Szafranski, 1995: 56). It is not inconceivable, for example, that cyber-terrorists might break into a state computer system and tamper with national insurance numbers or tax codes. An act such as this would not be detected immediately and could cause irreparable damage to relations between the public and the state; possibly destabilizing it. Indeed Sterling warned that: 'hackers in Amtrak computers or in air-traffic controller computers will kill somebody someday' (Sterling 1994: 185). At the present time these examples remain possibilities and it is perhaps of greater significance that they have not yet taken place. However, vigilance against cyber-spying and terrorism is going to become crucial as more and more state processes are run by computer and as more and more industrial processes are driven by central computer programs.

Cyber-theft

The second generic type of cyber-crime is cyber-theft, of which there are two types. The first is the appropriation of intellectual property. For example, pictures of a famous pop star might be appropriated from Internet images or scanned from physical sources. They would then be repackaged in a glossy and professional format with some explanatory text and sold on via a cyber-shopping mall to interested parties who purchase in good faith. The mall could be in the United States of America, but the payments made to an Australian bank account. The whole operation would take about two or three weeks and by the time the deception was detected the proceeds would have been removed from the bank account and the perpetrators gone. Another derivation of the appropriation and exploitation of intellectual properties currently taking place is the production of counterfeit products, direct copies of the original being made and sold through the cyber-shopping malls.[18]

The second type of cyber-theft is the appropriation of cyber-cash. The cyber-cash concept is developing rapidly and while the developers envisage the eventual establishment of a self-contained monetary system within cyberspace, current concepts of cyber-cash are related to the use of credit cards. A very common form of cyber-theft is the fraudulent use of appropriated credit cards to buy goods over the Internet from a cyber-shopping mall. The important issue here is that the offender does not actually need to have the credit card.[19] All of the relevant details are available from a discarded credit card receipt: number, name on the card, expiry date (Tendler, 1996a).

Cyber-obscenity

The Carnegie Mellon Survey (Rimm, 1995)[20] has suggested that as much as half of all Internet use may be related to the consumption of pornography, mostly in relation to the Usenet discussion groups. The methodology by which this estimate was calculated has subsequently been disputed and the true figure is thought to be less than one per cent. Nevertheless, there has been considerable discussion over the issue of pornography. However, much of this discussion has been unfocused and emotive because of the fact that pornography is defined by the laws of individual countries and definitions can vary from one country to the next (Itzin, 1993). In Britain, for example, individuals regularly consume images that might be classed as obscene in many Middle Eastern countries. And yet, what individuals consider to be obscene in the United Kingdom is acceptable in many Scandinavian countries. In seeking to clarify this issue the European Commission's *Green Paper on the Protection of Minors and Human Dignity in Audio-Visual and Information Services* highlighted the need to distinguish between illegal acts, such as child pornography which are subject to penal sanctions, and children gaining access to sites with pornographic content, which is not illegal, but may be deemed as harmful for children's development (European Commission Select Committee, 1996: ch. 1). This distinction still does not clarify the situation, rather it encourages the expression of a wide range of moral, political and policing agendas.

The discussion over cyber-pornography is dealt with more fully elsewhere (Akdeniz, 1996), but aspects of it are important for the discussion here because it is an important driving factor in the debate over the policing of the virtual community. Along with other types of cyber-crime, it also highlights the fact that future criminologies of cyberspace will have to reflect its unbounded nature and will have to accommodate a set of dynamics which both undermine conventional understandings of causality and cut across the traditional treatment of crime.

THE REGULATION AND CONTROL OF THE INTERNET: CYBER-POLICING

It will be some time before the arguments over jurisdiction and govern-ance are fully resolved but their outcome will eventually be very im-portant in defining who will police the Internet. However, at present no one group has formally been allocated responsibility for the Internet in the United Kingdom, so in order to inform understanding, there is a need to look at who is currently policing the virtual community and at what strategies they are using. Four main groups currently policing the Internet can be identified: they are state-funded non-police organ-izations; state-funded police organizations; Internet providers; and Internet users. The strategies employed by these various bodies provide a spec-trum of policing models although, given the nature of cyberspace, they can not be taken as a definitive list of examples.

State-Funded Non-Public-Police Organizations

The governments of Singapore, China and Vietnam have actively sought to control their citizens' use of the Internet, either by forcing users to register with the authorities or by directly controlling Internet traffic coming into their countries (Standage, 1996; Caden and Lucas, 1996: 87; Grossman, 1996). Within Europe, Germany has set up a regulatory agency, the Internet Content Task Force, and has passed new tele-communications laws requiring internet service providers to provide a back door so that security forces can read users' electronic mail if necessary (Grossman, 1996). The Internet Content Task Force also has powers to force German internet service providers to block access to certain materials, such as the Dutch site 'xs4all'. A similar organiza-tion is currently being planned by the French government which has also passed legislation to set up a central regulatory agency (Grossman, 1996). Moreover, in May 1996, the French prosecuted two leading Internet service providers.

The government of the United States of America has taken a slightly different tack by introducing a number of legal measures and techno-logical devices to regulate cyberspace in order to 'protect the interest of U.S. industry' (Reno, 1996). Since many of these measures seek to curb the freedom of the individual, it is therefore not surprising that much of the debate has revolved around the First Amendment of the United States Constitution, which guarantees freedom of speech, es-pecially during the constitutional challenge to the Communications

Decency Act 1996.[21] In addition to legislation there has been the development of technological censoring devices such as the 'V-chip technology' designed to filter out violence or pornography (Akdeniz, 1996) and the 'Clipper Chip' which is an 'escrowed encryption system' whereby the government retains the 'keys' to unscramble encrypted files (Reno, 1996). These keys would be released to any law enforcement officials who could demonstrate a need for them (Sussman, 1995: 54). These debates are discussed fully elsewhere (for example, Akdeniz, 1996; Sterling, 1994; Sussman, 1995: 54; Post, 1995: 8).

The policing of the Internet in the United States has also involved a broad range of state funded non-public-police organizations. The United States Postal Service, for example, was instrumental in investigating offences of pornography in *United States of America* v. *Robert A. Thomas and Carleen Thomas*, after a computer hacker from Tennessee filed a complaint about the contents of the pornographic bulletin board (Byassee, 1995: 205). The case was subsequently investigated by a United States postal inspector. In another incident the US Securities and Exchange Commission, which was 'anxious about the spread of cyber-fraud', brought a case against a publicly traded company for allegedly conducting a fraud through the Internet. The Commission noted that they anticipate that they 'will be addressing this kind of conduct on the internet more frequently' (Pretzlik, 1996).

The government of the United Kingdom has yet to assign responsibility for the Internet and whilst the National Heritage Committee has argued that the information superhighway is so important that a cabinet minister is required to control and represent its interests in government, it appears unlikely that this will happen (National Heritage Committee, 1996). Instead the policy of the United Kingdom is to encourage the Internet service providers to regulate their own services, particularly with regard to the dissemination of illegal materials. There have also been proposals to develop an Information Society Task Force to coordinate bodies involved in promoting the use of IT (Select Committee on Science and Technology, 1996).

State-Funded Public Police Organizations[22]

State-funded public police organizations are organized both locally and centrally. Whilst in the United Kingdom they have no formal mandate to police the virtual community, it is the case that various specialist groups of police officers are nevertheless monitoring the Internet within the areas of criminal law for which they are responsible. For example, a computer crime unit was established by the Metropolitan Police and a smaller but similar unit was set up by the Greater Manchester Police (McCormack, 1996b). Elsewhere, officers in the West Midlands Police[23] and the Metropolitan Police Clubs and Vice Unit have used the Internet to conduct investigations.

At a national level, the National Criminal Intelligence Service (NCIS)[24] has taken responsibility for serious offences such as child pornography which cross force and international boundaries. It has been implied that the National Crime Squad which is scheduled to start in England and Wales by April 1998 (Steele, 1996) will take over the investigative role in such cases (Burrell, 1996). This model is similar to that operating in the United States of America, where the Federal Bureau of Intelligence set up a National Computer Crime Squad to deal with cases where the investigation crosses regional police boundaries.[25] The organizations involved, with perhaps the exception of the latter, only seek to explore their specific areas of investigation rather than take on a generic policing role.

An interesting example of cross-boundary cyber-policing took place in the United States of America when Bill Baker, a police lieutenant from Jefferson County, Kentucky, broke a major child pornography ring in the United Kingdom, without leaving Kentucky. Baker received an 'e-mailed' pointer from a source in Switzerland which led him to an Internet site based at Birmingham University, England. After three months of investigation, Baker contacted Interpol, the Metropolitan Police and the West Midlands Police, who arrested the distributors (Sussman, 1995).[26]

The Internet Service Providers

Since the mid 1990s the prevailing mood towards the Internet has changed from wonderment to suspicion. The moral panic (Cohen, 1980; Chandler, 1996) now surrounding the Internet and the threat of legal action (Uhlig, 1996b) has forced Internet providers to consider the possibility of controlling some of the activities that are taking place on their servers: especially the news discussion groups. In August 1996, Mr Taylor, the Science and Technology Minister of the United Kingdom, warned that 'in the absence of self-regulation, the police will inevitably move to act against service providers as well as the originators of illegal material' (Uhlig, 1996b). This statement was quickly followed by a letter sent to Internet providers by Chief Inspector Stephen French of the Metropolitan Police Clubs and Vice Unit, warning that they could be liable for any illegal materials that were found to have been disseminated on their servers. Their response in September 1996 was to promote 'SafetyNet'; a mix of 'self-ratings', classification, user control, public reporting and law enforcement action (Grossman, 1996; Arthur, 1996). 'SafetyNet' was jointly endorsed by the Metropolitan Police, the Department of Trade and Industry (DTI), the Home Office and the associations of the Internet service providers: the Internet Providers Association and the London Internet Exchange (Uhlig, 1996c). In December 1996, 'SafetyNet' became 'Internet Watch' (Tendler, 1996b).[27]

The Internet Users

The final group who are involved in policing the Internet are the Internet community themselves. 'Virtual community policing' has yet to be formalized, but a number of examples have already occurred. In addition to the recently introduced complaint 'hotlines' and the development of software to screen out undesirable communications (Uhlig, 1996c)[28] there are a few recorded attempts to organize Internet users. The Internet Rapid Response Team (IRRT) is a voluntary group which polices the Internet to remove offensive material. They came to prominence when an email message advertising a collection of child pornography was received by thousands of Internet users all over the world (Uhlig, 1996a). The IRRT's response to the email messages, often referred to as 'Spam mail', was to barrage the New York Police with calls for an immediate investigation; the message had carried a New York address. The IRRT would appear to be organized along a 'guardian angel' model of policing. They argue that 'it is up to Internet users as much as anyone else to react quickly when something like this happens' (Uhlig, 1996a).

The various strategies described illustrate that cyberspace is already the subject of a form of multi-tiered governance. It is also interesting to note that the pluralistic model of policing cyberspace which emerges reflects the plurality of policing in late modern society, combining elements of both public and private models of policing. The next section attempts to apply the existing model of public policing to the Internet.

THE PUBLIC POLICING MODEL, CYBER-CRIMES AND THE TWENTY-FIRST CENTURY

As the population of cyberspace increases and the range of human activities carried out there expands, the incidence of cyber-crimes will rise considerably. A recent survey carried out by the National Computing Centre has revealed that the proportion of respondents reporting computer-related thefts rose by 60 per cent during the two years since its previous survey (National Computing Centre, 1996).[29] Whilst it is unlikely that the public police will be involved in the 'patrolling' of cyberspace, it is very probable that they will become involved in responding to complaints by members of the public against whom cyber-crimes have been committed. How will they respond? Most of the existing literature on the public police relates to changes within the police organization as it responds to the demands placed on it by late modernity, but there is very little literature on what the police actually do. It is therefore desirable to reflect upon current understanding of the public police in order to ascertain their capacity to deal with cyber-crimes. The following section will look at the public policing model and cyber-crimes.

It is anticipated that the forthcoming[30] study of the policing of computer crime by Thackray will show that out of five countries studied, Britain is the least sophisticated in its approach. Certainly 'the level of education and understanding of computer crime is far more advanced outside Britain' (McCormack, 1996b). In anticipating Thackray's findings it would appear that the root of the problem is a dissonance between the existing police occupational and operational cultures and the skills required to deal with cyber-crimes. He observes that British 'police forces are shying away from even attempting to investigate computer crimes. You see experienced detectives who lose all interest in pursuing cases where there are computers involved' (McCormack, 1996b: 3). Furthermore: 'We are far behind our own criminals on these matters. We only catch them when they get complacent and keep using old technology and old methods. If they simply keep up with current technology, they are so far ahead they are safe' (McCormack, 1996b: 3).

Thackray argues that the United Kingdom police responses to cyber-crimes are underresourced and suffer from a lack of support from other forces because of their general lack of interest in computer crimes. Thackray's observations support those of others; the Metropolitan Police Computer Crime Unit, for example, has suffered because of the limited number of cases that have been reported to it. Such a small number of cases, which underrepresents the total incidence of cyber-crimes (National Computer Centre, 1996), ensures that the police are not provided with the opportunity to develop their skills (Akdeniz, 1996b; Battcock, 1995). This observation finds a resonance in the DTI report on computer misuse which questioned whether or not the public police have the appropriate skills to investigate cases of computer crime (DTI, 1992: 29). Thackray argues for a more proactive organizational model for the policing of cyber-crimes which employs 'specially detailed officers who are educated in computer crime issues' (McCormack, 1996b).

The cultural dissonance observed between the public police model and the regulating of cyber-crimes does not appear to be limited to the United Kingdom. John Perry Barlow, the United States cyber-guru writing some years ago[31] recounts experiencing this while being interviewed by Special Agent Baxter about an alleged cyber-theft:

> I was the object of a two hour interview by Special Agent Richard Baxter, Jr. of the Federal Bureau of Investigation . . . Poor Agent Baxter didn't know a ROM chip from a Vise-grip when he arrived, so much of that time was spent trying to educate him on the nature of the thing which had been stolen. Or whether 'stolen' was the right term for what had happened to it . . . You know things have rather jumped the groove when potential suspects must explain to law enforcers the nature of their alleged perpetrations. (Barlow, 1990)

Barlow goes on to describe how Baxter's problem was not just related to information technology literacy. Rather he indicates the same cultural dissonance between cyber-culture and police operational culture that was described earlier.

> Agent Baxter looked at my list of Hacker's Conference attendees and read their bios . . . Their corporate addresses didn't fit his model of outlaws at all well . . . Why had he come all the way to Pinedale to investigate a crime he didn't understand which had taken place (sort of) in 5 different places, none of which was within 500 miles? (Barlow, 1990)

It is interesting to note that one of the approaches towards policing cyber-crimes that has been suggested for the United Kingdom is to pass the responsibility on to the National Criminal Intelligence Service (NCIS), thus removing the primary responsibility from the local police. Recent unpublished research into the role of NCIS found considerable animosity towards it from other police and police-related organizations,[32] thus rendering such policy problematic. The root of the problem appears to be that NCIS has failed to develop practical working relationships with local police forces (Burrell, 1996: 1). Of additional interest to the subsequent discussion is the fact that one of the main accusations against NCIS was the fact that it devoted its few resources to fighting sex tourism and 'disrupting sex tourists' activities rather than helping to secure convictions' (Burrell, 1996:1).

The above analysis raises a number of questions, not least of which is whether or not the cultural dissonance is merely a case of the public police getting used to a new set of issues or whether there is a more deeply rooted set of concerns, which might suggest that a different strategy should be employed. In order to get to grips with these issues, it is therefore necessary to look in more detail at the public policing model.

The policing tradition of the United Kingdom has been the archetype of policing models in many western countries, particularly in North America. It is based upon a locally organized public policing model that was formalized by Sir Robert Peel in the early nineteenth century (Critchley, 1967; Gash, 1961). The main function of the early full-time professional police was to keep the 'dangerous classes' off the streets, carrying a dual mandate to keep the peace and bring felons to justice (Manning, 1977; Reiner, 1992). One of the dominant characteristics of the public police organization since its inception has been its continual adaptation to the demands of modernity. Indeed, the very birth of the full-time police was motivated by the need to deal with the knock-on effects of rapid industrialization. It is therefore interesting to note that police commentators a century ago were engaged in anticipating what challenges new technologies[33] would pose for the police. The cartoon in Figure 9.1 is an imaginative impression of the police response to new technologies at that time.

However, what marks out cyberspace from previous technological eras is the disembedding of time, space and place, described earlier. Even the development of the automobile, telephone, radio and more recently the fax relied upon physical rather than purely electronic technologies. Cyberspace, by contrast, is a virtual environment and the links within it are virtually instant and purely electronic, which means that there are no physical boundaries to temper criminal activities. The police have never before experienced such a paradigmatic shift. It would be wrong, however, to interpret this shift as a break with the past, rather it should be seen as a rapid acceleration of the rate of change.

The police response to this change is somewhat contradictory. On the one hand they appear to have the capacity to respond quickly at an

Figure 9.1   The police embrace new technologies *circa* 1901

Source: *Punch*, 6 November 1901.

organizational level by setting up specialist units. However, on the other hand public policing practices have traditionally been moulded by the time-honoured traditions of policing and cannot respond to such rapid change. In fact, the basic principles of policing remain much the same as they were nearly two hundred years ago, despite the considerable social change that has taken place since. To illustrate the point in question, it is quite normal practice, whenever the theft of a computer occurs, to seek to prosecute the thief and recover the stolen property. The object of the theft is perceived to be the computer itself, which then forms the focus of the investigation (Wall, 1995). The criminal law in this instance relates to the theft of the computer and police practice relates to the apprehension and prosecution of the perpetrator and the restitution of the goods to the owner. As such, the motive for the theft is assumed to be the appropriation of the computer, an assumption which precludes any consideration of the value of the contents of that computer. Further examination of the police occupational and organizational cultures reveals the site of this dissonance.

Police occupational culture plays an important part in policing, more so, it is argued, than the letter of the law (McBarnet, 1979; Shearing and Ericson, 1991). It is police culture which enables the officer to make sense of the world which they have to police. Without this cognitive map they would have no understanding of their environment. So, when a police officer operates in cyberspace, it is argued, they interpret it in terms of their public police culture. Sterling commented in his influential work upon the policing of hackers that he felt that the 'police want to believe that all hackers are thieves' (1994: 63). Sterling was describing a phenomenon commonly found in studies of police culture whereby the police tend to change the meaning and common understanding of the areas in which they become involved. So, states Sacks: 'for the police, objectives and places having routine uses are conceived of in terms of favourite misuses. Garbage cans are places in which dead babies are thrown, schoolyards are places where mobsters hang out, stores are places where shoplifters go, etc.' (Sacks, 1972: 292; Shearing and Ericson, 1991: 490).

Applying Sacks's observations to policing the internet, it is possible to understand recent police statements which suggest that they see it not in terms of an exciting potential for the democratization of knowledge and the levelling of social boundaries, but rather as a place where pornographers ply their trade. This view is frequently supported by the citing of findings of the a foreman honed 1995 Carnegie Mellon University 'pornography study' which purported to identify '917,410 images, descriptions, short stories, and animations downloaded 8.5 million times by consumers in over 2000 cities in forty countries, provinces, and territories' (Rimm, 1995: 1849). It is no surprise then, to see statements made by the police which liken the internet newsgroups to 'libraries of pornography' (Uhlig, 1996c) and which set the agenda for forthcoming debate in which the police play a central role. It is also not surprising that in articulating what they see as the problem, the police draw from their experiences of the terrestrial world, conceiving of cyberspace as being 'like a neighborhood without a police department' (Sussman, 1995).[34] Moreover, the investigation of illegal pornography is recognized as a fairly traditional police activity and is therefore fairly unproblematic from a police point of view. Cyber-theft and cyber-trespass, by way of comparison, are very problematic for the police as they are not regarded as a traditional police activity, neither are they viewed as areas of concern within police management.

The cultural dissonance between traditional police and cyber-cultures can be illustrated by reference to new laws that have been introduced in the United Kingdom to deal with cyber-crimes. The Computer Misuse Act 1990 created three new criminal offences: unauthorized hacking; unauthorized access with intent; and unauthorized modification of the contents of any computer. However, the authors of this Act would appear to have given little thought to the difficulties of tracing and identifying hackers, and of being able to obtain enough evidence to put forward a convincing case (Charlesworth, 1995: 33). The police are not the only criminal justice agency which is experiencing problems with computer crime. The courts are currently having some difficulty in ascertaining the relative seriousness of computer thefts, as in the case of *R. v. Byrne*[35] (Wall, 1995), which suggests that they would have serious problems where the victim has not so much experienced a loss, but a dilution of the value of the original property because it has been duplicated.[36]

The preceding discussion has observed that a main source of the cultural dissonance lies in police occupational cultures. It is, however, also the case that police organizational cultures do little to facilitate broader change. The common response has been to create a specialist unit which concentrates available expertise. These units are subsequently vulnerable to the practice of rotating personnel and key staff are frequently moved elsewhere as soon as they acquire the requisite specialist skills. Based upon the principle of the 'gifted amateur' and designed to lead to the circulation of ideas whilst preventing the development of corruptive contacts, rotation policy has the counter-productive side-effect of reducing the residual knowledge base and reducing the effectiveness of (some) specialist units. It also compounds the issue by not only removing experienced personnel but also adding the problems associated with socializing and training new members. This point was flagged by Thackray who, after spending time conducting research into the area, was moved back into the uniformed branch (McCormack, 1996b). Ironically, once the police do develop an organizational response, the problem often appears to become worse due to the inevitable sensitization of the issue by the media and an increase in reported incidents.[37]

The above analysis highlights concerns about the practicalities of involving local public policing organizations in the policing of cyber-crimes. In fact the existing information suggests that extending the full jurisdiction of cyberspace to the public police would be counter-productive. Current law is still based upon traditional concepts of physical property and its protection. These laws are inadequate when the sort of crimes individuals are increasingly falling victim to are moving from physical to virtual reality. But the public police will nevertheless have a role to play in the policing of cyber-crimes, most likely as the first point of contact with the victim. However, for this involvement to be successful, aspects of police occupational culture need to be reinstitutionalized (Shearing, 1995: 60) to overcome the cultural dissonance which currently exists so that the police understand when to become involved, but also when not to become involved. The debates over police cultures have hitherto been less than optimistic because the literature suggests that they are fairly intransigent to change. However, much of the research which has informed those debates, especially in the United Kingdom, was conducted in the mid-1980s. It is encouraging that police officers appointed since then come from a broader social and educational background than their predecessors. At an individual level contemporary constables are not only more receptive to new ideas, but they now enter the police with a degree of literacy in information technologies. In addition, it could be argued that the British police now have a greater organizational capacity than they previously had to deal with new challenges. For example, the Association of Chief Police Officers (ACPO) has established itself as an important and influential central policy-making unit (Savage, Charman and Cope, 1996). This role enables the identification of emerging problem areas which will affect the police and provides a forum for central discussion of policy options.

CONCLUSION: POLICING, CRIMINOLOGY AND THE VIRTUAL COMMUNITY

Janet Reno, the Attorney General of the United States of America, recently highlighted what she sees as four major challenges for law enforcement in the twenty-first century arising from cyberspace (Reno, 1996). They are the preservation of government control over access to the internet in order to catch cyber-criminals; the training of government agents and prosecutors to respond to computer crimes; the increasing cooperation in the international law enforcement community to deal with trans-border issues; and finally the amendment of existing laws which have been drafted with physical objects in mind so that they cover intellectual properties (Reno, 1996). The issues raised by Reno are generally accepted as the way forward. However, whilst no one would deny that cyber-crimes degrade the quality of life, her interpretation of the various challenges is underpinned by an ideology in which regulation is presented as unproblematic and a natural development of the Internet. It must therefore be remembered that it is no coincidence that the debate over control has corresponded with the full realization of the commercial potential of the Internet and that the initiatives to introduce control have come from two directions: the state, whose sovereign interests are threatened (Johnson and Post, 1996), and commerce, who wish to gain monopoly over areas currently in the public domain of cyberspace. Thus, any cyber-policies must balance intrusion by the state with a respect for the needs of the virtual community. Without such a balance, it is possible that two situations could arise: on the one hand, an over-regulated cyberspace cluttered with so much 'official graffiti' (Hermer and Hunt, 1996: 455) as to prevent any meaningful activity taking place, and on the other a grossly under-regulated cyberspace in which every constructive activity would be immediately debased. The art of governance will lie in striking the right sort of balance.

The earlier analysis identified a number of existing models by which the regulation of cyberspace and policing of cyber-crimes are currently taking place. It is a system that is not dissimilar to the pluralistic models of policing operating already in late modern society. What this suggests is the impracticability and impossibility of one single body having a remit to police the virtual community. It also indicates that different generic types of behaviour should be policed by different means and also that different degrees of seriousness of outcome should influence the type of response. It would therefore be wrong to simply assume that all cyber-crimes should fall within the remit of the public police; they are quite different in nature and outcome and therefore need to become the responsibility of different groups. It is necessary to build upon existing resources to inform future strategies (Shearing, 1995). Some offences and behaviours, for example, are serious to the point that prosecution should be the only course of action. Other undesirable behaviours could be reasonably dealt with within cyberspace, for example, by denying access of entry or by restricting access to certain areas. It would therefore be imaginable that any formal policing model for cyberspace would be pluralistic and multi-tiered, and would include combinations of the elements that exist already: some state policing, some involvement by state-funded non-police organizations, and a degree of self-regulation by the internet providers combined with self-policing by Internet users.

To conclude, the emergence and development of cyberspace raises numerous issues as to the nature of crime, offending, policing and control at the end of the twentieth century. Indeed its unique characteristics and lack of boundaries raise serious implications not only for its regulation and control, but also for the discipline of criminology, a discipline which has for the most part relied upon common traditional conceptions of crime and control. As we approach the coming millenium, there is a clear need for more research to inform conceptual, theoretical and methodological debates about cyberspace, not only so that a realistic strategy for policing the virtual community may be reached, but also to inform criminological inquiry into the twenty-first century.

Notes

1. The following discussion focuses primarily upon policing in the United Kingdom, but draws upon the experiences of the United States and other jurisdictions where appropriate.
2. The term 'Internet' as used here is synonymously with 'World Wide Web' and the 'information superhighway'.
3. Also see the executive summary of the Information Warfare Tutorial at [http://144.99.192.240/usacs/iw/tutorial/exesum.htm].
4. [http://www.altavista.digital.com/].
5. Extending Braverman's (1976) hypothesis to the construction of social life (Wall and Johnstone, 1997).
6. Bauman (1992: 151) on Baudrillard.
7. Because of this the term 'hyperspace' might be a more appropriate description.
8. For a discussion of the policing and maintenance of intellectual property see Wall (1996).
9. 74 F.3d 701; 1996 U.S. App. Lexis 1069; 1996 Fed App. 0032P (6th Cir.); 43 Fed. R. Evid. Serv. (Callaghan) 969; 96 Cal.
10. The preliminary investigation in this case was carried out in the United States before it was handed over to the police of the United Kingdom. See Court of Appeal (Criminal Division) *The Times*, 3 October 1996.
11. As yet few test cases have reached the courts.
12. See [http://www.fbi.gov/compcrim.htm].
13. Pub. L. No. 99-474, 100 Stat. 1213 (1986) with the amending 18 U.S.C. § 1030.
14. For further discussion of the 'demonization' of the hacker see Chandler (1996), Duff and Gardiner (1996), Ross (1990: para. 4) and Sterling (1994).
15. For further details of 'Information Warfare', United States Airforce Fact Sheet 95-20, also see Szafranski (1995).
16. Also see Uhlig (1996d).
17. An example of computer spying was illustrated in the case of the Hanover Group (Hafner and Markoff, 1991; Young, 1995: 11).
18. This is part of the rapidly expanding business in counterfeit products, toiletries, designer labels and rock merchandizing.
19. See 'Credit Card Fraud Technique' at [http://www.echotech.com/ccfraud.htm].
20. The publicity arising from the publication of the Carnegie Mellon Survey was a major contributor to the development of the moral panic over the Internet.

21. *ACLU et al.* v. *Reno*, 12 June 1996, 929 f.Supp.824.
22. The roles of the various security services are not discussed here.
23. After 'Operation Starburst' the West Midlands Police identified a paedophile ring (Rose, 1995: 16).
24. Crime (Sentences Bill) HC 1996–7, no. 3.
25. This view is contrary to that of the previous Home Secretary, Michael Howard.
26. See *R.* v. *Fellows and R.* v. *Arnold*.
27. Internet Watch can be found at [http://www.internetwatch.org.uk/hotline/].
28. Various Internet service providers have promised to distribute free to customers (Uhlig, 1996c).
29. Questionnaires were sent to 9500 UK organizations and in-depth interviews were conducted with 25 organizations; 89 per cent of respondents reported at least one security breach (National Computing Centre, 1996).
30. Research conducted under the Police Research Group initiative which has yet to be published.
31. Although Barlow wrote this piece in 1990, over six years ago, it does nevertheless highlight the main processes involved in the paradigm shift.
32. For example, the United Kingdom Customs and Excise.
33. At this time the boundaries between science fiction and scientific fact were blurred by popular authors such as H. G. Wells.
34. Sussman (1995), citing the director of the Federal Law Enforcement Training Center.
35. *R.* v. *Byrne* (1993) 15 Cr App R(S) 34. This case was primarily about the theft of computers.
36. At present such a dispute would be resolved through the civil courts.
37. See the arguments made by Young (1974).

References

Akdeniz, Y. (1996a) 'Computer pornography: a comparative study of US and UK obscenity laws and child pornography laws in relation to the internet', *International Review of Law, Computers and Technology*, vol. 10, no. 2, pp. 235–61.

Akdeniz, Y. (1996b) 'Section 3 of the Computer Misuse Act 1990: An antidote for computer viruses', *Web Journal of Contemporary Legal Issues*, vol. 3,

Arthur, C. (1996) 'New crackdown on child porn on the internet', *The Independent*, 23 September.

Barlow, J. P. (1990) 'Crime and puzzlement: in advance of the law on the electronic frontier', *Whole Earth Review*, Fall, p. 44.

Barlow, J. P. (1994) 'The economy of ideas: a framework for rethinking patents and copyrights in the digital age (Everything you know about intellectual property is wrong)', *Wired*, vol. 2, no. 3, p. 84.

Battcock, R. (1995) 'Computer Misuse Act 5 years on' [http://www.strath.ac.uk/Departments/Law/student/PERSONAL/R_BATTCOCK/].

Bauman, Z. (1992) *Intimations of Post-Modernity* (London: Routledge).

Benedikt, M. (ed.) (1991) *Cyberspace: The First Steps* (Cambridge, Mass.: MIT Press).

Blakey, D. (1996) 'Policing cyberspace', *Policing Today*, vol. 2, no. 1, pp. 19–21.

Braithwaite, J. (1992) *Crime, Shame and Reintegration* (Cambridge, Cambridge University Press).

Braverman, H. (1976) *Labour and Monopoly Capital* (New York: Monthly Review Press).

Burrell, I. (1996) 'Leak reveals contempt for British FBI', *The Independent*, 11 October, p. 1.

Byassee, W. S. (1995) 'Jurisdiction of Cyberspace: applying real world precedent to the virtual community', *Wake Forest Law Review*, vol. 30, pp. 197–220.

Caden, M. L. and Lucas, S. E. (1996) 'Accidents on the Information Superhighway: on-line liability and regulation', *Richmond Journal of Law & Technology*, vol. 2, no. 1.

Chandler, A. (1996) 'The changing definition and image of hackers in popular discourse', *International Journal of the Sociology of Law*, vol. 24, pp. 229–51.

Charlesworth, A. (1995) 'Between flesh and sand: rethinking the Computer Misuse Act 1990', *International Year book of Law, Computers and Technology* (Oxford: Carfax Publishing) vol. 9, pp. 31–46.

Cohen, S. (1980) *Folk Devils and Moral Panics* (Oxford: Basil Blackwell).

Critchley, T. A. (1967) *A History of the Police in England and Wales 1900–1966* (London: Constable).

DTI (1992) *Dealing with Computer Misuse* (London: HMSO).

Duff, L. and Gardiner, S. (1996) 'Computer crime in the global village: strategies for control and regulation – in defence of the hacker', *International Journal of the Sociology of Law*, vol. 24, pp. 211–28.

Elmer-Dewitt, P. (1994) 'Battle for the soul of the Internet', *Time*, 25 July, pp. 50, 52.

Escobar, A. (1996) 'Welcome to Cyberia: Notes on the anthropology of cyberculture', in Z. Saradar and J. R. Ravetz (eds), *Cyberfutures: Culture and Politics on the Information Superhighway* (London: Pluto Press).

European Commission Select Committee (1996) *Green Paper on the Protection of Minors and Human Dignity in Audio-Visual and Information Services* (Brussels–Luxembourg).

Evans, J. (1994) 'Cruising the Internet: what's in it for lawyers?', *Cal. Lawyer*, July, p. 67.

Fraser, B. T. (1996) 'Computer Crime Research Resources', School of Library and Information Studies, Florida State University [http://mailer.fsu.edu/~btf1553/ccrr/search1.htm].

Gash, N. (1961) *Mr Secretary Peel* (London: Longman).

Gibson, W. (1984) *Neuromancer* (London: HarperCollins).

Giddens, A. (1990) *The Consequences of Modernity* (London: Polity Press).

Gottfredson, G. and Hischi, T. (1990) *A General Theory of Crime* (Stanford California: Stanford University Press).

Grossman, W. (1996) 'A grip on the new', *Electronic Telegraph*, 1 October, no. 496.

Hafner, K. and Markoff, J. (1995) *Cyberpunk: Outlaws and Hackers on the Computer Frontier* (New York: Simon & Schuster).

The Herald (1996) 'Inquiry into pornography on Tory students' Internet page', *The (Glasgow) Herald*, 19 August, p. 6.

Hermer, J. and Hunt, A. (1996) 'Official graffiti of the everyday', *Law and Society Review*, vol. 30, no. 3, pp. 455–80.

Itzen, C. (ed.) (1993) *Pornography: Women, Violence and Civil Liberties* (Oxford: Oxford University Press).

Johnson, D. and Post, D. G. (1996) 'Law and borders: the rise of law in cyberspace' [http://www.law.syr.edu/Course.Materials/Chon/borders.html].

Kumar, K. (1978) *Prophecy and Progress: The Sociology of Post-Industrial Society* (Harmondsworth: Penguin).

Lloyd, I. (1994) 'Shopping in Cyberspace', *International Journal of Law and Information Technology*, vol. 1, no. 3, pp. 335–48.

Mandel, T. F. (1993) *Surfing the Wild Internet*, SCAN; Business Intelligence Program, SRI International, Menlo Park, No. 2109, March.

Manning, P. K. (1977) *Police Work* (Cambridge, Mass.: MIT Press).

McBarnet, D. (1979) 'Arrest: the legal context of policing', in S. Holdaway (ed.), *The British Police* (London: Arnold).

McCormack, N. (1996b) 'Criminals slip through the net', *Electronic Telegraph*, 5 November, p. 3.

National Computing Centre. (1996) *The Information Security Breaches Survey 1996* (The National Computing Centre Limited).

National Heritage Committee (1996) *The Structure and Remit of the Department of National Heritage* (London: HMSO).

Post, D. (1995) 'Encryption vs. the alligator clip: the feds worry that encoded messages are immune to wiretaps', *New Jersey Law Journal*, 23 January, p. 8.

Pretzlik, C. (1996) 'Firm accused of fraud on the Internet', *Daily Telegraph*, 9 November.

Reiner, R. (1992) *The Politics of the Police* (Sussex: Wheatsheaf).

Reno, J. Hon (1996) 'Law enforcement in cyberspace', address to the Commonwealth Club of California, San Francisco Hilton Hotel, 14 June [http://pwp.usa.pipeline.com/~jya/addres.txt].

Rheingold, H. (1993) *The Virtual Community: Homesteading the Electronic Frontier* (London: Secker & Warburg).

Rimm, M. (1995) 'Marketing pornography on the information superhighway: a survey of 917,410 images, descriptions, short stories, and animations downloaded 8.5 million times by consumers in over 2000 cities in forty countries, provinces, and territories', *Georgetown Law Journal*, vol. 83, no. 5, pp. 1849–1934.

Rose, P. (1995) 'Internet police crack child porn network', *Daily Mail*, 27 July, p. 16.

Ross, A. (1990) 'Hacking away at the counterculture', *Postmodern Culture*, vol. 1, no. 1: [http://jefferson.village.virginia.edu/pmc/issue.990/contents.990.html].

Sacks, H. (1972) 'Notes on police assessment of moral character', in D. Sudnow (ed.), *Studies in Social Interaction* (New York: Free Press).

Saradar, Z. and Ravetz, J. R. (1996) 'Reaping the technological whirlwind', in Z. Saradar and J. R. Ravetz (eds), *Cyberfutures: Culture and Politics on the Information Superhighway* (London: Pluto Press).

Savage, S. P., Charman, S. and Cope, S. (1996) 'Police governance: the Association of Chief Police Officers and constitutional change', *Public Policy and Administration*, vol. 11, no. 2, pp. 92–106.

Schlozberg, S. (1983) *Computers and Penal Legislation* (Oslo: Norwegian Research Centre for Computers and Law).

Select Committee on Science and Technology (1996) *Information Society: Agenda for Action in the UK, Fifth Report, Select Committee on Science and Technology*, H. L. 1995–1996.

Shearing, C. (1995) 'Transforming the culture of policing: thoughts from South Africa', in D. Dixon (ed.), *Crime, Criminology and Public Policy*, Special Supplementary Issue of the *Australian and New Zealand Journal of Criminology* (Sydney: Butterworths).

Shearing, C. and Ericson, R. (1991) 'Culture as figurative action', *British Journal of Sociology*, vol. 42, no. 4, pp. 481–506.

Standage, T. (1996) 'Web access in a tangle as censors have their say', *Electronic Telegraph*, 10 September, no. 475.

Steele, J. (1996) 'Howard denies the national police squad will be like FBI', *Electronic Telegraph*, 3 July, no. 419.

Sterling, B. (1994) *The Hacker Crackdown* (London: Penguin Books).

Sterling, B. (1995) 'Good cop, bad hacker', speech to the High Technology Crime Investigation Association, *Wired*, vol. 3, no. 5, p. 122.

Sussman, V. (1995) 'Policing Cyberspace', U.S. News 38; World Rep., Jan. 23, 1995, at 54, Lexis, News library, Usenews file, 1995 WL 3113171.

Szafranski, Col. R. (1995) 'A theory of Information Warfare: preparing for 2020,' *Air Chronicles*, vol. 1, pp. 56–65 [http://www.cdsar.af.mil/apj/szfran.html].

Tendler, S. (1996a) 'Hi-tech cheats use supermarket cards to fake credit sales', *The Times*, 26 June, p. 6.

Tendler, S. (1996b) 'Public to help police curb internet porn', *The Times*, 2 December.

Tribe, L. H. (1991) 'The constitution in cyberspace: law and liberty beyond the electronic frontier', *The Humanist*, 26 March, p. 15.

Uhlig, R. (1996a) 'Hunt is on for Internet dealer in child porn', *Electronic Telegraph*, 23 October, no. 518.

Uhlig, R. (1996b) 'Minister's warning over Internet porn', *Electronic Telegraph*, 16 August.

Uhlig, R. (1996c) '"Safety Net" on Internet will catch child porn', *Electronic Telegraph*, 23 September, no. 488.

Uhlig, R. (1996d) 'Hackers sabotage Blair internet page', Electronic Telegraph, 10 December, no. 566.

United Nations (1995), *International Review of Criminal Policy No. 43 and 44 – United Nations Manual on the Prevention and Control of Computer-Related Crime* [http://www.ifs.univie.ac.at/~pr2gq1/rev4344.html#crime].

Wall, D. S. (1995) 'Technology and crime: increased capital investment in information technology and changes in victimisation patterns', *International Yearbook of Law, Computers and Technology*, vol. 9, pp. 97–109.

Wall, D. S. (1996) 'Reconstructing the soul of Elvis: the social development and legal maintenance of Elvis Presley as intellectual property', *International Journal of the Sociology of Law*, vol. 24, pp. 117–43.

Wall, D. S. and Johnstone, J. (1997) 'The industrialization of law: the impact of information technology upon the legal practice', *International Journal of the Sociology of Law*, vol. 27.

Wasik, M. (1991) *Crime and the Computer* (Oxford: Clarendon Press).

Young, J. (1974) 'Deviance amplification', in S. Cohen (ed.), *Images of Deviance* (Harmonsdworth: Penguin).

Young, L. F. (1995) 'United States computer crime laws, criminals and deterrence', *International Yearbook of Law, Computers and Technology*, vol. 9, pp. 1–16.

Index